Popularizing Anthropology

Anthropology written for a popular audience is the most neglected branch of the discipline. In the 1980s postmodernist anthropologists began to explore the literary and reflective aspects of their work. *Popularizing Anthropology* advances that trend by looking at a key but previously marginalized genre of anthropology.

The contributors, who are well-known anthropologists, explore such themes as:

- why so many popular anthropologists are women;
- how the Japanese have reacted to Ruth Benedict;
- why Margaret Mead became so successful;
- how the French media promote Lévi-Strauss and Louis Dumont;
- why Bruce Chatwin tells us more about Aboriginals than many anthropologists of Australia;
- how personal accounts of fieldwork have evolved since the 1950s;
- how to write a personal account of fieldwork.

Popularizing Anthropology unearths a submerged tradition within anthropology and reveals that, from its beginning, anthropologists have looked beyond the boundaries of the academy for their listeners. It aims to establish the popularization of the discipline as an illuminating topic of investigation in its own right, arguing that it is not an irrelevant appendage to the main body of the subject but has always been an integral part of it.

Jeremy MacClancy and **Chris McDonaugh** are Senior Lecturers at Oxford Brookes University.

Popularizing Anthropology

Edited by Jeremy MacClancy and
Chris McDonaugh

London and New York

First published 1996
by Routledge
11 New Fetter Lane, London EC4P 4EE
Transferred to Digital Printing 2003
Simultaneously published in the USA and Canada
by Routledge
29 West 35th Street, New York, NY 10001

Typeset in Garamond by Routledge

British Library Cataloguing in Publication Data
A catalogue record for this book is available from the British
Library

Library of Congress Cataloguing in Publication Data
Popularizing anthropology / edited by Jeremy MacClancy and
Chris McDonaugh.
  p. cm.
  Includes bibliographical references and index.
  1. Anthropology–Popular works. I. MacClancy, Jeremy.
  II. McDonaugh, Chris, 1953– .
  GN31.2.P66   1997
  301–dc20

                                              96-7567
                                              CIP

ISBN 0–415–13612–1(hbk)
ISBN 0–415–13613–X(pbk)

Towards the memory of Godfrey Lienhardt, 1921–1993

Contents

Notes on contributors

Jonathan Benthall is Director of the Royal Anthropological Institute.

Alan Campbell is a lecturer in Social Anthropology at the University of Edinburgh.

Dominique Casajus is an attaché de recherches, CNRS, Paris.

Philippe Descola is Directeur d'Études, École des Hautes Études en Sciences Sociales, Paris.

Joy Hendry is Professor of Social Anthropology at Oxford Brookes University.

Wendy James is a lecturer in Social Anthropology at the Institute of Social and Cultural Anthropology, Oxford University.

Jeremy MacClancy is a senior lecturer in Social Anthropology at Oxford Brookes University.

Christian McDonaugh is a senior lecturer in Social Anthropology at Oxford Brookes University.

William E. Mitchell is Professor of Social Anthropology at the University of Vermont.

Howard Morphy is Curator of the Pitt Rivers Museum, Oxford University.

Judith Okely is Professor of Social Anthropology at the University of Hull.

Preface

The original stimulus which led to this book was a series of evening conversations between ourselves, during which we came to realize both the importance of the topic and the fact that no anthropologist had so far focused attention on it. Words led to action: a seminar series held at Oxford Brookes University during the course of 1993, and a day conference held that summer at the Institute of Social and Cultural Anthropology, Oxford University.

Unfortunately, we were not able to include in this book all the papers given, and we would like to thank those who came to speak but whose words we have had 'to leave out here. Also, for their financial support and assistance, we wish to thank the British Academy, the British Council, the Institute of Social and Cultural Anthropology, Oxford University, Maison Française, and the School of Social Sciences, Oxford Brookes University.

Articles by Casajus and Descola were translated from their original French by McDonaugh.

We dedicate this book to the memory of Godfrey Lienhardt. Even though none of the contributors were formally taught by Godfrey, almost all of us have been influenced, in different ways, by his work and example. Godfrey would not have considered himself in any way a popularizing anthropologist, but the elegant, pellucid way in which he powerfully expressed his subtle ideas remains exemplary to any anthropologist who wishes his words to reach beyond the walls of academe.

Jeremy MacClancy
Christian McDonaugh

Chapter 1

Popularizing anthropology

Jeremy MacClancy

It is a perfect summer's day. The view across Idle Valley is marvellous. The house is impressive and, above all, expensive, befitting its owner, a writer of best-selling historical romances.

But Christopher Marlowe is bored. His suspect, the writer, is drunk, but not drunk enough to confess all. Instead, he ruminates out loud. Two paragraphs into his ponderings he turns anthropological. 'Ever read *The Golden Bough*? No, too long for you. Shorter version though. Ought to read it. Proves our sexual habits are pure convention – like wearing a black tie with a dinner jacket.'

(Chandler 1953: 212–13)

The terse comment exposes the worst fears of industrious, committed academics. Decades of work by a distinguished intellectual who painstakingly puts together an encyclopaedic series of tomes are smartly reduced to a single, misrepresentative phrase: 'proves our sexual habits are pure convention'. Any sense of subtlety or of shades of opinion is lost for the sake of a throwaway line, uttered by a drunk.

Not surprising, then, that so many anthropologists have been wary of attempts to popularize their discipline. They do not want to see their laborious efforts misused in a way which brings little credit to themselves, to their collective endeavour, or to the people they study. They have no desire to observe the crude ways their finely wrought concepts, generated in an academic environment, are transmitted to an alien audience. Not for them the populace applauding their ideas for non-scholastic reasons.

There is an additional reason, however, for this wariness towards the popular: career prospects. Kudos – and prestigious professorships – are won by those who make theoretical advances, not by those who play to the gallery. And for those budding lecturers who are not aiming so high, but merely for tenure, it is safer to confer quietly with colleagues and to produce learned volumes which can only be appreciated by the few than to run the risks of pandering to the public. Lévi-Strauss only wrote *Tristes Tropiques* because he thought he had failed as an academic. Though he had spent ten years working on the material for *Les Structures élémentaires de la parenté*, there had been little reaction to the book in Parisian circles. As he feared, when his travelogue was published, some of his peers were not pleased; among others, Paul Rivet, director of the Musée de l'Homme, refused to receive him.

The assumption underlying this sort of culturally snobbish behaviour is that academics should restrict themselves to academic work, and not concern themselves with 'lesser' matters (Grillo 1985: 15). Learned research is 'pure' and worthy of respect. Work on themes with popular appeal is considered close to sullying oneself, rarely deserving more than contempt. Better to remain within the cloisters than to go forth and dirty one's fingers, unless of course one is going to fashionably exotic settings. This attitude is not new. Andrew Lang (1936 [1907]: 12, 14) was able to praise Tylor's *Primitive Culture* – 'never sinking to the popular... [it] never ceases to be interesting' – but could only manage to speak of his peer's successful introduction to the discipline, *Anthropology*, by calling it 'a piece of *vulgarization*' (original emphasis). A similar attitude is evinced in the (most likely) apocryphal reply made by Marrett in response to a junior don's comment that he had committed a factual blunder in his popular work, *Anthropology*: 'Uhh!' the distinguished academic replied, 'Can't expect truth for a shilling!'

One consequence of these condescending attitudes is that the very topic of popularization has been ignored as much as the activity is looked down upon. Yet just because putting the word across to a non-academic audience may not be considered 'the done thing' by many does not, under any circumstances, mean that we should scorn it, either as an anthropological practice or as a subject of investigation. In fact, precisely because it may not be 'the done thing' may well be the best reason for doing it. Anthropologists are supposed to examine ideologies rather than reproduce them. This issue of popularization is especially pertinent today because of the postmodernist challenge to the traditional structure of the discipline (Clifford and Marcus 1986; Clifford 1988). These critics of the conventionally accepted question ethnographic authority and underline the irreducibly literary nature of ethnography. They call, among other things, for the creation of plural texts, the recognition of the need for reflexivity, the realization of the subversive potential of anthropology. According to their interpretation, the boundary between art and science is blurred, ethnography is an interdisciplinary product, and the production of ethnographic texts is a problematic enterprise.

What is so surprising, however, about their work is their focus on canonical texts to the exclusion of anything which smacks of the popular. Though keen to expose, and so help to undermine, the hegemonic strategies of the anthropological elites, they have overlooked the renowned texts by which the discipline is known beyond its boundaries. Popular texts might be popular, but they are still constructed texts and ones, moreover, which test the relation between anthropology and literature in ways the exclusively scholastic refuse to consider. The postmodernists' disregard of this corpus is curious because, for those who wish to heed their clarion call for the blurring of genres and the democratization of our subject, it is necessary to point out that a plenitude of examples already exists, as we shall see. Ironically, postmodernists, in bypassing popular works of anthropology, have reinforced some of the very attitudes which they take such pains to question. By neglecting these works, they have failed to challenge radically the reigning hegemonies. Instead, they have helped to perpetuate them; or rather, they attempt to replace them with another – their own.

The rapidly changing nature and ever-increasing degree of contact between peoples around the world would have forced a rethinking of the discipline, whether or not certain anthropologists had collectively constructed postmodernism. The concept of a culture as a clearly bounded entity is by now too patent a fiction to be maintained. No present-day fieldworkers can write about peoples without knowing that their words will be read by the indigenes, if not today then in the near future. As the number of graduates continues to rise in both the developed and the developing worlds, the once-privileged status of the intellectual (a status partly based on rarity) declines, as does the authority that went with the position. This increase in numbers broadens the ethnic and sexual base of the anthropological constituency, transforming it in the process. The old clubbishness is going. Members of previously under-represented groups increasingly speak up. In this context of constant flux and self-questioning, reflexivity and the search for appropriate modes of expressing contemporary realities do not appear as options. They are perceived as necessities.

At the same time, anthropologists are also being challenged by changes within academe: the rise of new technologies, cutbacks in funding and faculty budgets, an increase in student loads, and, in the United States, the introduction of computerized exams with a consequent reduction of the discipline to memorized lists of exotica. A shift in students' interests heightens this sense of flux. Kinship loses its place as a central subject of great theoretical import. Fieldwork away from 'home' becomes not the rule but tends towards the exceptional. In North America, some departments of anthropology shrink or disappear. 'Cultural studies', drawing acknowledged inspiration from the discipline, continues to rise and rise, without apparent limit. Its sustained success comes to be seen as a threat to the very existence of anthropology.

These changes, both global and parochial, force anthropologists to consider how the knowledge they produce can be made accessible to a wider and perhaps different group of listeners. In the process they come to realize that the space between the academic and the popular is not a one-way street but an arena of voices where each may inspire the others. As the example of Ruth Benedict's *Chrysanthemum and the Sword* shows, that space is potentially one of productive dialogue rather than patronizing monologue. Popular anthropology need not be a downmarket derivative of 'the real stuff'. It is not a cheapened version of a high-quality product which has been allowed to 'trickle down' (a patronizing metaphor of treacly hierarchy). It is an integral, contributory part of the discipline, broadly conceived. It may be as serious-minded as academic anthropology. Indeed, at times, it may have loftier aims, a successful popular book helping to influence the attitudes of many while a run-of-the-mill ethnography may solely add to the lengthening bookshelf on 'the X'. This is not to devalue expertise but to recognize its different types, and the particular contribution each can make. The overly scholastic, who sneer at popular style, fail to appreciate that their own discourse is merely one variant, and that each has integrity within its own frame. The unattractive consequence of all this is that anthropologists who stubbornly resist the issue and the lessons of popularization face the prospect of marginalizing themselves, ultimately to their own detriment. Unless we are prepared to take seriously the power, place and meaning of popular anthropology, we may lose the ability to negotiate our intellectual position in the world at large.

On all these grounds, the study of popular anthropology is not peripheral but focal. For exactly who and what has become popular when, how, in what ways, for what reasons, and to what effect, are all themes which starkly illuminate the nature of the anthropological enterprise, its reception, its institutional development, and its possible futures. Hence this book.

We chose not to strait-jacket the discussion by imposing a singular definition of popularization. The 'academic' and the 'popular' are not rigid categories. They are fluid, multifarious terms whose meanings have changed as the discipline has evolved. They are only presented as a dichotomy in the rhetoric of self-interested players who wish to stake out their own position and polarize the opposition. (For examples of this strategy in other disciplines, see Dolby 1982; Gieryn 1983.) Our object is not to further binarism but to promote plurality. Instead of prescriptively confining the object of our interest, we wished contributors to explore the diversity of the topic and give some idea of the terrain that might be covered: its audiences, its foci, its styles, its varieties, its publishing contexts, its possible perils.

In a broad sense, there are as many different ways to 'popularize' anthropology as there are audiences for it. Besides the general book-reading public, we might list policy-makers (Hinshaw 1980), development consultants, management trainers (Chapman 1994), impresarios of corporate initiation ritual (e.g. Rae 1995), academics in other disciplines who wish to adopt ethnographic techniques (Chambers 1987: 313), artists whose knowledge of anthropology informs the vision of the world they project (Cowling 1989; Rhodes 1994: 177–92; Weiss 1995), viewers of television (Singer 1992; Banks 1994), nationalist politicians (MacClancy 1993; Efron 1994; Dubow 1995), advocates of sexual plurality (e.g. Bornstein 1995; Spencer 1995), folklore revivalists (Chandler 1993: 9, pers. comm.), socialist theorists (Trautmann 1987: 251–55), Neopagans, New Agers and Modern Primitives (Jencson 1989; Vale and Juno 1989; Grant 1995), Neoshamans (Atkinson 1993: 322–33; Vitebsky 1995), first-year students (James, in this volume), style analysts (e.g. York 1994), novelists (e.g. Huxley 1936; Cartwright 1993; Dooling 1995), nutritionists (Easton, Shostak and Konner 1989), and teachers of modern languages who want their students to do some 'fieldwork' during their study year abroad (Street 1992b). Furthermore, different styles of anthropology practised by the anthropologists of different nations may well produce variant ways of popularizing the discipline.

We have tried to represent some of these diversities within this volume but, like the editors of any collection, we were limited by the people we knew, the people we heard of, and the people we were able to contact and who responded positively. One restriction we felt forced to impose from the very beginning, in order to ensure that speakers might address overlapping issues, was a concern with literary forms of popularization. This is not to imply that we think the popularization of the discipline via other established media – such as museums (Karp, Kreamer and Lavine 1992) and television (Jenkins 1986; Ginsburg 1992; Turton 1992), multimedia, or new computer technologies less important or revelatory – but simply that the study of these modes of disseminating knowledge deserves books in its own right. There was not space in the original seminar series and conference to investigate adequately the issues they raised, so we excluded them. Though the resulting book does not represent in a comprehensive manner the diversities of popularization, the range of papers published still gives some idea of the potential breadth of the topic. Our aim, after all, was not to compile a definitive volume but to stimulate an overdue debate.

A BRIEF HISTORY OF POPULARIZATION

From the very beginning of an anthropology recognizable as such to modern anthropologists, its practitioners were concerned with popularization. But the chronicles of its evolution in the three main centres of modern anthropology – Britain, the United States, France – are revealingly different. For that reason, I trace each separately.

The Ethnological Society of London, founded in 1844, made its sole object the promotion and diffusion of ethnological knowledge. It held both special meetings, where 'popular' topics were discussed, and ordinary meetings, at which 'scientific' subjects were debated in more technical terms and to which women were not admitted. John Lubbock, president of the Society in the mid-1860s, wrote both of his books, *Pre-historic Times* (1865) and *The Origin of Civilization* (1870), in such a clear, engaging prose that they were extremely successful and reached a remarkably wide audience (Riviere 1978: xiv–xvi). A breakaway organization, the Anthropological Society, founded in 1863, gained over 500 members within the first two years of its existence, embarked on an ambitious publishing programme, and even put out a *Popular Magazine of Anthropology* (Stocking 1987: ch. 7). Its dynamic president, James Hunt, also established an 'Anthropological Lecturing Club', whose object was 'to diffuse a knowledge of Anthropology amongst all classes of society'.

These pioneers, whether styling themselves 'ethnologists' or 'anthropologists', had a broad conception of their subject as one embracing prehistory, archaeology, physical anthropology and the study of the customs of contemporary non-urban peoples, in both the West and beyond. However, the ruling groups of both societies tended to come from different backgrounds, to have somewhat different goals, and to rely on different sources of information. Most leading members of the Ethnological Society, who came from dissenting middle-class families, upheld liberal, humanitarian and utilitarian ideals, and maintained the utopian belief that the sustained efforts of education and science would result in a better society. Darwinian evolutionists, they drew upon archaeological and ethnographic data in their endeavour to elucidate historically the single common origin of all human groups (ibid.). In contrast, James Hunt and his clique were conservatives who came from marginal positions within more traditionally established social backgrounds. Polygenists keen to detail the supposedly fundamental differences between the races of humankind, they stressed the value of physical anthropology. Unlike the 'Ethnologicals', these heterodox Tories were quite prepared to win popularity by being extreme, using anthropological theories as direct support for their political views and provoking discussion on controversial issues: cutting back funds for African missions, defending the brutal suppression of the Jamaican Rebellion of 1865, and arguing against female emancipation (Rainger 1978). However, Hunt's club incurred increasing debts and its membership began to decline. After his death in 1869, the new president of the 'Anthropologicals' agreed to compromise and, in 1871, the two societies amalgamated into 'The Anthropological Institute of Great Britain and Ireland', which the old 'Ethnologicals' soon came to control.

All the members of the fledgling Institute were either gentlemen amateurs, or professionals engaged in other areas of scholarly or scientific activity. None of them regarded themselves as 'anthropologists' but as intellectuals who occasionally studied anthropological themes: Lubbock was a natural scientist, politician, financier and social reformer; Maine was a professor of jurisprudence and a colonial administrator. Those whom we may regard as the first true anthropological professionals only emerged in the last decades of the century, from the small group of full-time paid curators entrusted with the care of ethnographic collections.

At that time in Britain, self-education was an accepted means of upward mobility among the middle and upper working classes, and museums were the most successful centres for the popularization of academic knowledge (Van Keuren 1984: 172). Ethnographic curators, who had to compete against the attractions of travelling shows of exotic peoples staged by entrepreneurs and at least one anthropologist (George Catlin), were keen to justify their positions by claiming that their institutions provided 'rational amusement', and that they were visited by members of all social classes, and especially by a large section of the working class (Altick 1978: 268–87; Street 1992a). To that end they tried to make their collections as accessible as possible. The curators of the Horniman Museum in London, for instance, held a regular series of lectures open to the general public and took great pains to make explicit the rationale behind their selection and display of material. Public demand was so great that, within a few years of opening its doors, the Horniman was receiving over 90,000 visitors a year (Coombes 1994: 113, 154). This initial cohort of professionals also assisted in the presentation of anthropological materials in national and international exhibitions, which were then, like museums, a major means of popular education and the largest of which could attract tens of millions of visitors. For example, in 1908 Haddon organized the anthropological section of the grand Franco–British Exhibition and supervised a display on comparative religion in the London Missionary Society exhibition 'The Orient in London', writing an erudite introduction to the handbook for its 'Hall of Religions' (Haddon 1909; Coombes 1994: 204).

Tylor in the 1870s and Haddon two decades later furthered the name of their subject by writing and reviewing for a variety of major periodicals and by lecturing widely (Quiggin 1942: 115–21; Leopold 1980: 19). To this end they were assisted by the prolific Andrew Lang, whose articles and reviews in the press and prestigious journals generated great general interest in anthropology, and, more indirectly, by popular British authors of the period whose novels made contemporary anthropological theories 'deeply actual' (De Cocq 1968: 127; Street 1975). Haddon, who lacked tenure for much of his life, also wrote several popular books. His bestseller, *Evolution in Art* (1895) gained wide attention because leading art historians saw it as a challenge, which deserved reply, to their view of art as a work of individual, inspired genius.

As the title of that work suggests, Victorian and Edwardian anthropologists were able to sell so many books and to fill lecture-halls so easily because they contributed to one of the great public debates of their time: the status and practical consequences of evolutionary theory. Lubbock's brand of evolutionism, with its euphoric ideas on the advantages of 'scientific' anthropology and the future of humankind, was 'very congenial to many of his contemporary readers' (Riviere 1978: xlii). Tylor proclaimed anthropology to be a 'reformer's science' which could be employed, among other ways, to identify illiberal survivals fit only for elimination. Pitt Rivers, arguing from an opposite political position, thought an anthropology museum laid out on evolutionist lines would demonstrate the necessity of gradualistic change and so help to dissuade workers from heeding the calls of revolutionaries (Van Keuren 1984: 187). These evolutionist anthropologists were all aware of the great role their discipline could play in the running of the Empire. As Henry Balfour, first curator of the Pitt Rivers Museum at Oxford, argued, 'the proper understanding of native races and their relationship to each other is a matter of vital importance to us, if we are to govern justly and intelligently the very heterogeneous peoples who come under our sway' (Balfour 1904: 13). But the repeated attempts to convince the British Government to create a Bureau of Anthropology or to fund the training of colonial officers came to nothing. Similarly, though the criminological work of anthropologists such as Cesare Lombroso influenced popular culture and informed political debate, the Government chose not to implement its findings (Pick 1989). For British anthropology to survive, it had, for the time being, to rely on the support of fellow academics and on the indirect benefits of public interest.

Some anthropologists of this period classified their work as either 'technical' or 'popular', but the distinction between these categories was usually negligible. Though some of their writings might assume more knowledge on the readers' part than others, almost everything they wrote could be understood by any informed person of their time. Their discourse, after all, was the same as that of their educated contemporaries. Giving public lectures or writing books did not involve any gross oversimplification of complex theories or tortuous translation from some erudite dialect. To that extent, the promoters of the discipline were not so much concerned with popularization (in the sense of being a distinctive practice markedly different from contemporary scholastic endeavour), as with dissemination of their ideas and materials to increase people's acquaintance with the subject. Of course, some Victorian anthropologists were much less popular than others, partly because they did not present their arguments in an effective manner. Who today remembers, for instance, the work of Charles Staniland Wake (Needham 1967: xiv), a learned, imaginative anthropologist yet one who only wrote for readers almost as knowledgeable about kinship and marriage as he, and whose prose, compared to the attractive clarity of Tylor's, is stilted and unrewarding?

In several ways Sir James G. Frazer marks both the highpoint and the endpoint of the historical period that I have related so far. Frazer marks the highpoint, for he remains today the most famous, and certainly the most financially successful, of all British anthropologists. His books are still in print and his influence astonishingly widespread: his ideas have made themselves felt in almost every area of the humanities and the social sciences while, within literature, Conrad, Eliot, Pound, Yeats, Synge, Lawrence, Iris Murdoch, Saul Bellow and Norman Mailer are only the most illustrious among the generations of writers indebted to him (Fraser 1990). Indeed, given his effect on the content, structure and rhetoric of twentieth-century novels and poems, one literary historian has gone so far as to argue that *The Golden Bough* is 'in a very real measure, responsible for the form and shape of modern literature' (Vickery 1973: 120; also Manganaro 1992). By the 1920s it had become essential reading for anyone with claims to an education or a critical attitude to life; hundreds wrote to its author thanking him for opening their eyes and changing their lives (Howarth 1978: 131; Ackerman 1987: 3).

Frazer marks the endpoint, for he was the last prominent member of those generations of anthropologists who tried in their writings to establish a closeness between themselves and their readers. In contrast, Malinowski's contemporaries and students wished to bracket off their ethnography as a professionally distinct form of intellectual exercise which, by using their experience of fieldwork as a legitimating device, created simultaneously a distance between themselves and their readers, and a closeness between themselves and the societies they studied (Strathern 1987). Lubbock, Tylor, Frazer and their peers spoke as though from their armchairs, to people who were in a similar position. Malinowski and his peers spoke as though from the village hut, to people who had never been in a similar position. Yet the number of anthropologists was still so low that those of the interwar generation, like their predecessors, had to write their books with both academic and non-academic audiences in mind. To that extent the functionalist ethnographies of the 1920s and 1930s may be regarded as works of 'popular' (i.e. relatively non-technical) anthropology.

Frazer's career also marks the transition from a broad conception of anthropology, produced by well-educated amateurs and museum curators, to a more fragmented form of the discipline, produced by tenured academics who specialized in one of its branches: most social anthropologists studied the behaviour of present-day peoples, most physical anthropologists studied the biological dimensions of humankind and their evolution. Prehistory and archaeology became separate disciplines, ones of marginal interest to most modern anthropologists. The leading proponent, and most skilled promoter, of a self-defined modern form of social anthropology, one marked off from historically related intellectual endeavours, was Bronislaw Malinowski. Since evolutionism was by then falling out of popular favour (and with its decline went much of the market for anthropology), Malinowski was much concerned with ways of making his new brand of the discipline known to the general public and of winning respect for it within intellectual circles (Firth pers. comm.; Malinowski 1967: 160). In the process of attempting to achieve these aims he would aggrandize himself to an extent that has yet to be equalled by a modern British anthropologist.

On returning, jobless, from fieldwork in the Trobriand Islands, the unknown anthropologist tried to establish his reputation – and make a little money – by writing a readable book acceptable to a commercial publisher. Shortly after *Argonauts of the Western Pacific* (1922) was published and he had gained the financial security of a permanent lectureship at the London School of Economics, Malinowski diversified his attempts to spread his name beyond the confines of his chosen discipline. In 1923, his essay 'On the Problem of Meaning of Primitive Language' was appended to Ogden and Richards's highly successful *The Meaning of Meaning*, so bringing his work to the attention of, among others, philosophers, linguists, psychologists and literary critics (Leach 1965: 35). Almost immediately afterwards, Malinowski made his bid to revise Freud, by using the evidence of his Trobriand material to question the supposed universality of the Oedipus complex (Stocking 1986). Though orthodox Freudians summarily rebuffed his challenge to their position, his controversial endeavour gave him an immediate entree to the intellectual left-wing circles of London social life, where he soon made his mark. His views became slogans of progressive morality and education, and won him influential friends, such as Bertrand Russell and Julian Huxley. Havelock Ellis became an especial friend (Russell 1929: ch. 2, 1968: 195–6; Mitchison 1979: 54; Leach 1965; Grosskurth 1980: 380; Firth 1981: 114).

Malinowski's main anthropological competitors at this time were the diffusionists, centred around Grafton Elliot Smith who held a professorship at University College London. Elliot Smith, keen to raise public support for his approach, was an assiduous correspondent to *The Times* and prestigious weeklies on matters diffusionist; edited a series of books entitled 'In the Beginning of Things', mainly written by academics, aimed at the popular market; and managed to attract a number of colonial administrators and cadets to his courses (Kuklick 1991). In order to counter Elliot Smith's attempt to win disciplinary supremacy, to broaden acceptance of his kind of anthropology, to gain funding for his students and for posts, and to improve his chances of enlightening government policy towards colonized peoples, Malinowski began in the late 1920s and 1930s to preach the pragmatic benefits of his functionalism (Symonolewicz 1955: 49; Strenski 1987a: 42–69), even if it meant moving away from the immediately popular:

> More and more modern anthropological research is being directed to such aspects of human civilization as economics, education, law, demography, hygiene and systems of nutrition, which are apparently commonplace and drab, but nevertheless fundamental ... This change of front in anthropological research is mainly due to the fact that, like every other science, anthropology has had to show its practical utility or become disqualified as an idle mental game.
>
> (Malinowski 1934: xvii–xviii)

To that discipline-saving end, Malinowski contributed to non-academic periodicals a host of articles which trumpeted the virtues of anthropology and its usefulness for the solution of moral and practical quandaries: he was particularly concerned about problems of sex and marriage, and of social change, especially in Africa (Firth 1988: 35; Stocking 1991: 53, 60). At the same time, and for much the same purposes, he welcomed to his famous LSE seminars a variety of non-academics, such as visiting missionaries, colonial officials, merchants, Africans (most notably Jomo Kenyatta) and the founders of Mass Observation (Robeson 1945: 14–15; Delf 1961: 99; Murray-Brown 1972: 188–9; Huxley 1985: 195–7; Berman and Lonsdale 1989: 160–1; Kuklick 1991: 212). They all felt there was something practical they could learn from the subject.

In the last decade of his life Malinowski maintained his place in the public arena by writing forewords for books by colleagues and associates, not just in anthropology but in psychoanalysis, analytical psychology and political studies as well; by sitting on the editorial boards of progressive journals such as *The Realist*; and, above all, by employing his anthropological knowledge to argue in numerous public lectures, several popular articles, and one book against fascism and modern warfare.

Malinowski's efforts paid off. Colonial administrators came to regard the intensive study of peoples under their tutelage as much more potentially pertinent to their needs than anthropometry or diffusionist theories. Indeed, the idea of fieldwork was such a winning innovation that the Rockefeller Foundation stopped funding the research of diffusionists *because* they did not live with the peoples they studied. Instead, together with the Carnegie Foundation and various British colonial and European governments, it financially supported the establishment and underwrote the running costs of the International Institute for African Languages and Cultures. This body, later renamed the International African Institute, was dominated by British interests and provided the grants for a whole host of Malinowski's students to do fieldwork (Kuklick 1991: ch. 5; Stocking 1992: 193–207).

Malinowski's popularizing efforts also paid off, acquaintance with his fieldwork-backed form of anthropology becoming part of the assumed cultural knowledge of educated Britons. In 1932 Q. D. Leavis referred to her *Fiction and the Reading Public* as an 'anthropological' study of English culture; when, five years later, Mass Observation started to recruit assistants, the idea of the need for an 'anthropology at home' had already become common (Calder n.d.: 91). Two years before that, Charles Duff, a successful satirist, had chosen to couch his needle-sharp lampoon of the hypocritical mores of suburban Londoners in the form of an ethnography 'based totally on fieldwork'. According to this intrepid observer, fear was the basis of locals' morality, money the only religion, birth, marriage and death 'Important Financial Events', and artists taboo. The pen-name which Duff gave himself for this sustained piece of irony was Professor V. Chernichewski.

As this back-handed compliment suggests, Malinowski had successfully turned himself into a very well-known figure. By the time of his death, Kluckhohn (1943: 208) went so far as to claim that 'Certainly no anthropologist has ever had so wide a popular audience. Thousands of laymen in many countries came to entertain with fervour the attitude of an anthropology whose methods, purposes and results had at last become intelligible.' When, in August 1936, he was invited as one of the distinguished guests to the Harvard Tercentenary

Celebrations, Malinowski's name drew such a large audience to his lecture (on 'Culture as a Determinant of Behaviour'), 'that the very large commodious hall filled long before the time scheduled for the lecture to begin, in spite of the fact that Sir Arthur Eddington and other world-renowned scientists were lecturing in nearby halls at the same time' (Montagu 1942: 148).

The majority of British social anthropologists, however, secure in recently founded university posts, did not adopt Malinowski's general approach. Evans-Pritchard, hegemon of British anthropology from the 1940s on, was not interested in broadening the audience for anthropology. Essentially a very private man not given to Malinowskian excess, he had no wish to make a space for himself in the public arena. His students and most of his peers evinced little desire to occupy that space themselves. Unlike Malinowski, they were not 'easily drawn into the seductive but somewhat elusive field of reflection' on matters of public concern (Firth 1981: 125). Their research funding assured, through their effective control of the British Government's Colonial Social Science Research Council, they proceeded to carry out studies which were decreasingly relevant to the requirements of colonial administrators (Kuklick 1991: 191). On the whole, postwar British anthropologists, if offered the chance to extend the reach of their subject, preferred to enlighten colleagues in related professions, such as medicine and health. They also showed little enthusiasm for the promotion of the teaching of anthropology in secondary schools, as it was thought that the discipline required students with reasonably mature minds, ones capable of handling fairly abstract conceptions. Otherwise the subject would end up being taught as merely a variant of human geography or descriptive ethnography. For the professoriate of the period it was far more attractive to stage graduate seminars in a Socratic manner than to simplify the subject for schoolchildren.

Until the 1930s, most anthropological articles and books could be read by any educated person with a sense of dedication. But within two decades the language of university-based anthropologists had become sufficiently abstruse and their analyses sufficiently arcane as to bar the majority of readers who had not been trained in the subject. In 1928, Elliot Smith and Malinowski had aired their opposed views in a small book intended for a general audience (Elliot Smith *et al.* 1928). By the late 1940s, such a book had become almost inconceivable. In this postwar context of disciplinary specialization, where the gap between the scholastic and the popular grew ever greater, writing a book for the extra-academic market was no longer a matter of choosing the appropriate literary style but had become a testing exercise in translation from one discourse into another. And most anthropologists were not interested in the job, or not up to it.

Since Malinowski had already done the groundwork for his students, establishing the value of a fieldwork-based functionalism at academic, practical and popular levels, they and their peers chose to narrow their vision to an almost totally scholastic one and made their highest priority writing the sort of books 'which could help to construct the foundations of theoretical analysis in a new mode' (Firth 1975: 3; also Evans-Pritchard 1946). Though they were prepared to give the occasional public address, to speak on the radio when requested (e.g. Evans-Pritchard 1951), to teach extra-mural students from time to time, and to produce introductory books when asked to do so (e.g. Beattie 1964; Lienhardt 1964; Pocock 1975; Lewis 1976), they were on the whole far more concerned with developing their own discipline than with imparting the results to a wider audience. (The one, striking, exception was the almost irrepressible Edmund Leach, whose prestigious position, clarity of style and network of contacts enabled him to write for a broad range of popular weeklies.) Haddon (1903: 21) might have complained that anthropologists were too little concerned with popular exposition, but most of his successors disagreed. As far as they were concerned, theory was to come first. Popularization could come later.

While social anthropologists were unprepared to popularize their discipline, ethologists were not so reticent. In fact, their books have sold so well that large sectors of the British public now regard the ethologists' work as being as representative of 'anthropology' as that carried out by their fieldworking colleagues. In social gatherings in Britain today, saying one is an anthropologist usually leads to some jokey comment about 'naked apesters'. What Konrad Lorenz (1966), Desmond Morris (1969), Robert Ardrey (1967; 1976), and Lionel Tiger and Robin Fox (1972), among others, did was to revive the evolutionary paradigm which post-Victorian anthropologists had worked so hard to counter. Oversimplifying their material for the sake of their potential audiences, these biological determinists interpreted social behaviour in neo-Darwinian terms, often tying their evolutionary narrative down with a single explanatory thread: in Ardrey's case, territory (later, hunting); in Lorenz's, aggression; in Tiger and Fox's, 'biogrammar'. Perhaps the only significant difference between these latterday social evolutionists and their Victorian predecessors was that the former had nonhuman (but anthropomorphized) primates play the same explanatory role which 'primitives' had had to play before.

The reaction to the male-centred and generally conservative tone of these ethological writings came in a series of popular books from academics, such as Goodall (1971) and Montagu (1968), and non-academics, such as Morgan (1972) and Reed (1975). But, as Haraway (1992: 127) observes, neither Morgan nor Reed were a match for their credentialled opponents, while Montagu's prose could not compare with that of Lorenz, Morris, or Tiger. Sperling (1991: 14), in a review of the work of these male authors, has claimed that the influence of their models 'on popular perceptions of the relationships of humans to animals and of the meanings of the gender divisions has been profound'. Yet a public lecturer (Towers 1972) who toured halls in the United States and Britain in the late 1960s found, to his surprise, that most people had read Morris's *The Naked Ape* purely for amusement and general interest: few appeared to have accepted its reductionist thesis. My own personal experience, as a teacher of social anthropology, is that a high percentage of introductory students, when asked to account for a particular social behaviour, provide biologistic explanations, and it can prove very difficult indeed to persuade them to rethink their approach or to expand their vision. Though the popular fashion for ethology has passed, to be partially replaced by sociobiology, the more popular works of sociobiologists (e.g. Wilson 1975; 1978; Dawkins 1976) appear to have had relatively little specific effect on the public. Rather, they seem to have bolstered, in a general manner, people's predispositions to comprehend their social lives along evolutionist lines.

The seemingly idyllic situation of British social anthropology changed dramatically in the late 1970s as the Government began to reduce severely its contribution to university budgets and its funds for research (Riviere 1989). One reaction to this threat to the British anthropological community was the creation of voluntary organizations concerned with various forms of applied anthropology, most of which in 1988 combined to constitute the British Association for Social Anthropology in Policy and Practice (Shore and Wright n.d.). But while some British anthropologists have been prepared, in this way, to find new justifications for the continued existence of their discipline, almost none has attempted to broaden its popular audience. The only significant exception here is Nigel Barley (see Chapter Eleven). His lampoons of fieldwork, however, have been as heavily criticized within the anthropological community as they have been praised beyond it.

By this time, television had become as important as books and articles in popularizing the discipline. According to a recent survey, the most common way that anthropology students become aware of the subject is through ethnographic films and anthropological programmes on television ('Report on RAI questionnaire', *Anthropology Today*, February 1990; also Loizos 1980: 577). Thus we could characterize the evolution of the popularization of anthropology as a development from primarily visual means – in museums and international exhibitions – in the nineteenth and early twentieth centuries, by way of predominantly literary means – in books and articles – in the period from 1920s to the mid-1970s, to, once again, mainly visual means – television.

The course of American anthropology over the same period somewhat mirrored that of its British counterpart: a wide-ranging subject, primarily reliant on gentlemen scholars and museum staff, developed into a set of separate but related disciplines run by professionals and based in universities. During the nineteenth century, the premier anthropological institution in the country was the National Museum, founded for the 'increase and diffusion of knowledge among men'. Its pious curators, who regarded themselves as the moral educators of their visitors, sought to confirm the divine purpose for this world by demonstrating the ordered evolution and diversity of humankind, a message they furthered at World's Fairs where they were frequently given whole buildings to display their exhibits, and where they were permitted to take anthropometric measurements of the exotic peoples on show (Hinsley 1981; Benedict 1983; Rydell 1984). The 'tribal villages' created at these expositions inspired circuses to enlarge their own displays of exotic peoples. The featured attraction of Barnum and Bailey's 1893–5 show was 'the Great Ethnological Congress', a assembly of 74 non-Western people displayed in the menagerie tent (Bogdan 1988: 185). Whatever the worthy curators thought of these cheap exhibits, a change in government policy in the 1900s forced them to shift their Museum's focus from educating the public to entertaining it. In consequence, over the next two decades the role of museums as centres for anthropology began to be overshadowed by the rise of academic departments, whose fieldworkers were financed by research councils and private foundations. The most prominent of these departments was that at Columbia, headed by Franz Boas.

Boas, patriarch of modern American cultural anthropology, was by conviction a progressive, committed both to a rationalistic understanding of the world and to the need to defend the validity of alternative cultural visions of the world (Stocking 1992: 97). Opposed to a rigid evolutionism which prematurely classified peoples into distinct races, he spent much of the later part of his career researching into, writing popular articles on, and publicly battling against the racist confusion of physical and cultural attributes. In Britain, it was biologists who led the scientific campaign to discredit racism (Malinowski played only a minor role in its public refutation); in the United States, it was anthropologists, headed by Boas, who led the crusade (Barkan 1992). In the process, Boas educated a sector of the public in the difference between the older, broad-based anthropology and the newer, more narrowly defined cultural version of the discipline which he, his colleagues and their students were propounding.

Though the Boasian message of cultural relativity was promoted by many of his circle (e.g. Herskovits [Merriam 1964; Jackson 1986]) in a variety of newspapers and weeklies, it was spread much, much wider, to almost all sections of the American literate public, by a single book produced by one of his former students. Ruth Benedict's *Patterns of Culture* (1934), perhaps *the* bestselling work of American anthropology, also served to popularize the broader notion of 'culture' as not just the 'higher' arts but as a people's whole way of life. Six years later she, as progressive as her mentor, again transmitted some of Boas's ideas to a wider public in her *Race, Science and Politics* (Caffrey 1989). The pamphlet she produced with Gene Weltfish on the same topic, *The Races of Mankind* (1940), went into millions of copies, and was then made into a film, a comic and a children's book (Mead 1949: 460). Her last book, *The Chrysanthemum and the Sword*, another publishing success, was one of the bestselling anthropological works of the postwar world.

It was another of Boas's students, however, who was to achieve the most extensive, most consistent popularization of cultural anthropology. Unlike her friend Benedict, who was primarily interested in changing people's values, Margaret Mead was primarily interested in winning, and maintaining, fame. By making each of her books provide an answer to a topical question of current interest and by lecturing from every podium to which she could gain access, she soon achieved her desire. By doing so, the 'Grandmother of the World' kept anthropology in the public eye right up to the year of her death in 1978, demonstrating that there was almost no social problem on which she (and by implication, others in the discipline) could not pronounce.

The number of departments of anthropology in America had already begun to rise in the 1930s, but it was in the postwar decades that they went through a period of spectacular growth. Universities established hundreds of posts, while the National Institute of Mental Health, the National Science Foundation, and, from the 1960s on, the Ford Foundation funded a broad range of research. Applied anthropology, whose heyday had been the war years, languished during this period. Unlike Boas, the leading anthropologists of the postwar years did not believe that the pursuit of rationalistic approaches would almost inevitably lead to social progress; they were less interested in trying to influence contemporary issues of public import than in elaborating the theoretical sophistication of the discipline. But in the 1970s, as the period of expansion came to an end in the universities, as the supply of government funds was cut back, and as an increasing number of practitioners became dissatisfied with an anthropology that seemed primarily turned in upon itself, more and more began to spend their time utilizing their distinctive methodologies to study problems in education, medicine and related areas. Yet no anthropologist with anything like the public stature of Mead has emerged in this period. No one has been able to put the anthropological message across, to a comparable extent, to non-academic audiences. In fact the two most popular American social anthropologists of the last twenty years – Carlos Castenada and Michael Harner (Atkinson 1993: 322) – have, unlike Mead, not been concerned with topics such as the relevance of anthropology in the formulation of public policy. Instead they have appealed, through their espousals, respectively, of ritualized drug-taking and neo-shamanism, to those who reject a Western-based rationalistic approach to the world.

The development of the subject in France followed a somewhat different course compared to its evolution in Britain or the United States. In the nineteenth century, learned societies of gentlemen scholars interested in a wide-ranging (but predominantly physical) anthropology were founded whose members, like their Anglo-Saxon counterparts, participated in the establishment and running of anthropological museums, sponsored public lectures, and assisted in, and so helped to legitimate, popular ethnographic exhibitions (Bender 1965; Schneider 1982: ch. 6). However, unlike the British and American anthropologies of that time, which were not seen to constitute a grave threat to the established moral order, French anthropology was popularly identified very strongly with anti-authoritarianism and anticlericalism. In 1859 Paul Broca was only allowed, after much negotiation, to found the Société d'Anthropologie on the condition that a plainclothes policeman attend its meetings to ensure that the discussion did not move on to seditious or morally outrageous themes. In the later decades of the century, Broca's intellectual successors blended left-wing politics with evolutionism in order to produce a combative anthropology with which to fight against the forces of reaction and to promote social change (Hammond 1980).

Given these sorts of predecessors, it is perhaps unsurprising that, in 1913, Marcel Mauss (1969 [1913]) and his colleagues were lamenting the lack of interest displayed by the government of the day in funding research or posts; Mauss had argued for the establishment of a Bureau d'Ethnologie on the grounds of its potential theoretical and practical importance (for the efficient administration of French colonies), but his attempts had come to nothing. If official attitudes were to be reversed, it was necessary, Mauss and his peers thought, to popularize the discipline. The contemporary vogue for astronomy among the general public was, to a great extent, due to the popularizing work of the Parisian scientist Flammarion; what was now needed, one of them argued, was a Flammarion of anthropology. Yet, unlike Boas, Mauss and his circle did not try to correct public prejudices about the racist muddling of biological and social factors, and the only exception to this rule, Henri Hubert (Strenski 1987b), buried his work in learned journals.

Shortly after the end of the First World War, Paul Rivet, a physical anthropologist and director of the Musée d'Ethnographie du Trocadero, took advantage of the recent fashionable interest in *le primitif* (stimulated by the work of Picasso and other Modernists), to raise money for the founding of the Institut Français d'Ethnologie, for ethnographic expeditions, and for the reorganization of his dilapidated, shambolic museum, which he wanted to be a 'marvellous instrument of popular education'. 'Let us open the doors of culture' became his clarion call. The results are plain: the Institut, backed financially by the Minister of Colonies and the governors of several colonial governments, held its inaugural classes in 1925; the first of what was to be a long series of well-publicized field trips started out the following year. The Colonial Exposition of 1931, in which anthropologists participated, greatly stimulated public interest in the subject, and the new Musée de l'Homme finally opened its doors in 1937 (Riviere 1968; Clifford 1988; Fournier 1994: 502–12, 595–612).

Despite the well-publicized efforts of Rivet and his peers, however, a distinctively *social* anthropology remained a marginal discipline. In 1929 the rather unworldly Mauss had tried to attract Rockefeller money for the establishment of a grand institute of social science, broadly defined; one of its first tasks would be an ethnographic study of Paris which, he thought, would popularize the discipline and the institute. But the Rockefeller directors had regarded his proposal as utopic, and had given their money to a French economist instead (Fournier 1994: 547–51). It was not until the 1950s that the government began to create a substantial number of teaching and research positions (Karady 1972; 1981; n.d.)

Though the subject was institutionally peripheral, it was, and has been, kept in the public eye, of at least the educated sectors of the French populace (who study philosophy in their final years at secondary school), partly because many of its practitioners since the time of Mauss and Lévy-Bruhl have regarded its findings as of direct relevance to contemporary philosophical debate. In this century, one version or another of French social anthropology has never been far from the interests of the avant-garde.

The great postwar exemplar of this tradition is Lévi-Strauss, who was prepared to criticize Sartre, was happy to engage in public debate with philosophers, and remains ready to pass general comments on ultimate questions. In many ways a *philosophe* and *moraliste* in the true eighteenth-century manner (Crozier 1964; Hughes 1968), his best-selling *Tristes Tropiques* may be regarded as an extremely skilful weaving together of autobiography, ethnography and philosophical reflection posing under the genre of travelogue. After Sartre's death, he became the latest intellectual hero and master-thinker of his country (roles unknown in contemporary British or American culture); yet even before then, structuralism had already replaced existentialism as the dominant intellectual fashion (Pace 1986). Some French journalists (see Chapter Seven), however, have criticized Lévi-Strauss because they found his methodology too 'scientific' to be of assistance in answering the big questions of their day. Though it is true that he, unlike Sartre, has not offered the educated French public a metaphysics with moral worth, but an ultra-formal method of seemingly limited relevance beyond the *laboratoire*, and though most intelligent lay persons cannot comprehend the intricacies of his, at times, arcane analyses, the popular prestige of his structuralism is almost unassailable, while the power of his prose and the brilliance of his vision have been strong enough to attract dozens of budding intellectuals into the discipline. Indeed Needham (1984) has argued that the popularity of Lévi-Strauss does not rely on the content of his intellectual endeavours, but rather on the idiosyncrasies of the man himself:

> the 'poetic' quality in his writing; his very obscurities can be seen as enigmatic and hence profound; there are intimations of great mysteries, refractions of perennial insights, echoes of oracular utterances. His vision is hermetical, and his writings have prospered because they promise to reveal what is hidden, the occult factors by which human experience is shaped.
>
> (Needham 1984: 393)

On this interpretation, Lévi-Strauss, who joined the circle of exiled surrealists in wartime New York, emerges as the Last of the Great Surrealists, whose almost cabbalistic writings 'evoke a response liberated from the confinements of exactitude and logic' (ibid.).

FOCUS

The reasons why anthropology is popular at any particular moment are various and changing. A central factor is people's perennial curiosity about 'the exotic', a labile, evolving category, which may simultaneously represent the industrialized West both as its hegemonic opposite and as its counter-hegemonic realization, both as an inversion of publicly promoted values and as an example of privately recognized counter-values. 'The exotic' is at one and the same time a source of both repulsion and attraction, of both horror and fascination, and, properly presented, it sells. The more fluently written of the mid-Victorian anthropological literature on the varieties of kinship and marriage, for instance (Tuzin 1994), attracted such a wide readership partly because their authors' accounts of 'primitive promiscuity', alternative connubial arrangements, and other such matters helped to satisfy the sublimated sensuality of their contemporaries. Though 'the exotic' is historically contingent, some topics seem to have a long-standing allure. Hunters and gatherers in tropical climes have especially intrigued romanticizing Westerners (e.g. Van der Post 1958) who perceive them as living examples of a primal, authentic humanity now irrevocably lost by Euro–Americans. Shamanism, with its appeal of wildness and transgression, has long interested those reacting to the hierarchies and institutions of more organized religions (Thomas and Humphrey 1994: 2).

While the importance of popular interest in the foreign, the wondrous and the strange is not to be underestimated, those anthropologists whose writings have sold particularly well have been above all those who, whether intentionally or not, have been best able to cater to the particular interests of their lay contemporaries. Most of those academics successful in the extra-academic market have been those most capable of dealing, directly or indirectly, in a convincing manner with subjects central to some of the main social, religious and scientific issues of the day. If 'Where have we come from? What are we? Where are we going?' are queries raised whenever the answers provided by established faiths seem insufficient, there have usually been some anthropologists ready to formulate new responses, ones of great appeal to large sections of the public.

A key reason for the spectacular success of Frazer was that he was both encyclopaedic of ethnographic data and eclectic of contemporary intellectual fashions. According to Vickery (1973: 4–6, 33–4), he wove together the central strands of thought of his age – J. S. Mill's rationalism, Matthew Arnold's historicism, and T. H. Huxley's evolutionary and scientific outlook – with the contemporary passion for classical and other mythologies. By exploring the interrelated ways of the Ancients, rural Europeans and tribal peoples, he simultaneously civilized the apparently savage and subtly savaged the supposedly civilized. At a time when the unchecked forces of industrialization and imperialism were violently changing the nature of British society and its place in the world, at a time when Britons' conceptions of the rural and the urban, the past and the present, the indigenous and the foreign, the religious and the secular, were all undergoing radical revision, Frazer's works proposed a learned but readable response to the questions people posed and to the doubts they harboured. Instead of relying on the old verities, he proffered a cultured agnosticism as the only appropriate attitude to adopt in his time. And, just as possession of the Golden Bough had enabled Virgil's Aeneas to enter the underworld and return, so could Frazer's book act as a vade-mecum for those who wished to tour the Other and learn from the experience (Beard 1992: 223). As the historian of Greek religion Jane Harrison put it, 'Sir James has a veritable genius for titles . . . at the mere sounds of the magical words "Golden Bough", we heard and understood' (Harrison 1925: 82).

The main reasons for Ruth Benedict's success are formally similar to those for Frazer's: she was an exceptional synthesizer and her moral concerns echoed those of an increasing proportion of the population. Writing at a time when (and contributing to the process whereby) anthropology was replacing natural history as a source of scientific moral authority in the United States, she demonstrated the changeability of convention from society to society, and so questioned both the authority of tradition in the America of her day and the degree to which people's behaviour is inherent. In place of a rigid Victorian morality, whose underpinnings had already been weakened by philosophers, physicists and artists, she put forward a more supple ethics, one based on relative, not absolute values, one where chaos and order could coexist, where self and society could come to a harmonious compromise (Caffrey 1989). Benedict offered her readers, in sum, a moral position from which to judge, and act in, the world.

The Chrysanthemum and the Sword was a bestseller not only in the English-speaking world but also, rather unexpectedly, in Japan itself, as many Japanese thought it an acute, if provocative, characterization of themselves. If the 1987 survey quoted by Hendry (see Chapter Four) can be believed, maybe as many as *twenty million* Japanese have read Benedict's book. Even though she never learnt the language nor visited the country, her book sparked off a national debate, which continues to this day, about the nature of Japanese identity. Even though her work, especially her distinction between shame and guilt, suffered in translation, it is still regarded as genuine source material and as a classic which must be confronted by any indigenous scholar wishing to discuss the nature of Japanese uniqueness. In this unforeseen manner *The Chrysanthemum and the Sword* has become an integral part of the indigenous way of life itself, influencing its trajectory and its members' conceptions of themselves. It is the first, and perhaps still the only, example of a deliberately popular ethnography being transformed into an ethnographic text of which subsequent ethnographers of the area must take account. It is the clearest instance yet of an anthropological book fomenting dialogue between the populace and the academy, between subjects and anthropologists, between texts and readers.

Like Benedict, Margaret Mead regarded anthropology as a potentially positive force for social change which, properly transmitted, could influence people's values and beliefs. Unlike Benedict, who was a very shy person, Mead was a particularly forceful personality who was almost always prepared to opine publicly, in an at times very direct manner on matters of general interest, whether it were child-rearing, disarmament, race relations, feminism, or the drug culture which arose in the 1960s (Gardner 1996). As one of her colleagues put it, 'She had a fine sense of what was current and was often diligent in thinking about and publishing readable books and articles on what was coming up in the many shifting preoccupations of her lifetime' (quoted in Howard 1984: 167). Another portrayed her more sharply as 'proffering ideas like mannequins in a fashion book, pausing when she recognized that she had touched a responsive chord' (quoted in Grosskurth 1988: 65). In *Coming of Age in Samoa*, Mead contested the notion that adolescence was necessarily a period of stress and strain independent of local cultural conditions; in *Growing up in New Guinea* she questioned the belief in the natural creativity of children and claimed to have demonstrated that they needed to be given freedom in order to evolve rich ways of life for themselves; in *Sex and Temperament in Three Primitive Societies*, she argued against the dominant sexual ideology, grounded on a bogus biology, of men as born aggressors and women as naturally passive. While prepared to attack values and practices she disagreed with, Mead was ready to shower praise on some behaviours, ones which many Americans held dear, such as caring and friendship, and she liked to reassure her audiences with optimistic messages, such as that failure was only the inability to think positively (Grosskurth 1988: 75). Never a gloomy doomsayer, she transmitted to audiences her unshakeable conviction that any of them could choose to develop themselves in more or less the way they wished, and they cleaved to her belief in their possibilities.

Malinowski never achieved anything like the degree of popularity enjoyed by Frazer, Benedict, or Mead. Though he was prepared to speak out on the radio or in brief articles, in none of his major works did he *directly* address the moral issues of his day or offer an alternative ethics for a renovated society. Some of his ethnographies, however, did gain a certain renown, or even notoriety, among the more literate members of the public. While Malinowski did win something of a reputation among certain circles as a moral crusader, the primary basis of his popularity seems to have been educated laypersons' interest in authoritative, authentic accounts of the exotic, especially with respect to the varieties of sexual experience. By presenting his potentially sensationalist material in an academically respectable manner, he allowed otherwise respectable people to indulge the more private realms of their fantasies.

Malinowski was himself well aware of the ways that anthropologists could broaden the audience for their books. Introducing Reo

Fortune's *Sorcerers of Dobu* (Malinowski 1932a: xvii), he stated, 'The most spectacular chapter of the book, and the one which will attract not only the anthropologist but a wider public, is the account of sorcery, and Dr Fortune has shown a shrewd appreciation of his book's appeal in choosing his telling title.' He named his own works flamboyantly: *Crime and Custom in Savage Society* (1926), *Sex and Repression in Savage Society* (1927), and, most notoriously, *The Sexual Life of Savages* (1929). While on a visit that year to the United States, he wrote to his wife: 'The English edition of my book is sold on the boulevards alongside *The Well of Loneliness*, *Lady Chatterley's Lover* (a porno-gramme by DH Lawrence) and Frank Harris's *My Life and Loves*, so that sounds hopeful' (in Wayne 1995: 143–4).

Despite the titillatory promise of its title, *The Sexual Life of Savages* is in fact an erudite account of Trobriand domestic life. Nevertheless, the book, which was reprinted three times in as many years, quickly generated much controversy. Firth (1981: 114) remembered that 'When people said of Malinowski, "Ah yes, I've read *his* book," one never needed to ask which book.' Reviewers for the prestigious British weeklies chose to concentrate, in a tone of astonished scepticism, on the Trobrianders' ignorance of the biology of procreation and on the local girls' apparent ability to fornicate freely without getting pregnant (*The Spectator* 16 March 1929, p. 427, *New Statesman* 4 May 1929, p. x). The prurient were fascinated by the detailed and explicit accounts in the book of Trobriand sexual behaviour. Others were not so approving. The novelist Elspeth Huxley (1985: 195) covered her copy in brown paper so as not to offend visitors to her flat. A Scots writer deplored the fact that his compatriots were more familiar with Trobrianders' sex lives than with their own history: 'Of what interest was the Gael without sexual attraction? Only if there arose a Malinowski of the Gael might they shew interest' (Barke 1936: 81). Robert Graves (Graves and Hodge 1940: 92) complained of anthropologists who 'could not disguise their bawdy relish in the sex habits of primitives' and who published their reports 'as refined erotic reading than as stern works of research'. The Governor-General of Tanganyika (quoted in Huxley 1985: 255) urged that Colonial Service Cadets should not have to study 'the eccentricities of remote Papuans, the scars they make on their bottoms and their unsavoury sexual habits scarcely any anthropologist can keep off'.

Malinowski had gone too far, and he realized it. As he admitted, he had fed public interest a little too eagerly: 'We are enjoying now a surfeit of sex – I alone have to plead guilty to four books on the subject, two of which have the name "sex" on the title-page. Sex has been emphasized for many reasons, some very good, some rather extraneous' (1932b: x). In a 'Special Foreword to the Third Edition' of the book (1932c: xix), he strove to reorient readers by emphasizing that he had wanted the book 'to be regarded as an achievement in field-work and in methods of exposition . . . But this experimental and ambitious aim has not, so far as I can judge, received the attention which I wished it to receive.' However, it appeared people were less interested in accounts of functionalism than of fornication. The book continued to sell. Indeed, it is still in print today.

Malinowski's interest in gaining the attention of the public was such that he was, at times, prepared to expurgate his own books. Havelock Ellis was 'really alarmed and shocked' when Malinowski confessed to him that he had toned down certain details – particularly the subject of unpleasant smells – in order not to offend the sensibilities of his readers. In a letter to his friend, Malinowski tried to justify his self-censorship:

> I would prefer *not* to shock. So in my more scientific work, while seeking to say everything necessary to be said in simple bald uncoloured words (avoiding the use of any Latin, which I regard as a most offensive practice), I have always omitted any crude and repellent details which do not seem to me necessary for the comprehension of the matter in hand, while in my personal writings I seek to express the shocking things in a quiet, suave, matter-of-course way, sugar-coating the pill. (Some of my shocking things have never been discovered!) I do not mean that I regard the sugar-coating as indispensable, but merely that I prefer to use it so far as possible. Only, when used, it must not be visible! It seems to me a serious error to show even the *slightest* consciousness that one is shocking. Any excuse or apology is fatal.
>
> (quoted in Grosskurth 1980: 383–4)

Malinowski wanted to educate, not to lose, his public, and so hid the fact that he was hiding anything.

Some anthropologists have gained popularity, not by explaining the course of humanity or the present problems of the West in anthropological terms, nor by writing sexually explicit ethno-graphies, but by penning personal accounts of fieldwork itself. Anthropology is a peculiar discipline, one in which the researcher is the key instrument of research. Though some have instituted 'objective' research methods in their effort to reduce the effects of this individuality, the central tool of ethnography is still the sole ethnographer. Their books are not reports of twiddling knobs to ensure the instrument is working properly but accounts of individuals getting to know other, very different people, in arduous but exotic circumstances. They are meant to be authentic and authoritative, for their authors are supposed to be intellectuals and, now that explorers no longer have anywhere to 'discover', they feed an already established public demand (Riffenburgh 1994) for the narratives of heroic adventurers in foreign places. As I argue in my own contribution to this book (see Chapter Eleven), the content and format of successful fieldwork accounts have, like other popular works of anthropology, changed in tune with the development of the authors' own society. Among accounts of fieldwork by British-trained anthropologists, Laura Bohannan's *Return to Laughter*, which presented time spent among exotic Others as a spiritual quest for oneself, was particularly appropriate for her postwar Oxford peers who either filled the ranks of the Christian Union or adopted *Being and Nothingness* as their Bible. Three decades later the books by Nigel Barley were a timely puncturing of Susan Sontag's pretentious, sexist and, by then, widely-accepted trope of the 'anthropologist as hero'. In the United States, the first volumes in Castaneda's 'Don Juan' series appealed to members of the drug culture seeking 'alternative realities', especially those which could be entered without undergoing a laborious initiatory period of formal instruction and rational argumentation; his later books, in which women come to the fore, chimed with the rise of feminism (Needham 1985: 190–1).

Most books about fieldwork, such as those by Bohannan and Barley, are about time spent in the field, not about the intellectual process of fieldwork itself. Rather than detail what their authors were trying to do there, they dwell lovingly on their protagonists' experience: the blunders they make, the friendships they forge, the dramas they witness, the self-realizations they come to, the tears they shed on departure. Philippe Descola's *Les lances du crépuscule* reverses this trend. As he describes in his chapter, his book is not just another chronicle of tribulations in an exotic setting, but an anthropological whodunit. It represents the fieldwork of himself and his wife as a series of steps by which they slowly came to comprehend, in their own terms, something of the Amazonians they were living with. Deliberately imitating the writers of detective novels, he leaves a trail of clues through his text. When, for example, he comes to interpret shamanic trance, or when in his account the identity of a murderer is finally clarified, astute readers will already have put together much of the relevant information themselves. At the same time, he portrays the way he and his wife – fellow sleuths on a trail of their own making – continued to sift their confused and ambiguous material until they were able to construct interpretations they found coherent and satisfying. In this Agatha-Christiean mode, Descola provides a new portrait of practitioners: the fieldworker as gumshoe.

STYLE

Popularizers have popular style. They are wordsmiths forging phrases of extra-academic appeal, for people who are not paid to read, but who pay to read, in the free time they have available. Their audience cannot be assumed. It has to be won. Like other academics, popularizers employ a rhetoric which they consider appropriate to their readership. But, as Campbell argues in a strongly polemical manner in this volume (see Chapter Two), unlike many other academics they do not confuse the erudite with the dull, nor the popular with the frivolous, and they question the conventionally accepted opposition of the scholarly versus the accessible. As far as they are concerned, obscure, difficult prose is only for those who do not know how to express themselves. Good ideas do not have to be couched in esoteric mannerisms or be burdened with endnotes[1] and other tired emblems of supposed scholarship. As the limpid styles of, for instance, Evans-Pritchard and Godfrey Lienhardt demonstrate, just because one's prose is fluent and easy to read does not necessarily mean that one's ideas are thereby any the less serious, subtle or complex. If an idea has any power or any potential, its promise need not be confined only to those who are prepared to struggle through laboured prose. Marrett in his day commented, 'So long as he who writes on such topics is profuse in facts, vivid in style, and not too technical in language – this last condition being not the least important – he may confidently reckon on a fair sale' (Marrett 1910: 299). Popularization, in other words, is about openness, not about closing the university gates to all those who lack letters after their name.

Part of the reason for Frazer's remarkable success was his ability to convey his views, without distorting them, in a language free of technical jargon and obscure expression. Preferring eloquent elegy to clumsily formulated dogma, he did not present his arguments in a doctrinaire manner, but skilfully blended modesty of statement with a grand literary style, one sprung with biblical and Latinate rhythms

(Lienhardt 1992: 7). The weighty result he leavened with irony, humour and an artful, sustained use of concrete imagery. Frazer, in other words, was not trying to batter his readers with the power of bald logic, but to persuade them with the appeal of his rhetoric (Vickery 1973: 20–32). As the record of his sales shows, if he did not always manage to win over his enormous audience, at the very least they were prepared to read his words.

Malinowski, taking Frazer as one of his two main literary models (the other was Conrad), used the same elegiac tone and similarly framed his work as an odyssey into another world with himself as the readers' expert guide: 'Let us imagine that we are sailing along the South coast of New Guinea towards its Eastern end...' (1922: 33). Heeding the example of his mentor, Malinowski detailed the land-scape and ambience of his exotic island 'home' in compellingly vivid terms. 'I found', he wrote to Frazer, 'That the more scenery and "atmosphere" was given in the account, which you had at your disposal, the more convincing and manageable to the imagination was the ethnology of that district' (Malinowksi Correspondence 25/10/1917, LSE, quoted in Thornton 1985: 7). His prose, which seldom strays into the highly abstract, is thick with adjectives of colour, tone, feeling and size. He employs what Payne calls a 'Syntax of Agency': his preferred tense is the present, and his favoured voice the active; things have not 'been done', Trobrianders (and Malinowski) 'do' them. As an exotic-yarn-spinner, with a rare tale to tell, Malinowski at times blurs the line between mytho-poetic fiction and what is drawn from actual experience. He also classes his characters archetypically: the indigenes, with their mysterious but explicable ways; the cramp-minded colonial residents, who always get the locals wrong; the Ethnographer-as-Hero, who sets our understanding straight (Payne 1981; Stocking 1983). And, just in case readers failed to observe the correspondences between his style and Frazer's, Malinowski gave his cleverly crafted work a similarly classical title and even had the great man preface it. He wanted *Argonauts of the Western Pacific* to be seen, in part, as a *Golden Bough* for his times. As he wrote to his wife, 'May it really be a golden fleece!' (in Wayne 1995: 26).

Many of Malinowski's academic successors did not approve of his literary style (nor that of Firth's 'belletristic' *We, The Tikopia* [Hocart 1937]). Wishing to regard anthropology as a science which investi-gated normative social systems, they disliked the romantic streak within his works. Evans-Pritchard (1951: 93) branded his *Argonauts* as 'journalistic', while others thought he contextualized events too widely and detailed them too vividly (Kaberry 1957: 85). They were also well aware that the internal unity of his books relied less on logical organization than on his skill as a writer. As Firth acknowledged, Malinowski was not a systematist, rather a representative of a romantic mode of thought who was impatient with 'the neat verbal definition' (quoted in Symmons-Symonolewicz 1958). Even he, the most loyal of Malinowski's students, has described his mentor's book against modern war as 'politically naive' and its philosophical analysis of the word 'freedom' as 'homespun' (Firth 1988: 36). Kluckhohn (1943: 211), lamenting the lack of Boasian austerity and of a sustained note of high seriousness in Malinowski's writings, charged him with being 'frequently wordy, often flippant, occasionally trivial, pretentious, even cheap'. It was difficult for an anthropologist of Kluckhohn's temperament to take seriously a colleague who could write in the foreword to one of his major ethnographies:

> Let me confess at once: the magnificent title of the Functional School of Anthropology has been bestowed by myself, in a way on myself, and to a large extent out of my own sense of irresponsibility... The only thing which I can claim in extenuation of this act of self-appointment was that it was not done without some sense of humour.
>
> Oh, I am the cook and the captain bold,
> And the mate of the *Nancy* brig:
> And the bo'sun tight
> And the midship mite
> And the crew of the captain's gig...
>
> (Malinowski 1932c: xxix–xxx)

Trobrianders might have remembered Malinowski as 'The Man of Songs' (Hogbin 1946), but his successors did not share his taste in ditties from Gilbert and Sullivan, nor did they imitate his irreverent example. These sober characters preferred to remain within their academic confines. Rather than run the risk of detailing the imponderabilia of actual life and of thus being thought 'impressionistic and subjective' (Kaberry 1957), they preferred to write ethnographies which were much more analytical, relatively lifeless and totally humourless. The only attempt at a joke Evans-Pritchard (1940: 13) ever made in print was to say that after a few weeks of associating solely with the stubbornly unforthcoming Nuer, 'one displays, if the pun be allowed, the most evident symptoms of "Nuerosis'".

Malinowski had wanted to flesh out his accounts and to put blood into his characters. His successors were content to provide a much more dry, skeletal framework, illustrated with filigree-like diagrams of kinship and clan structure. Indeed, the concern with ethnographic formality became such that Evans-Pritchard's students learnt to write their accounts of individual societies according to a standard format with a set series of one institution per chapter, supposedly to aid a rather mechanical form of comparison. Though Evans-Pritchard did advise his doctoral students freshly back from the field to write their theses like novels 'with a strong beginning, a solid middle and a good end', he did not want them to produce evocative representations of the exotic, but dispassionate, formalized, structural analyses tied to a narrative peg. Mead's *Coming of Age in Samoa* he crabbed as a 'discursive, or perhaps I should say chatty and feminine, book with a leaning towards the picturesque, what I might call the rustling-of-the-wind-in-the-palm-trees kind of anthropological writing, for which Malinowski set the fashion' (1951: 96).

Like Malinowski, Benedict employed artistic devices in her prose, mainly because she was deliberately aiming her books at a mass market. The audience she wished to reach was what she called 'Macy shoppers': those 'ordinary' men and women who, according to her, created a culture. Benedict felt strongly that if she was to move this category of reader, she, a published poet, had to use a literary style which would make the lessons of her book both enjoyable to learn and meaningful in day-to-day experience. She was also particularly concerned about the production and promotion of *Patterns of Culture*. She debated with friends and her editor the merits and demerits of over fifty titles for the book, worried about the colour of its cover, rewrote its blurb several times, insisted that its price be as low as possible, and got Mead to publicize it in conversations and reviews (Modell 1983: 208–12).

Mead, whose literary talents were not as great as those of Benedict, was equally anxious that her books should be highly readable. *Coming of Age in Samoa* is set in a seemingly timeless ethnographic present, and written in a patently romantic style, by an apparently all-knowing ethnographer who is not troubled by doubts – and who relegated methodological and historical aspects of her study to appendices. Even in *New Lives for Old. Cultural Transformations – Manus, 1928–1953* (1956), written twenty-five years later and which took historical change as its central theme, Mead, although by then much more methodologically sophisticated, continued to employ a romanticizing mode and to present herself as an untroubled, omnicompetent witness: 'the short tropical twilight' continues to 'close down on us' and there is still 'bright moonlight, without a ruffle of wind' (Mead 1956: 35, 42). Evans-Pritchard and other British theorists may have disliked the literary expressiveness of her work, but she was less interested in impressing them than her public. To ensure that her readers could always understand her message, she used to lay stress on actual people and recognizable relationships: as she once said to Radcliffe-Brown, 'For me the most important thing is to study reality – real objects and real events – and to talk about them in terms of abstractions, but not to treat abstractions as though they were realities' (quoted in Grosskurth 1988: 65).

Some popularizers do not only know how to write. They also know how to perform, catching the attention of their audience with the cultivated tricks of their personal style as much as with the power of their arguments. Though Margaret Mead, as Mitchell reveals in his poignant portrait of his former teacher, was a passionate and lively speaker (her advice to those unskilled in the art was 'Begin with something very startling, prove that it was wrong, say something outlandish, and be alliterative' [Howard 1984: 374]), in her later life she did come partly to rely on patently theatrical props. Cutting a distinctive figure, she would march up to the lectern cloaked in a brocaded cape and wielding a shoulder-high forked staff, which she would stamp if she felt it necessary. Mead revelled in looking like a prophet and well knew the effect her costume had. Fellow anthropologists might carp at such seemingly non-academic behaviour, but that, of course, does not mean that many of the more successful among them are not themselves performers, albeit in a somewhat different, possibly less blatant mode.

Malinowksi was similarly not scared of being polemical, and vigorously engaged on public platforms with other intellectuals about the issues of his day. As a shrewd missionary advised Audrey Richards (1943: 4), 'Invite Malinowski to the opening session of a conference: half the audience will disagree with him violently, but the discussions will go with a swing from the start.' His personal style, however, failed to impress many of his colleagues. If many British anthropologists had little time for popularization, they had even less for someone who acted as his own popularizer. Evans-Pritchard, who praised Tylor for avoiding the 'stage-making proclivities' of most of his contemporaries, thought Malinowski 'a bloody gas-bag' (Evans-Pritchard 1951: 31; Goody 1995: 74). Beyond a reduced circle of disciples centred around his seminar, few were enamoured of Malinowski's at times extravagant ways. Several were infuriated by his fondness for harlequinade (Lowie 1938: 241; Kluckhohn 1943: 208; Firth 1957: 10–11; Barkan 1992: 125). Like the angry critics of Mead who thought that her desire for public prominence led her at times to trivialize the findings of the discipline, they considered that a discipline as worthy as theirs deserved more responsible emissaries to the extra-mural world.

THE VARIETIES OF POPULARIZERS

So far I have discussed only popular works by academic anthropologists who sought, or seek, to reach a wider readership. Yet only a relatively small number of practising anthropologists popularize their discipline. Most have neither the gift nor the inclination, while some are scared that writing a popular work will lead to them being ostracized by their more strait-laced peers. Not surprising then, that a large number of the books aimed at the popular market which deal with anthropology in one way or another are in fact written not by academic anthropologists, but by either: those who, though trained in anthropology, did not remain (or did not remain solely) in academic life; knowledgeable lay persons curious about other ways of life; educated people who have learnt some anthropology and wish to propagate its practice among the populace, or scholars from other disciplines who are perceived as anthropologists by their non-academic readers.

A significant group here consists of those female graduates of anthropology who did not enter the university hierarchy. Okely argues (see Chapter Nine) that one reason why these educated women became popularizers is that they were interested in topics, such as menstruation, sexual behaviour, birth and childcare, which were not generally considered appropriate subjects of academic study until the 1980s. Though there was a considerable popular market for books on these themes, anthropological enquiry being a usefully genteel means of conveying, for example, rudimentary sexual instruction (Bennett 1995: 28), there was very little demand within the universities for research into them. Furthermore, since a disproportionately low number of female anthropology students went on to lectureships, let alone professorial posts, the women who wrote on these topics were most likely untenured. Thus, by producing works for the only market open to them – the non-academic public – these women, already bordering on the margins, tended to confirm in the eyes of their more well-established colleagues their marginal status. In effect, the marginalized were forced to practise a professionally marginal activity: popular anthropology. There they were joined by feminists, such as Germaine Greer, who found in ethnographies some of the material they were seeking with which to question the contemporary Western conventions of sexually appropriate behaviour.

There is also a heterogeneous group of trained anthropologists who have not followed the traditional trajectory of academic anthropology and who would not, most likely, consider themselves popularizers, yet whose writings have served to popularize interest in the subject. Otherwise unclassifiable, independently-minded characters, whose careers cannot be pigeonholed in a conventional manner, such as Michel Leiris and Francis Huxley, fit in here. Leiris entered anthropology via surrealism, studied with Mauss, and travelled with Griaule. Throughout his life he was both a professional ethnographer and a writer, winning distinguished prizes for his volumes of poetry and autobiography. If there is anything approaching a unity to the corpus of his work it lies in his desire to explore the resources of language and, in his own words, 'to enlarge our understanding of humanity' (quoted in Jamin 1991: 414). He regarded his autobiography as a form of self-ethnography, and his ethnographies as, partly, studies in a rigorous subjectivity. Rejecting the idea that anthropology served any purpose and changed anything, he was only prepared to admit that his writings had 'helped a few people see things a bit more lucidly' (in Price and Jamin 1988: 170).

Francis Huxley might phrase his work in similar terms. In the course of his life, he has moved from social anthropology – his accounts of fieldwork in the Amazon (1956) and Haiti (1966) are not catalogues of his own tribulations but attempts, through the use of anecdotes, to let the locals 'speak for themselves' – via the work of R. D. Laing and Lewis Carroll (1976) into illustrated books on the anthropology of religion (1974) and esoteric symbolism (1986; 1990). In the process, he has in some ways followed the example of his uncle, Aldous, in wishing to investigate alternative realities, and that of his father, Julian (who wrote several successful books of popular science), in not wishing to restrict the work of academics to academic readerships. If there is anything common to his work and that of Leiris, it is a sustained dissatisfaction with a narrowly erudite discourse and with the parcelling off of domains of knowledge within purely scholastic terrain. Unlike Malinowski, Benedict and Mead, these idiosyncratic individuals have not chosen to be popularizers of anthropology for the sake of making the discipline better known and understood; rather, they have not wished to bolster a distinction between the academic and the non-academic. Of course, in doing so, they have indirectly helped to popularize the subject.

Perhaps this is the point at which to mention Patrick Putnam (1904–1953), a Bostonian who spent his adult life on the edge of the Zairean rainforest, where he built and ran an infirmary, a tourist hotel and a reserve for exotic local animals. The main attraction of the area for Putnam and his monied visitors, however, were the pygmies who periodically resided at the camp and whom he hired to stage spectacles of 'pygmy customs'. Putnam, who had attended classes in anthropology at Harvard, did not popularize the pygmies in print, but he did take financial advantage of their perennial appeal to others. His eccentric status as 'King of the World in the Land of the Pygmies' relied on his ability to facilitate their popularization by visiting journalists and film-makers and the young Colin Turnbull, whom he greatly encouraged (Mark 1995). Such resident anthropologists *manqués*, though popularly represented as anthropologists, are not so much popularizers in their own right but key intermediaries in the popularization of indigenes by others. They are crucial enablers in the process, rather than manufacturers of the final product.

The more narrow-minded of academic anthropologists look down upon popular works, though their authors are often able to describe certain activities and domains better than their more hide-bound brethren. Ethnographies written by professional practitioners of the genre cannot cover every aspect of a way of life, and those not included may well be described – maybe even, in some ways, better described – by non-academics and amateur ethnographers, such as missionaries (e.g. Leenhardt [Clifford 1982]), white settlers (e.g. Asterisk 1923; Jamin 1979; Young 1992), colonial administrators (e.g. Man 1885; Robertson 1897) and visiting novelists. In the Australian case, for instance (Morphy; see Chapter Eight), the Queenslander Bill Harney, who spent his entire life working with or among the indigenes, portrays in his books something strikingly absent from the texts of most anthropologists: the now-past cross-cultural interface, where Aboriginal men sold their labour to ranchers and Aboriginal women sold their bodies to those with cash, where white workers could see themselves as forming, together with the Aborigines, an underclass opposed to the cattle barons, police and government officials. In more recent times, the British novelist Bruce Chatwin has written about the modern version of that intercultural border. Since entrance through this nebulous boundary is now negotiated by a variety of Aboriginal 'advisers' (a group which includes ethnographers), it is not perhaps surprising that so many Australian anthropologists have criticized his book so much. For they themselves have, for once, been treated as 'informants'. Instead of studying other peoples, they have been studied, like other peoples, by an outsider, and the process has made them feel uncomfortable. Yet if one aim of anthropology is to portray and analyse the varieties of social practices, then the frontier – a culture of its own – is as appropriate an object of investigation as any other. Just because anthropologists are themselves members of that society is no reason for not studying it. We're not special.

In my experience and that of several of my colleagues, many people regard the (highly successful) work of scholars such as Joseph Campbell (e.g. 1960) and Mircea Eliade (e.g. 1960; 1964) as eminently anthropological. Though the former is a comparative mythologist, who held a post in a department of literature, and the latter a historian of religions, both fill their books with analyses of ethnographic material. Both employ eclectic methodologies (drawing on, among others, psychology [especially Jungianism], diffusionism and modern social anthropology). Both organize their material according to their own pre-established typologies, take their world as their limit, and display almost encyclopaedic pretensions. For some of these reasons, they might be classed as 'neo-Frazerians'. Indeed, reviewers of their books have compared the projects of both of them with that of Frazer, while Eliade virtually parrots his predecessor when he states (1960: 14) that his ultimate aim is to be 'our guide upon those far journeys, and . . . serve as interpreter in our encounters with the most "alien" among the "others"'. Like the present market for *The Golden Bough* (which is being kept in print in Britain by two separate publishing houses), the main readership for these authors today seems to be New Age mystics and prospective members of that loosely defined movement.

Perhaps one of the most sustained, and potentially one of the most radical, attempts to popularize the practice of social anthropology was that of Mass Observation (MacClancy 1995). Its organizers thought that, by training volunteers to become systematic observers of their own and others' lives, and by publishing synoptic reports of these observations, they could help people to empower themselves. But this popularizing endeavour by a team of independently-minded, boundary-blurring researchers, none of whom had received a formal education in anthropology, was not approved of by the majority of British social anthropologists who at that time (the mid-1930s) were primarily concerned with establishing a common set of disciplinary conventions. Many Victorian anthropologists had been keen to promote the practice of ethnography among educated expatriates. Their successors were not so happy to see amateur fieldworkers on their own doorstep. Evans-Pritchard called Mass Observation 'bilge' (Goody 1995: 74). Its leaders, however, were not out to please the professors but to inform the British public, and they continued, despite academic criticism, to practise and to promote their own (very popular) brand of anthropology. Indeed the organization still continues.

What the examples of Campbell, Eliade and Mass Observation also reveal is the tension between academic and popular definitions of 'anthropology'. For, while university-based scholars may wish to restrict its application to those texts and practices of which they approve (and thereby indirectly legitimate their own defining position with the anthropological hierarchy), others may wish to use a more plural, less restrictive conception of the term, one which attempts to broaden its membership and serves to accommodate a democratic variety rather than narrow its audience and sharpen a hegemonic singularity. This tension is not new. In 1898, Haddon (1898: v) wrote in the introduction to one of his popular works that 'my wish is not merely to interest my readers, but to induce them to become workers'. The next year, C. H. Read (1900: 9) stated the opposite view in his presidential address to the Anthropological Institute: 'While it would be doing good work to popularize anthropology, I doubt whether it would benefit anthropology to be popular, as a science.'

PUBLISHERS

An account of the popularization of social anthropology with any pretension to roundness would have to include a study of the structure of the publishing industry: what sorts of anthropology can be printed when, where (in books or magazines?), how easily, by what sort of publishing house, and to what effect? Such a study has yet to be carried out (see, e.g. Tebbel 1987; Feather 1988), and all I can do here is to indicate the very barest outlines such an investigation might take.

It was not until well into the 1930s that university presses began to produce books of anthropology. Up to that time, anthropologists had given their manuscripts to commercial publishers, usually ones with a tradition of printing scholarly monographs. Macmillan published all of *The Golden Bough* (1890–1915) – valuing it for the authors it drew to the imprint (Morgan 1944: 173) – and all of Westermarck's multivolume works (1906, 1921, 1926), while Routledge's stable included Reo Fortune, Audrey Richards and Malinowski. Even as late as 1942, Chatto and Windus were prepared to print such a monumental tome as Layard's *Stone Men of Malekula* – over 800 pages of small type and intricate kinship diagrams. In the late Victorian and Edwardian period, anthropologists such as Haddon also contributed to the various popular series produced by British publishers, such as the *Harmsworth History of the World*, which purported to be encyclopaedic and 'scientific' in the presentation of the Empire (Coombes. 1994: 205). In the interwar years, series of pocket books provided anthropologists with another outlet for their abilities, and for gain: Watts and Co.'s 'Thinker's Library' produced shorter books by Elliot Smith, Frazer and Haddon, and reprinted Tylor's *History of Anthropology* in two volumes; Elliot Smith edited 'In the Beginning of Things' for Gerald Howe Ltd.; Kegan Paul, Trench and Traubner included two essays by Malinowski (1926; 1927) and a debate between him and Elliot Smith (Elliot Smith *et al.* 1928) in its 'Psyche Miniatures' series; Nelson had Firth write *Human Types* (1938) for its 'Discussion Books'. But the war ended production of these series while, by the late 1940s, ethnographies had become so technical and arid in style that they were only put out by university presses and those commercial houses (such as Routledge, and Cohen and West) which maintained a speciality in academic publishing.

Since that time, in Britain and America, anthropologists who have wanted their books to reach beyond a market of fellow academics and students have been hampered by the almost rigid distinction which has arisen, and has been maintained by publishers and booksellers, between specialist and 'trade' books, i.e. between books sold by catalogue or in specialist outlets, and books which, while not aimed at the mass market, are intended for a broad readership and sold in commercial booksellers. Which category a book fits into influences the discount offered to its seller, the rate of returns, its shelf life, the budget devoted to its presentation, and the possibility of its author receiving an advance. Attempts during the boom in higher education in the 1960s and early 1970s to cut across this divide almost all failed.

The Penguin 'Anthropology Library', which published paperback versions of basic texts such as Mary Douglas's *Purity and Danger*, closed within a few years, as did the Paladin paperback series which included works by Bateson, Roy Willis, and Tiger and Fox. What has been successful is the paperback series of précised ethnographies, 'Case Studies in Cultural Anthropology', put out by Holt, Rinehart and Winston since 1961, edited by the Stanford anthropologists George and Louise Spindler, and designed to meet the burgeoning market of introductory students in the social sciences. The series, still expanding, now runs to over fifty titles, Chagnon's paperbacks on the Yanomamo (1983) being the most famous, and their heady mixture of sex, drugs and violence in an exotic setting appealing strongly to undergraduate audiences.

In the last decade the specialist/trade distinction has become even sharper, with the virtual end of reviews in the quality press of ethnographies and academic anthropology, the decline of smaller publishers, who were able to maintain a foothold in the specialist or academic fields, and the ascendancy of accountancy and marketing practices within the larger commercial houses. Books attempting to overcome this economic divide are now rare, a possible recent example being Adam Kuper's (1994) book on the contemporary debates between biological and social anthropologists, which has already been bought by an American book club. The only popular series in which anthropologists are now able to participate are the 'partworks' (e.g. *Man, Myth and Magic*) produced by mass market publishers such as Marshall Cavendish.

From the Victorian period up to the beginning of the Second World War, many anthropologists both in Britain and America were prolific contributors to literary weeklies and monthlies. Indeed, in the late nineteenth century, the London-based *Fortnightly Review* 'published essays by the major sociocultural evolutionists which, in terms of their content and style of argument, could just as well have appeared in the *Journal of the Anthropological Institute*' (Stocking 1987: 325). In the 1960s and 1970s a few British anthropologists (above all, Leach) did write brief essays for weeklies such as *New Society* and *The Listener*. But both of those journals, and many others like them, have since folded, and today the only significant outlets for anthropologists with pretensions to literary journalism are *The London Review of Books*, *The New York Review of Books*, and the book review section of *The New York Times*.

In the early 1980s (see Benthall, Chapter Six) the Royal Anthropological Institute tried to bridge the gap between anthropologists
and non-specialists by producing a bimonthly, *Anthropology Today*. The
original objective was to produce an anthropological equivalent of
Encounter, providing an anthropological perspective on contemporary
social issues (Houtman and Knight 1995). But the economic risks of
distributing the journal through booksellers and newsagents were so
great that it is still only obtainable by subscription. As such, its main,
present function appears to be informing anthropologists (and some
people in associated fields) of some of the sorts of work being done in
the name of anthropology of which they would otherwise be unaware.
In other words, Benthall introduces us to a further variety of
popularization, that *within* the academy of anthropologists.

This rather bleak picture of a cumulative anthropological confine-
ment, a compound of academic practice and the economics of the
marketplace, does not apply to the French publishing and newspaper
industries. There, anthropologists such as Marc Abélès write regularly
for the quality press and have their latest works fully reviewed (see
Casajus, Chapter Seven). When Jack Goody, then the professor at
Cambridge, visited l'Ecole des Hautes Etudes to give a series of
lectures, *Le Figaro* ran a pair of full pages on him and his work for three
consecutive days. It is extremely hard to imagine *The Times* or *The New
York Times* acting in a similar manner if his Parisian equal came to
speak at Oxford or Columbia.

In France, the divide between specialist and trade books is
traditionally much less wide, while the continuing contiguity
between anthropology and the avant-garde has ensured that all but
the most technical of ethnographies may be seriously considered by
commercial publishers. Even such an intellectually demanding
account as Remo Guideri's *La Route des mortes* (1981) was published
by a non-academic press, Editions Seuil. Perhaps the most dramatic
example of this almost seamless spectrum from the popular to the
most rigorously scholastic is the success of 'Terre Humaine' (Casajus,
Descola), whose over fifty titles have so far sold more than five million
copies. Started in 1955 at Editions Plon by Jean Malaurie, an
anthropologist of the Arctic, his aim was not to produce, as in the
Anglo–American tradition, a series – one confined to a particular
academic speciality or genre of literature – but a *'collection'* of eye-
witness accounts of ways of life by novelists, poets, writers, social
anthropologists, and 'indigenous authors'. In his own words,

While we do publish studies of societies and peoples, 'Terre Humaine's' main originality is to do with the fact that its authors are from very different countries and backgrounds, with a wide range of political commitments and of approaches to human phenomena. These approaches are, in sum, complementary. In my opinion, the writing of first-hand documentary testimony can belong to great literature. . . . We were the first to put top people and supposedly lower-rank people on the same literary level: Lévi-Strauss and a Turkish primary-school teacher or Russian peasant. We have taken rural thought out of the university museum and folklore studies in which it was bogged down. *Le Cheval d'Orgueil* by Pierre-Jakez Hélias, the autobiography of a Breton peasant sold 2 million copies and was like a clap of thunder in French publishing. To start with, it showed townspeople that peasants were not the idiots they thought them to be, but bearers of a complex thought. And then, every Frenchmen discovered that he had in his father or grandfather some peasant ancestry. The French intelligentsia discovered its own mental, religious and mythic substrate in European peasant civilization. And a number of books in the 'Terre Humaine' collection are used in baccalaureate and university courses.

(in Benthall 1987: 8–9)

Instead of precariously straddling a well-marked divide, as would be the case for a British or an American editor, Malaurie has exploited the richness of the meeting-place between literature and social anthropology. In the process, he has produced books which can be read for enjoyment by intellectuals, urban-dwellers and schoolchildren.

THE PERILS OF POPULARIZATION AND THE PRESS

Books such as Benedict's *The Chrysanthemum and the Sword* and Bohannan's *Return to Laughter* may be regarded as the 'quality' sector of the market for popular anthropology, where academics try hard and conscientiously to communicate to the public some of the lessons their discipline may teach. There is also what we might call a 'tabloid' sector to this market, where anthropologists popularize their and others' work in an unscrupulous, sensationalist manner. Castaneda fits in here, as do Colin Turnbull, Derek Freeman and a whole gallery of unattractive others.

Turnbull's caricature of the Ugandan Ik, *The Mountain People* (1972), was such a bestseller that it has even been turned into a ballet (see James, Chapter Three), where the Ik are held up to the public as a dramatic, exotic example of the way poverty can corrode all aspects of moral life. Yet the book is such a throughgoing misrepresentation of Ik ways that they later told a visiting linguist (Heine 1985, also de Waal 1993) that should Turnbull ever dare to return to their land they would force him 'to eat his own faeces'. It is not too fanciful to suggest that Turnbull, who felt that anthropologists had a duty to popularize their findings because of their unique moral significance (Middleton 1994), wanted to repeat the success of *The Forest People* (1961). This romanticizing portrayal of the Mbuti pygmies as unselfish hunter-gatherers wandering contentedly through the rainforests of Zaire was used to contrast with what he saw as the self-centred and calculating ways of Westerners. It seems that by the 1970s his desire to produce an equally vivid portrayal of a different people, from which another, clear moral message could be drawn, led him to misreport the Ik so grossly that the ensuing controversy destroyed much of his reputation as an ethnographer.

Freeman (1983) is a somewhat different, and in many ways more interesting, case because he criticized Mead's *Coming of Age in Samoa* on the grounds of ethnographic misrepresentation for a popularizing end, though being guilty of precisely the same himself (Brady 1983; Scheper-Hughes 1984). Both in fact provided an oversimplified account of Samoan life: Mead, for the sake of questioning the simple-minded biological determinism of her time, Freeman, for the sake of lauding a universal, biological 'maternal instinct'. Perhaps the most important outcome of this debate was the reminder that ethnographers are not the providers of eternal verities, but of partial truths and, unless they can be shown to be culpable of deliberate, gross misrepresentation, cannot be flatly accused of being totally 'wrong' or unreservedly praised for being completely 'right'. In the process, it is the public who are misled, and, once the heat of debate has cooled, left with the awareness that anthropologists may not be as authoritative or honest as many of them would like to claim.

A comment on the Holt, Rinehart and Winston series may also fit into this section on the perils of popularization, as the potential dangers of using these potted ethnographies as class texts are very real (see James, Chapter Three). For in order for each of these accounts to be distinctive, and therefore to sell, authors need to emphasize cultural singularity at the expense of other approaches, such as drawing out the nature of and similarities between social systems among different groups. Thus lecturers, by using these précised accounts of other peoples as substitute teaching texts for full-length ethnographies, can well end up exaggerating cultural difference for the sake of contrast and argument, as well as typecasting peoples in the process. The Yanomamo become aggressive brinkmen, the Senoi mystical dreamers, the Mbuti peace-loving Greens *avant la lettre*, and so on. The richness of these various peoples' ways of lives is reduced to a gallery of stark portraits (*Patterns of Culture* was criticized in similar terms), as though they constituted a pedagogical exhibition arranged by the course instructor. They have been oversimplified into exemplars of personality archetypes, and their characters transformed into caricatures. In the case of *Anthropology Today*, the market closed off certain of its options; in the context discussed by Okely, publishers exploited a market eschewed by the academy: in contrast, in the case James provides, the market acts in concert with the academy, to their mutual benefit, and commoditizes cultures in the process.

Some anthropologists are wary of popularization because they are worried about the ways others may use their words. Comments such as those made by one reviewer of Malinowski's *Argonauts* would only confirm their fears: 'The author's infinitely careful scientific method makes the material he has collected so completely trustworthy that it is possible to use it for all sorts of purposes for which it was not directly intended' (*The Spectator*, 16 September 1922). In 1977 two distinguished British anthropologists even declined to contribute to a book, proceeds from which would go to the Royal Anthropological Institute, of recipes culled during fieldwork because they thought styles of cooking could not be transferred from their original ecological setting (Kuper 1977: 9–10). The sad truth, however, which must be communicated to such cautious characters as this pair, is that if anthropologists are not prepared to popularize their own work, then others will do the job for them, sometimes to ridiculous effect, as in the tabloids (Peterson 1991), sometimes to nefarious effect, as by political groups (e.g. Gordon 1992). As Campbell so cogently argues, rather than disparaging the press for not always representing them and their work in exactly the way they might wish, anthropologists should praise, in a suitably discriminating manner, journalists' efforts to publicize fieldworkers' reports about what is happening, for example, to indigenous minorities in oppressive states, to rainforest dwellers invaded by aggressive gold-prospectors, or to tribals threatened by illconceived 'development' plans.

Instead of turning away from the fourth estate, anthropologists should use it to inform the public of their work, and of its value, especially if, in a time of shrinking public funds, they wish their subject to survive. (For a 'how-to' guide, see Lepowsky 1994a; b; 1995.) As William Beeman (1987: 2), perhaps the only university-based anthropologist who writes regularly for national newspapers in the United States, has argued, 'The American public is most often led to believe that the prime motivators of human action are economic necessity and threat of force. The position that religion, ideology, or cultural belief could be a comparable basis for human action is not well represented in the press.' It is, above all, anthropologists who should be able to demystify the actions of individuals whose cultural practices are different to those of the Western mainstream; the most appropriate places for them to do so, in America at least, are on the 'op-ed' (opposite editorial) pages of daily newspapers and in journals of opinion. In Brazil, a host of anthropologists, with their own newspaper columns or spaces on radio shows, already act as cultural commentators on the events of the day. It is said that one even accompanied the national football team in a recent World Cup tournament (P. Riviere pers. comm.) To those academics who think such popularizing is not a legitimate activity for intellectuals, Beeman contends that what he is advocating is not popularization but public service. (On a more self-interested note, anthropologists who learn how to work with the media may also end up supplying themselves with the material for their next ethnography – one on the media industry.)

Funding bodies are well aware of the need for researchers to press home their findings. The recently formulated 'Communications Policy' of the British Economic and Social Research Council stresses 'both the contractual obligation upon researchers to disseminate their work and the ethical responsibility to communicate with the people who ultimately provide the money for research – the public' (ESRC 1994). In this context it is, perhaps, reassuring to note that at the end of a seven-month-long debate conducted in the columns of the *AAA Newsletter* during 1992, its editor (Givens 1992) could report that not one member of the American Anthropological Association who contributed to the discussion felt that publicity was bad for the discipline. As he dramatically put it, the present predicament that all anthropologists had to face was, 'Project – or perish'.

What the individual essays in this volume collectively suggest is that anthropologists bypass the topic of popularization at their peril. It is, quite simply, too important an activity for us to scorn.

The prejudiced have regarded popular anthropology as tantamount to descent into the marketplace. Marrett (1910: 300) called it 'that vain thing'. The less blinkered have preferred to see popularization as a complementary practice, related in many different, and some unexpected, ways to more academically conventional pursuits. As the essays collected here demonstrate, there is no hard and fast line separating popular and scholastic work but, rather, a constant intermingling of the two. Some anthropologists may have at times wished to demarcate sharply, for internal institutional reasons, the acceptable boundaries of their discipline, but the efforts of their popularizing contemporaries have repeatedly thrown into relief the essentially arbitrary nature of this line-drawing. Popular anthropology is not some unlikeable, distasteful appendage to the main body of the subject, but an integral part of it.

Some anthropologists criticized the postmodernists' textual approach to ethnographies as a disengagement from the real world. This kind of navel-gazing might be all very well. But the navel is not very deep and, once its profundities have been checked out, it is time to raise one's eyes and face the world. The analysis of popular anthropologies as texts is not open to the same censure. For this neglected corpus provides us with a plethora of suggestive examples (generated by or satisfying popular demand) for a renovated, genuinely radical anthropology, one which holds the promise of enabling a more plural, egalitarian form of the discipline. If anthropology is to do more than enrich the common vocabulary ('rites of passage', 'cargo cult', etc.), then its practitioners need to engage with contemporary realities, in ways meaningful to subjects and readers and which tempt them to participate. At a time when professional expertise is greeted with increased scepticism, and new forms of disseminating knowledge are constantly invented, anthropologists should not cower behind the university walls, but dare to lower the drawbridge.

Arguing from similar premises, Downey and Rogers (1995) call for 'partnering' between academics and the popular market they serve, while Grimshaw and Hart (1994: 253) extol the potential contribution of 'the amateur', 'a person motivated by affection and genuine commitment rather than by the goals of professional reward and recognition'. Broadening the anthropological constituency by opening our ranks to amateurs does not mean the end to our criterion of excellence, but its renovation and the admission that there may be diverse criteria. Grimshaw and Hart raise the part-time anthropologist W. H. R. Rivers as their standard. The founders of Mass

Observation are an even better choice, for their democratizing
programme won mass support and promised to recast the subject in
the process. It is from such beginnings that a reinvigorated,
authentically popular anthropology could emerge.

ACKNOWLEDGEMENTS

I am grateful to Sir Raymond Firth for generously agreeing to be
interviewed, and to Chris Holdsworth, Chris McDonaugh, Peter
Parkes, Peter Riviere and, especially, Routledge's readers for comments, some of which I heeded.

NOTE

1 Like this one.
  Some academics, it is true, seem to prefer obscurity, as though in
  some way it validated the nature of their enterprise. The point was made
  in a recent discussion between three intellectuals broadcast by the BBC:

  Paris [Ernest Gellner said], was 'the world capital of obscurity. The
  production of obscurity in Paris compares to the production of motorcars
  in Detroit in the great period of American industry.'
    'Why, then,' asked chairman Colin MacCabe, 'have Foucault, Derrida,
  Barthes *et al.* been so influential all over the world?'
    'Because,' replied the imperturbable Gellner, 'there is a demand for
  obscurity.' At this, MacCabe turned helplessly to Dr George Steiner. 'I
  don't think Ernest means that,' said the Doctor benignly. 'I do,' replied
  Gellner and rested his case.

  (Naughton 1992)

REFERENCES

Ackerman, R. (1987)*J. G. Frazer. His Life and Work*, Cambridge: Cambridge
  University Press.
Altick, R. (1978) *The Shows of London*, Cambridge, Mass.: Belknap.
Ardrey, R. (1967) *The Territorial Imperative. A Personal Inquiry into the Animal
  Origins of Property and Nations*, London: Collins.
—— (1976) *The Hunting Hypothesis*, New York: Atheneum.
Asterisk (pseudonym of R. J. A. G. Fletcher) (1923) *Isles of Illusion*, Bohun
  Lynch (ed.), London: Constable.
Atkinson, J. M. (1993) 'Shamanisms Today', *Annual Review of Anthropology*
  21: 307–30.
Balfour, H. (1904) 'The Relationship of Museums to the Study of
  Anthropology', *Journal of the Anthropological Institute* XXXIV: 10–19.
Banks, M. J. (1994) 'Television and Anthropology: An unhappy marriage?',
  Visual Anthropology 7, 1: 21–45.

Barkan, E. (1992) *The Retreat of Scientific Racism. Changing Concepts of Race in Britain and the United States Between the Two World Wars*, Cambridge: Cambridge University Press.

Barke, J. (1936) *Major Operation*, London: Collins.

Barnard, A. (1989) 'The Lost World of Laurens van der Post?', *Current Anthropology* 30: 104–14.

Beard, M. (1992) 'Frazer, Leach, and Virgil: The popularity (and unpopularity) of *The Golden Bough*', *Comparative Studies in Society and History* 34: 203–25.

Beattie, J. (1964) *Other Cultures. Aims, Methods and Achievements in Social Anthropology*, London: Routledge and Kegan Paul.

Beeman, W. O. (1987) 'Anthropology and the Print Media', *Anthropology Today* 3: 2–4.

Bender, D. (1965) 'The Development of French Anthropology', *Journal of the History of the Behavioural Sciences* 2: 139–51.

Benedict, B. (1983) *The Anthropology of World's Fairs. San Francisco's Panama Pacific International Exposition of 1915*, London: Scolar.

Bennett, C. (1995) 'Sex! Sex! Sex! How dull can it possibly get?', *The Guardian 'Weekend'*, 16 September: 28–33.

Benthall, J. (1987) 'Terre Humaine. Interview with Jean Malaurie', *Anthropology Today* 3, 4: 8–10.

Berman, B. J. and Lonsdale, J. M. (1989) 'Louis Leakey's Mau Mau: A study in the politics of knowledge', *History and Anthropology* 5, 2: 143–204.

Bogdan, R. (1988) *Freak Show. Presenting Human Oddities for Amusement and Profit*, Chicago: Chicago University Press.

Bornstein, K. (1995) *Gender Outlaw: On men, women and the rest of us*, London: Routledge.

Brady, I. (ed.) (1983) 'Speaking in the Name of the Real: Freeman and Mead on Samoa', *American Anthropologist* 85, Special Section: 908–47.

Caffrey, M. M. (1989) *Ruth Benedict. Stranger in this Land*, Austin: University of Texas Press.

Calder, A. (n.d.) *The Mass Observers 1937–1949*, Unpublished ms.

Campbell, J. (1960) *The Masks of God. Volume I: Primitive Mythology*, London: Secker and Warburg.

Cartwright, J. (1993) *Masai Dreaming*, London: Macmillan.

Chagnon, N. A. (1983) *Yanomamo: The Fierce People* (3rd edition), New York: Holt, Rinehart and Winston.

Chambers, E. (1987) 'Applied Anthropology in the Post-Vietnam Era: Anticipations and ironies', *Annual Review of Anthropology* 16: 309–37.

Chandler, K. (1993) *"Ribbons, Bells and Squeaking Fiddles". The Social History of Morris Dancing in the English South Midlands, 1660–1900*, Publications of the Folklore Society: Tradition 1, Middlesex: Hisarlik.

Chandler, R. (1953) *The Long Good-bye*, London: Hamish Hamilton.

Chapman, M. (1994) 'Social Anthropology and Business Studies – mutual benefit?', *Anthropology in Action* 1: 12–15

Chernichewski, V. (pseudonym of C. Duff) (1935) *Anthropological Report on a London Suburb*, London: Grayson and Grayson.

Clifford, J. (1982) *Person and Myth. Maurice Leenhardt in the Melanesian World*, Berkeley: University of California Press.

—— (1988) *The Predicament of Culture. Twentieth-Century Ethnography, Literature, and Art*, Cambridge, Mass.: Harvard University Press.

Clifford, J. and Marcus, G. (eds) (1986) *Writing Culture: The poetics and politics of ethnography*, Berkeley: University of California Press.

Coombes, A. E. (1994) *Reinventing Africa. Museums, Material Culture and Popular Imagination*, New Haven: Yale University Press.

Cowling, M. (1989) *The Artist as Anthropologist. The Representation of Type and Character in Victorian Art*, Cambridge: Cambridge University Press.

Crozier, M. (1964) 'The Cultural Revolution: Notes on the changes in the intellectual climate of France', in S. R. Graubard (ed.) *A New Europe?*, London: Oldbourne.

Dawkins, R. (1976) *The Selfish Gene*, Oxford: Oxford University Press.

De Cocq, A. P. L. (1968) *Andrew Lang. A Nineteenth-century Anthropologist*, Utrecht: Uilg Zwijsen Tilburg.

Delf, G. (1961) *Jomo Kenyatta. Towards Truth about 'The Light of Kenya'*, London: Gollancz.

de Waal, A. (1993) 'In the disaster zone. Anthropologists and the ambiguity of aid', *Times Literary Supplement*, 16 July: 5–6.

Dolby, R. G. A. (1982) 'On the Autonomy of Pure Science: The construction and maintenance of barriers betwen scientific establishments and popular culture', in N. Elias, H. Martins and R. Whiteley (eds) *Scientific Establishments and Hierarchies*, Dordrecht: Reidel.

Dooling, R. (1995) *White Man's Grave*, London: Sinclair-Stevenson.

Downey, G. L. and Rogers, J. D. (1995) 'On the Politics of Theorizing in a Postmodern Academy', *American Anthropologist* 97: 269–81.

Dubow, S. (1995) *Scientific Racism in Modern South Africa*, Cambridge: Cambridge University Press.

Easton, S. B., Shostak, M. and Konner, M. (1989) *The Stone-Age Health Programme. Diet and Exercise as Nature Intended*, London: Angus and Robertson.

Economic and Social Research Council (ESRC) (1994) *Pressing Home your Findings. Media Guidelines for ESRC Researchers*, Swindon: ESRC.

Efron, J. M. (1994) *Defenders of the Race. Jewish Doctors and Race Science in Fin-de-siècle Europe*, New Haven: Yale University Press.

Eliade, M. (1960) *Myths, Dreams and Mysteries*. London: Harvill.

—— (1964) *Shamanism. Archaic Techniques of Ecstasy*, trans. W. R. Trask, Bollingen Series LXXVI, New York: Bollingen/Pantheon.

Elliot Smith, G., Malinowski, B., Spinden, H. J. and Goldenweiser, A. (1928) *Culture: A Symposium*, Psyche Miniatures, General Series, London: Kegan Paul, Trench and Traubner.

Evans-Pritchard, E. E. (1940) *The Nuer*, Oxford: Clarendon Press.

—— (1946) 'Applied Anthropology', *Africa* XVI: 92–101.

—— (1951) *Social Anthropology*, London: Cohen and West.

—— (1981) *A History of Anthropological Thought*, edited by Andre Singer, London: Faber.

Feather, J. (1988) *A History of British Publishing*, London: Croom Helm.

Firth, R. (1957) 'Malinowski as Scientist and as Man', in R. Firth (ed.) *Man and Culture. An Evaluation of the Work of Bronislaw Malinowski*, London: Routledge and Kegan Paul, pp. 1–21.

—— (1975) 'An Appraisal of Modern Social Anthropology', *Annual Review of Anthropology* 4: 1–25.

—— (1981) 'Bronislaw Malinowski', in S. Silverman (ed.) *Totems and Teachers. Perspectives on the History of Anthropology*, New York: Columbia University Press, pp. 100–39.

—— (1988) 'Malinowski in the History of Social Anthropology', in R. Ellen, E. Gellner, G. Kubica and J. Mucha (eds) *Malinowksi between Two Worlds. The Polish Roots of an Anthropological Tradition*, Cambridge: Cambridge University Press, pp. 12–42.

Fournier, M. (1994) *Marcel Mauss*, Paris: Fayard.

Fraser, R. (ed.) (1990) *Sir James Frazer and the Literary Imagination. Essays in Affinity and Influence*, London: Macmillan.

Freeman, D. (1983) *Margaret Mead and Samoa. The Making and Unmaking of an Anthropological Myth*, Cambridge, Mass.: Harvard University Press.

Gardner, H. (1996) *Leading Minds. An Anatomy of Leadership*, London: Harper Collins.

Gieryn, T. F. (1983) 'Boundary work and the Demarcation of Science from Non-Science: Strains and interests in professional ideologies of science', *American Sociological Review* 48: 781–95.

Ginsburg, F. (1992) 'Ethnographies on the Airwaves: The presentation of anthropology on American, British and Japanese television', in P. Hockings and Y. Omori (eds) *Cinematographic Theory and New Dimensions in Ethnographic Film*, Senrie Ethnological Studies No. 24, Osaka: National Museum of Ethnology, pp. 31–66.

Givens, D. B. (1992) 'Publish or Perish', *American Anthropological Newsletter* 37, 5: 1.

Goodall, J. (1971) *In the Shadow of Man*, Boston: Houghton Mifflin.

Goody, J. (1995) *The Expansive Moment. Anthropology in Britain and Africa 1918–1970*, Cambridge: Cambridge University Press.

Gordon, R. J. (1992) *The Bushman Myth. The Making of a Namibian Underclass*, Boulder: Westview.

Grant, L. (1995) 'Written on the Body', *The Guardian 'Weekend'*, 1 April: 12–20.

Graves, R. and Hodge, A. (1940) *The Long Weekend. A Social History of Great Britain 1918–1939*, London: Faber.

Grillo, R. (1985) 'Applied Anthropology in the 1980s: Retrospect and prospect', in R. Grillo and A. Rew (eds) *Social Anthropology and Development Policy*, ASA Monographs 23, London: Tavistock.

Grimshaw, A. and Hart, K. (1994) 'Anthropology and the Crisis of the Intellectuals', *Critique of Anthropology* 14, 3: 227–61.

Gross, J. (1969) *The Rise and Fall of the Man of Letters*, London: Weidenfeld and Nicolson.

Grosskurth, P. (1980) *Havelock Ellis. A Biography*, London: Allen Lane.

—— (1988) *Margaret Mead. A Life of Controversy*, Harmondsworth: Penguin.

Haddon, A. C. (1898) *The Study of Man*, London: Bliss and Sands.

—— (1903) 'Anthropology: Its position and needs', *Journal of the Royal Anthropological Institute*: 11–23.

—— (1909) 'Anthropological Notes', *Man* 9: 128.

Hammond, M. (1980) 'Anthropology as a Weapon of Social Combat in Late

Nineteenth-century France', *Journal of the History of the Behavioural Sciences* 16: 118–32.

Haraway, D. (1992) *Primate Visions. Gender, Race, and Nature in the World of Modern Science*, London: Verso.

Harrison, J. (1925) *Reminiscences of a Student's Life*, London: Cape.

Heine, B. (1985) 'The Mountain People: Some notes on the Ik of north-eastern Uganda', *Africa* 55: 3–16.

Herbert, C. (1991) *Culture and Anomie. Ethnographic Imagination in the Nineteenth Century.* Chicago: Chicago University Press.

Hinshaw, R. E. (1980) 'Anthropology, Administration, and Public Policy', *Annual Review of Anthropology* 9: 497–522.

Hinsley, C. M. (1981) *Savages and Scientists. The Smithsonian and the American Indian*, Washington: Smithsonian institution.

Hocart, A. M. (1937) 'Cinematic Anthropology', *Nature* 139, Supplement, March 13: 447–8.

Hogbin, I. (1946) 'The Trobriand Islands', *Man* XLVI: 72.

Houtman, G. and Knight, J. (1995) 'The Royal Anthropological Institute and the Popularization of Anthropology', *Practicing Anthropology*, 17: 37–41.

Howard, J. (1984) *Margaret Mead. A Life*, London: Harvill Press.

Howarth, T. E. B. (1978) *Cambridge Between Two Wars*, London: Collins.

Hughes, H. S. (1968) *The Obstructed Path: Social Thought in the Years of Desperation, 1930–1960*, New York: Harper and Row.

Huxley, A. (1936) *Eyeless in Gaza*, London: Chatto and Windus.

Huxley, E. (1985) *Out in the Midday Sun. My Kenya*, London: Chatto and Windus.

Huxley, F. (1956) *Affable Savages*, London: Hart-Davis.

—— (1966) *The Invisibles*, London: Hart-Davis.

—— (1974) *The Way of the Sacred*, London: Aldus.

—— (1976) *The Raven and the Writing Desk*, London: Thames and Hudson.

—— (1986) *The Dragon, Nature of Spirit, Spirit of Nature*, London: Thames and Hudson.

—— (1990) *The Eye. The Seer and the Seen*, London: Thames and Hudson.

Jackson, W. (1986) 'Melville Herskovits and the Search for Afro-American Culture', in G. W. Stocking (ed.) *Malinowski, Rivers, Benedict and Others. Essays on Culture and Personality*, History of Anthropology 4, Madison: University of Wisconsin Press, pp. 95–126.

Jamin, J. (1979) 'Preface', to *Iles-Paradis, Iles de Illusion: lettres des Mers du Sud* (Translation of Asterisk 1923) pp. 3–15.

—— (1991) 'Michel Leiris' in P. Boute and M. Izard (eds) *Dictionnaire de l'ethnologie et de l'anthropologie*, Paris: Presses Universitaires de France, pp. 413–14.

Jencson, L. (1989) 'Neopaganism and the Great Mother Goddess. Anthropology as midwife to a new religion', *Anthropology Today* April, 5, 2: 2–4.

Jenkins, A. (1986) '*Disappearing World* goes to China. A production study of anthropological films', *Anthropology Today* June 2, 3: 6–13.

Kaberry, P. (1957) 'Malinowski's Contribution to Field-work Methods and the Writing of Ethnography' in R. Firth (ed.) *Man and Culture. An*

Evaluation of the Work of Bronislaw Malinowski, London: Routledge and Kegan Paul, pp. 71–92.

Karady, V. (1972) 'Naissance de l'ethnologie universitaire', *L'Arc* 48: 33–40.

—— (1981) 'French Ethnology and the Durkheimian Breakthrough', *Journal of the Anthropological Society of Oxford*, XII: 165–76.

—— (n.d.) 'Academic Ethnology in France from Mauss to Lévi-Strauss: The social organization of a marginal discipline'. Unpublished paper.

Karp, I., Mullen Kreamer, C. and Lavine, S. D. (eds) (1992) *Museums and Communities: The Politics of Public Culture*, Washington, DC: Smithsonian Institution.

Kluckhohn, C. (1943) 'Bronislaw Malinowski 1884–1942', *Journal of American Folklore* 56, 221: 208–19.

Kuklick, H. (1991) *The Savage Within. The Social History of British Anthropology, 1885–1945*, Cambridge: Cambridge University Press.

Kuper, A. (1994) *The Chosen Primate. Human Nature and Cultural Diversity*, Cambridge, Mass.: Harvard University Press.

Kuper, J. (1977) *The Anthropologists' Cookbook*, London: Routledge and Kegan Paul.

Lang, A. (1936) 'Edward Burnett Tylor', in B. W. Friere-Marreco (ed.) *Anthropological Essays Presented to Edward Burnett Tylor in Honour of his Seventy-fifth Birthday, October 2 1907*, Oxford: Clarendon Press.

Leach, E. (1965) 'Frazer and Malinowski. On the "Founding Fathers"', *Encounter* 25, 5: 24–36.

—— (1967) *A Runaway World? Reith Lectures 1967*, London: BBC.

Leopold, J. (1980) *Culture in Comparative and Evolutionary Perspective: E. B. Tylor and the Making of Primitive Culture*, Berlin: Dietrich Reimer.

Lepowsky, M. (1994a) 'Writing for Many Audiences', *Anthropology Newsletter*, November: 48.

—— (1994b) 'An Anthropologist in Media Land', *Anthropology Newsletter*, December: 27.

—— (1995) 'Getting the Word Out', *Anthropology Newsletter*, January: 37, 44.

Lewis, I. M. (1976) *Social Anthropology in Perspective*, Harmondsworth: Penguin.

Lienhardt, R. G. (1964) *Social Anthropology*, Oxford: Oxford University Press.

—— (1992) 'Frazer's Anthropology: Science and sensibility', *Journal of the Anthropological Society of Oxford* 24, 1: 1–12.

Loizos, P. (1980) 'Granada Television's *Disappearing World* Series: An appraisal', *American Anthropologist* 82: 573–94.

Lorenz, K. (1966) *On Aggression*, New York: Harcourt, Brace and World.

Lowie, R. (1938) *The History of Ethnological Theory*, London: Harrap.

Lubbock, J. (1865) *Pre-historic Times, as Illustrated by Ancient Remains, and the Manners and Customs of Modern Savages*, London.

—— (1870) *The Origin of Civilization and the Primitive Condition of Man*, London.

MacClancy, J. V. (1993) 'Biological Basques, Sociologically Speaking', in M. Chapman (ed.) *Social and Biological Aspects of Ethnicity*, Oxford: Oxford University Press.

—— (1995) 'Brief Encounter. The meeting, in Mass Observation, of British

Surrealism and Popular Anthropology', *Journal of the Royal Anthropological Institute* (n. s.) 1, 3: 456–74.

Malinowski, B. (1922) *Argonauts of the Western Pacific. An Account of Native Enterprise and Adventure in the Archipelagoes of Melanesian New Guinea*, London: Routledge and Kegan Paul.

—— (1923) 'The Problem of Meaning in Primitive Language', in *The Meaning of Meaning* by C. K. Ogden and A. I. Richards (eds), London: International Library of Psychology, Philosophy, and Scientific Method, pp. 451–510.

—— (1926) *Myth in Primitive Psychology*, London: Kegan Paul, Trench and Traubner.

—— (1927) *The Father in Primitive Psychology*, London: Kegan Paul, Trench and Traubner.

—— (1932a) 'Introduction' to *Sorcerers of Dobu. The Social Anthropology of the Dobu Islanders of the Western Pacific* by R.F. Fortune, New York: Dutton, pp. xi–xxviii.

—— (1932b) 'Preface' to *Hunger and Work in a Savage Tribe. A Functional Study of Nutrition among the Southern Bantu* by A. I. Richards, London: pp. ix–xvi.

—— (1932c) 'Special Foreword to the Third Edition' of *The Sexual Life of Savages*, London: Routledge and Kegan Paul, pp. xix–xxxi.

—— (1934) 'Introduction' to *Law and Order in Polynesia. A Study of Primitive Legal Institutions* by I. Hogbin, London: Christophers, pp. xvii–lxxii.

—— (1947) *Freedom and Civilization*, London: Allen and Unwin.

—— (1967) *A Diary in the Strict Sense of the Term*, London: Routledge and Kegan Paul.

Man, E. H. (1885) *On the Aboriginal Inhabitants of the Andaman Islands*, London: Royal Anthropological Institute.

Manganaro, M. (1990a) 'Textual Play, Power, and Cultural Critique: An orientation to modernist anthropology', in M. Manganaro (ed.) *Modernist Anthropology. From Fieldwork to Text*, Princeton: Princeton University Press, pp. 3–47.

—— (ed.) (1990b) *Modernist Anthropology. From Fieldwork to Text*, Princeton: Princeton University Press.

—— (1992) *Myth, Rhetoric, and the Voice of Authority. A Critique of Frazer, Eliot, Frye, and Campbell*, New Haven: Yale University Press.

Mark, J. (1995) *The King of the World in the Land of the Pygmies*, Lincoln: University of Nebraska Press.

Marrett, R. R. (1910) 'The Present State of Anthropology', *The Athenaeum*, 12 March, 4298: 299–300.

—— (1941) *A Jerseyman at Oxford*, Oxford: Oxford University Press.

Mauss, M. (1969) 'L'Ethnographie en France et a l'étranger', *Oeuvres 3. Cohesion sociale et divisions de la sociologie*, edited by V. Karady (orig. published 1913 in *Revue de Paris* 20), pp. 395–436.

Mead, M. (1949) 'Ruth Fulton Benedict', *American Anthropologist* 51: 457–63.

—— (1956) *New Lives for Old. Cultural Transformations – Manus, 1928–1953*, London: Gollancz.

Merriam, A. P. (1964) 'Melville J. Herskovits', *American Anthropologist* 66: 83–109.

Middleton, J. (1994) 'Out of Order in Africa' (Obituary of Colin Turnbull), *The Guardian* 10 August.

Mitchison, N. (1979) *You May Well Ask. A Memoir 1920–1940*, London: Gollancz.

Modell, J. S. (1983) *Ruth Benedict. Patterns of a Life*, Philadelphia: University of Pennsylvania Press.

Montagu, A. (1942) 'Bronislaw Malinowski (1884–1942)', *Isis* (Harvard) 24, Pt. 2 No. 94; 146–50.

—— (ed.) (1968) *Man and Aggression*, Oxford: Oxford University Press.

Morgan, C. (1944) *The House of Macmillan (1843–1943)*, London: Macmillan.

Morgan, E. (1972) *The Descent of Woman*, New York: Stein and Day.

Morris, D. (1969) *The Naked Ape*, London: Jonathan Cape.

Murray, Sir Herbert (1930) 'Introduction', *Orakaiva Society*, Oxford: Clarendon Press, pp. xix–xxiii.

Murray-Brown, J. (1972) *Kenyatta*, London: Allen and Unwin.

Naughton, J. (1992) 'Admiral Plays a Blinder', *The Observer* 18 October.

Needham, R. (1967) 'Editor's Introduction' to *The Development of Marriage and Kinship* by C. Staniland Wake (orig. published 1889), Chicago: Chicago University Press.

—— (1984) 'The Birth of the Meaningful', *Times Literary Supplement*, 13 April: 393.

—— (1985) *Exemplars*, Berkeley: University of California Press.

Pace, D. (1986) *Claude Lévi-Strauss. The Bearer of Ashes*, London: Routledge and Kegan Paul.

Payne, H. C. (1981) 'Malinowski's Style', *Proceedings of the American Philosophical Society* 125, 6: 416–40.

Peterson, M. A. (1991) 'Aliens, Ape Men and Whacky Savages. The Anthropologist in the Tabloids', *Anthropology Today* 7, 5: 4–8.

Pick, D. (1989) *Face of Degeneration. A European Disorder, c.1848–c.1918*, Cambridge: Cambridge University Press.

Pocock, D. (1975) *Understanding Social Anthropology*, London: Hodder and Stoughton.

Price, S. and Jamin, J. (1988) 'A Conversation with Michel Leiris', *Current Anthropology* 29: 157–174.

Quiggin, A. H. (1942) *Haddon the Head Hunter. A Short Sketch of the Life of A. C. Haddon*, Cambridge: Cambridge University Press.

Rae, S. (1995) 'Selling Down the River', *Independent on Sunday 'Magazine'*, 24 September: 44–5.

Rainger, R. (1978) 'Race, Politics and Science: The Anthropological Society of London in the 1860s', *Victorian Studies* 22: 51–70.

Read, C. H. (1900) 'Presidential Address', *Journal of the Anthropological Institute* XXX: 3–17.

Reed, E. (1975) *Woman's Evolution*, New York: Pathfinder.

Rhodes, C. (1994) *Primitivism and Modern Art*, London: Thames and Hudson.

Richards, A. (1943) 'Bronislaw Malinowski', *Man* XLIII: 1–4.

Riffenburgh, B. (1994) *The Myth of the Explorer. The Press, Sensationalism and Geographical Discovery*, Oxford: Oxford University Press.

Riviere, G. H. (1968) 'My Experience at the Musée d'Ethnologie', *Proceedings of the Royal Anthropological Institute*: 17–21.

Riviere, P. (1978) 'Introduction' to *The Origin of Civilization and the Primitive Condition of Man* by John Lubbock (orig. published 1870). Chicago: Chicago University Press, pp. xiii–lxiv.

—— (1989) 'New Trends in British Social Anthropology', *Cadernos do Noreste* II: 1–17.

Robertson, Sir George Scott (1897) *The Kaffirs of the Hindu Kush*, London: Lawrence and Bullen.

Robeson, E. G. (1945) *African Journey*, New York: John Day.

Russell, B. (1929) *Marriage and Morals*, London: Allen and Unwin.

—— (1968) *The Autobiography of Bertrand Russell*, vol. 2, London: Allen and Unwin.

Rydell, R. W. (1984) *All the World's A Fair. Visions of Empire at American International Expositions, 1876–1916*, Chicago: University of Chicago Press.

Schapera, I. (1940) *Married Life in an African Tribe*, London: Faber.

Scheper-Hughes, N. (1984) 'The Margaret Mead Controversy: Culture, biology and anthropological Inquiry', *Human Organization* 43: 85–93.

Schneider, W. H. (1982) *An Empire for the Masses. The French Popular Image of Africa, 1870–1900*, Westport, CT: Greenwood.

Shore, C. and Wright, S. (n.d.) 'Colonial Gaze to Critique of Policy: British anthropology in policy and practice', in M. Baba and C. Hill (eds) *The Global Practice of Anthropology* (forthcoming).

Singer, A. (1992) 'Anthropology in broadcasting', in P. I. Crawford and D. Turton (eds) *Film as Ethnography*, Manchester: Manchester University Press, pp. 264–73.

Slocum, S. (1975) 'Woman the Gatherer' in R. R. Reiter (ed.) *Toward an Anthropology of Women*, New York: Monthly Review Press, pp. 36–50.

Spencer, C. (1995) *Homosexuality. A History*, London: Fourth Estate.

Sperling, S. (1991) 'Baboons with Briefcases: Feminism, functionalism, and sociobiology', *Signs* 17: 1–27.

Stocking, G. W. (1983) 'The Ethnographer's Magic: Fieldwork in British anthropology from Tylor to Malinowski', in G. W. Stocking (ed.) *Observers Observed. Essays on Ethnographic Fieldwork*, History of Anthropology 1, Madison: University of Wisconsin Press, pp. 70–120.

—— (1986) 'Anthropology and the Science of the Irrational. Malinowski's encounter with Freudian Psychoanalysis', in G. W. Stocking (ed.) *Malinowski, Rivers, Benedict and Others. Essays on Culture and Personality*, History of Anthropology 4, Madison: University of Wisconsin Press, pp. 13–49.

—— (1987) *Victorian Anthropology*, New York: Free Press.

—— (1991) 'Maclay, Kubary, Malinowski: Archetypes from the Dreamtime of anthropology', in G. W. Stocking (ed.) *Colonial Situations. Essays on the Contextualization of Ethnographic Knowledge*, History of Anthropology 7, Madison: University of Wisconsin Press, pp. 9–74.

—— (1992) *The Ethnographer's Magic and Other Essays in the History of Anthropology*, Madison: University of Wisconsin Press.

Strathern, M. (1987) 'Out of Context: The persuasive fictions of anthropology', *Current Anthropology* 28, 3: 251–82.

Street, B. V. (1975) *The Savage in Literature. Representations of 'Primitive' Society in English Fiction 1858–1920*, London: Routledge and Kegan Paul.

—— (1992a) 'British Popular Anthropology: Exhibiting and photographing the other', in E. Edwards (ed.) *Anthropology and Photography*, New Haven: Yale University Press, pp. 122–31.

—— (1992b) 'Anthropology and Higher Education,' Paper presented at Oxford Brookes University.

Strenski, I. (1982) 'Malinowski: Second positivism, second romanticism', *Man* 17: 766–70.

—— (1987a) *Four Theories of Myth in Twentieth-century History. Cassirer, Eliade, Lévi-Strauss and Malinowski*, Basingstoke: Macmillan.

—— (1987b) 'Henri Hubert, Racial Science and Political Myth', *Journal of the History of the Behavioural Sciences* 23: 353–67.

Symmons-Symonolewicz, K. (1958) 'Bronislaw Malinowski: An intellectual profile', *The Polish Review* III, 4: 55–76.

Symonolewicz, K. (1955) *Bronislaw Malinowski: A Sociological Analysis*, Ann Arbor: University Microfilms.

Tebbell, J. (1987) *Between Covers. The Rise and Transformation of Book Publishing in America*, New York: Oxford University Press.

Thomas, N. and Humphrey, C. (1994) 'Introduction' to N. Thomas and C. Humphrey (eds) *Shamanism, History and the State*, Ann Arbor: University of Michigan Press, pp. 1–12.

Thornton, R. J. (1985) '"Imagine Yourself Set Down...": Mach, Frazer, Conrad, Malinowski and the role of imagination in ethnography', *Anthropology Today* 1, 5: 7–14.

Tiger, L. and Fox, R. (1972) *The Imperial Animal*, London: Secker and Warburg.

Towers, B. (1972) 'Preface to the Second Edition' of *Naked Ape or Homo Sapiens?* by John Lewis and Bernard Towers (1st edition 1969), London: Garnstone, pp. ix–xiv.

Trautmann, T. R. (1987) *Lewis Henry Morgan and the Invention of Kinship*, Berkeley: University of California Press.

Turton, D. (1992) 'Anthropology on Television: What next?' in P. I. Crawford and D. Turton (eds) *Film as Ethnography*, Manchester: Manchester University Press, pp.283–99.

Tuzin, D. (1994) 'The Forgotten Passion. Sexuality and anthropology in the ages of Victoria and Bronislaw', *Journal of the History of the Behavioural Sciences* 30: 114–37.

Urry, J. (1993) *Before Social Anthropology. Essays on the History of British Anthropology*, Reading: Harwood.

Vale, V. and Juno, A. (1989) *Modern Primitives*, San Francisco: Research Publications.

Van der Post, L. (1958) *The Lost World of the Kalahari*, London: Hogarth Press.

Van Keuren, K. (1984) 'Museums and Ideology: Pitt Rivers, anthropology

museums and social change in Victorian Britain', *Victorian Studies* 28: 171–89.
—— (1989) 'Cabinets and Culture: Victorian anthropology and the museum context', *Journal of the History of the Behavioural Sciences* 25: 75–93.
Vickery, J. B. (1973) *The Literary Impact of The Golden Bough*, Princeton: Princeton University Press.
Vitebsky, P. (1995) 'From Cosmology to Environmentalism. Shamanism as local knowledge in a global setting', in R. Fardon (ed.) *Counterworks. Managing the Diversity of Knowledge*, London: Routledge, pp. 182–203.
Wallis, W. D. (1957) 'Anthropology in England Early in the Present Century', *American Anthropologist* 59: 781–90.
Wayne, H. (ed.) (1995) *The Story of a Marriage. The Letters of Bronislaw Malinowski and Elsie Masson*, Vol. 2, London: Routledge.
Weiss, P. (1995) *Kandinsky and Old Russia. The Artist as Ethnographer and Shaman*, New Haven: Yale University Press.
Wilson, E. O. (1975) *Sociobiology: The New Synthesis*, Cambridge, Mass.: Harvard University Press.
—— (1978) *On Human Nature*, Cambridge, Mass.: Harvard University Press.
York, P. (1994) 'The Dead Beat of the Street', *The Independent on Sunday*, 24 November: 24.
Young, M. W. (1992) 'Gone Native in Isles of Illusion: In search of Asterisk in Epi', in J. G. Carrier (ed.) *History and Tradition in Melanesian Anthropology*, Berkeley: University of California Press.

Chapter 2

Tricky tropes
Styles of the popular and the pompous

Alan Campbell

The main point I want to make is that the assumed contrast between scholarly and popular won't do. The associations go: 'popular' means accessible work in simple prose; 'scholarly' means specialized work presented in difficult prose. The background idea is that scholarly prose is obscure and inaccessible because it's dealing with complex ideas and requires intricate contortions of idiom while struggling with these ideas. Popular prose is just so because it leaves something out – it simplifies; it lacks subtlety and depth; it's superficial. This distinction is not helpful.

It would be wrong to underestimate how ingrained is the general process of thinking in terms of such distinctions. Binaries like that are cute; they are slick; and they let us all off the hook. This particular binary is a received idea. Here are two brief examples of the distinction in operation – and watch for the way that, once made, the distinction relieves us from further thought. First: 'Popular writers aren't interested in publicizing ideas, they are interested in publicizing themselves.' Hence their ideas need not be taken seriously since they are no more than a vehicle for the person to be a show-biz star. The background assumption here is that serious writers are, with pure conviction, interested in publicizing the ideas, and are consequently swaddled in commendable self-effacement. The distinction is seductively simple. From an academic point of view it is a comforting judgement. But it's nonsense; *as if* academics weren't up to *exactly* the same game of self-publicity. If you doubt that, ask the Derrida question of why people in academia put their names to something they publish.

Here's a second sound-byte on the same theme: 'An entertainer wants to give you exactly what you want ... An artist wants to give you what you *don't know* you want' (director David Cronenberg,

Rolling Stone, quoted in *The Guardian*, 23 January 1992). Translate this: 'The popular writer wants to give you exactly what you want... The scholarly writer wants to give you what you *don't know* you want.' The contrast is between: 'Lie back and enjoy it', and 'Come on, make the effort'. Well, you don't need to know about Thomas Kuhn's scientific paradigms to appreciate how much academic work is the complacent reiteration of what is already familiar, churning out the same thing again and again; nor how common are those exaggerated responses of hostility and defensiveness towards work that is seen as stepping out of line.

If we agree that the binary distinction is not helpful, we might be tempted to think that the problem could be solved by introducing more categories, or subdividing each of the original categories. Instead of these two, we might produce a classification of three, or four, or five, or else some sort of more sophisticated tree-diagram typology – various sub-types of the scholarly, sub-types of the not-so-scholarly, and sub-types of the popular. None of that is going to get us anywhere.

I think the better way to go is to look for principles of judgement, fashions of thought, conventions of writing. The exercise then is not to take a piece of work and ask which category it belongs to, and assign it to one, but to look at the work in terms of the various conventions it might be using, and also to consider the various kinds of judgement that might be brought to bear on the work.

I'll certainly use distinctions, but as temporary marking points; places from which to move on to something else or to change direction. As a prefatory hint, if you compare David Pocock's *Understanding Social Anthropology* (1975), a piece of work intended for schools or for introductory first-year university courses, a book that was explicitly aimed at a *sort of* popular audience; if you compare it with Pierre Bourdieu's *Outline of a Theory of Practice* (1977), I'd say that Pocock's is a brilliant piece of work – it's a gem of control, of balance, of effective prose, of lucidity; whereas Bourdieu's is verbiage, mutton dressed as lamb – and demonstrably so.

When first considering the opening distinction – differences between the popular and the scholarly – it struck me that the second category carried many more dubious assumptions along with it than the first did. But the question isn't usually presented like that. 'Popular' in this contrast would refer to nefarious influences that would be better avoided. 'Scholarly' would represent the most cherished values of academia. Those producing specialist work might secretly crave the fame of popularity, but if that were not forthcoming, they could comfort themselves with the thought that it's the sophistication of their technical work that denies them a wider audience. On the other hand, few people working in universities would feel comfortable if their work was described as unscholarly. Hence, by setting up the terms in opposition, there's already a defensive reflex written in, protecting the scholarly against the popular. So my question becomes: What, precisely, is being upheld?

LES CLERCS

The question is not just parallel with, but simply part of, twentieth-century arguments about the place of the intellectual. Isaiah Berlin thinks that the word 'intelligentsia' is not identical with the word 'intellectuals'. He demotes the word 'intellectuals' to those who 'simply want ideas to be as interesting as possible' (Berlin 1990: 148) – aesthetes of ideas. Paul Hollander (1981: 43), on the other hand, says that the words 'intellectuals' and 'intelligentsia' are interchangeable, except for a slight shift of emphasis due to historical fact. The slight shift of emphasis is this. 'Intelligentsia', as Isaiah Berlin explains, is a Russian word, referring to that movement, during the 1840s,

> of educated, morally sensitive Russians, stirred to indignation by an obscurantist Church, a brutally oppressive state indifferent to the squalor, poverty and illiteracy in which the great majority of the population lived; by a governing class which they saw as trampling on human rights and impeding moral and intellectual progress . . .
> (Berlin 1990: 149)

Its cognate, 'intellectual', emerges into general use in France during the Dreyfus affair. The Dreyfusards (involving, among others, Emile Zola, Durkheim and Lévy-Bruhl) themselves adopted the word as their auto-denomination in their *Manifeste des intellectuels* published in 1898. The counter-attack, led by people like Maurras and those associated with *Action française*, used the word as a term of abuse against the Dreyfusards.

It's a commonplace that the word 'intellectual' designating a class is out of place in English usage. It's a word more at home in Weimar Germany or pre-Franco Madrid and, of course, quintessentially in a Parisian café. Pierre Bourdieu's point (1980) in his reflection on Sartre's death is that the category 'intellectual', from that point on, is moribund in Paris. 'Glittering prizes of the media, the cultural goods market, and governmental bureaucracy' are, he says, threatening the autonomy of intellectual institutions and threatening to put an end to that most distinctive characteristic of an intelligentsia – to say 'non' to worldly power and privilege and to worldly authority. Sartre refused the offer of a Nobel Prize.

It's obvious why the word doesn't slip easily into English usage. The world of scholarship, books, literature, ideas, art, is in English society (as opposed to British society) a comfortable part of established institutions. Whereas the most privileged echelons of French academic, scholarly and arty life were said to form their own privileged but sealed society over against the institutions of political power, the most privileged levels of English academic, scholarly and arty life have intimate and ancient connections with Whitehall, the Inns of Court, wealth, snobbery, as well as the more recent glittering prizes of the media. (The M40 and the M11 motorways were not built to boost the national economy. They were built for reasons of privileged convenience. There's no motorway yet to Felixstowe and Harwich.) Not even the celebrated barbarism and anti-intellectualism of the English aristocracy is any counter to this area of life, since all privileged echelons are gravitating towards the same centre by different routes, and one area is not seen to compete with or threaten another. Hence, academic, scholarly and arty life is not saying 'non' to very much at all. Oxford University's refusal of an honorary degree to Margaret Thatcher is hardly an indication of an intelligentsia in full and flagrant revolt against the deep structures of privilege and power in the country at large.

I wouldn't be surprised if it was said that there still is, in Paris, an after-image of *les intellectuels* and that there's still a place for such values in public life there. I don't know. I suspect it's more likely that Britain and France are now homogenized – Chantal Cuer over there and Sarah Dunant (of *The Late Show*) here seem to make a good pair. It's the cultural commodity market, all packaged and glitzy, where presentation comes before anything else. Again, as a quick comparison, think of the contrast between Brian Moser's early *Disappearing Worlds* films (thoughtful, careful, clever) and the recent one on the Kogi of the Sierra Nevada in Colombia which was such a popular success, using the soft-focus approach where 'nice English explorer finds mysterious tribe who say some right-on ecological things'. A proper account of the history of ethnographic film would have a lot more to say about the comparison, but it suggests to me that it's not just lack of financial support that undermines the possibilities of producing thoughtful ethnographic film and good documentary. It's the present political and cultural climate too. Frivolity, shallowness and profit rule the airwaves. I'm sure the best television these days must be the Open University, but I don't have the viewing habits to keep up with it.

If I'm right about that state of affairs on television, and if you'd agree with me that the quality of public debate on television, radio and in the newspapers is dismal, then there are two sides to this predicament. We can look at it in one way and be insouciant: 'It doesn't matter,' we could say. If twenty million people watch *Coronation Street*, *Neighbours*, and those awful game shows, we don't have to. That's the easy response.

The darker side is brought out by Raymond Williams meditating on the book *Nineteen Eighty-Four* in the year 1984, assessing how far its prophecies were accurate. In George Orwell's novel the tyrannical system is mostly concerned with controlling the intellectual minority, neglecting the ignorant 85 per cent of the population. Williams says that almost the exact opposite has happened. It may be different in existing totalitarian regimes, but in capitalist democracies there is 'intense and continuous attention to the state of mind of the eighty-five per cent ... and a relative indifference to what "intellectuals" – already marked off as peculiar – believe or do' (Williams 1984: 121). Thinking particularly about history he suggests that, for the purposes of manipulating public opinion, it's not necessary to go to the trouble of rewriting the history books. 'Facts of the past' are left safely to 'research', to the lucubrations and ruminations of an impotent minority, 'to the obsessive and to the dry-as-dust' (ibid.: 122). Academia, scholarship, intellectuals are simply irrelevant.

On the one hand I'd accept that that is so, particularly following more than a decade of Thatcher and free market dogmas which have devastated so much of what was decent in these countries we live in, including all aspects of education; primary, secondary and tertiary. On the other hand, the universities are not entirely innocent victims. The impotence and marginalization of scholarly work is also to a large extent the fault of what goes on within academia. If you deliberately make yourself obscurantist, you will be obscured. So much of the obscurantist nonsense that's going on all around us at the moment is just inexcusable, particularly if you compare it with what was going on in, say, the late 1950s when E. P. Thompson, Eric Hobsbawm, Richard Hoggart, Raymond Williams and others were appearing.

RE-SEARCH

In *Real Presences*, George Steiner (1989: 34ff.) offers a clever explanation for the esoteric impulse in twentieth-century music, literature and the arts. He's pointing to the vacuous use of the word 'research' in universities when applied to the humanities. Looking particularly at literature he states that 'research' in this field refers to philology, to the emendation and recension of texts, to lexical and grammatical annotation – all in all a bundle of scrupulous, exact and exacting procedures for getting down to work on manuscripts and documents. He's comfortable with the word 'research' being used as a label for such procedures.

But the situation now is that there's nothing much left of this kind of work to do. It's all been done. But the *business* has to go on. So, on and on it goes; hundreds and hundreds of articles and dissertations and books on all sorts of subjects: on metaphor in Scott Fitzgerald, on the narrative grace of Chaucer, on E. M. Forster's avoidance of the tragic. All this is funded, presented and classified as 'research'. But, he says, all this 'grey morass' isn't 'research' at all. They are statements of personal intuition, declarations of taste, more or less novel, more or less ingenious, more or less productive of debate. *And there's nothing wrong with that as such*. But it's misleading to label these endless acts of 'secondary discourse', however well done, as 'research'.

He explains the process of using the idea of 'research' to make this smoke screen by adducing two causes: (1) the business aspect of university faculties, that they have to keep doing something; and (2) a point that's old hat to the discipline of anthropology: viz. nineteenth-century positivism, scientism, the aspirations to exact *Wissenschaft* – to knowledge that is scientific.

Steiner's concluding remarks are not very demanding: that making judgements about poems, paintings or pieces of music is not a cumulative procedure – we don't *do better* than Aristotle on Euripides, than Sam Johnson on King Lear, than Sainte-Beuve on Racine. We try again. We reinterpret. The image is a spiral, not an arrow. That's easy – even a bit banal.

But he throws in a nice twist to the argument. After a few comments on the way universities incorporate the living arts within themselves by the institution of writers in residence and 'workshops' (how very 1960s), of composers, *cinéastes*, playwrights, he goes on to say: look at the way that writers, poets, artists, composers, become *aware* of academic attention and academic expectations, and begin to create according to these expectations.

Steiner suggests, and I have no idea if this is accurate, that W. H. Auden can be recognized as one of the first of these; someone who began to write the type of poem that would reward the structural analyses of college and university classes. I'm not sure who was the first that ever burst into this cacophonous sea. But you can easily notice how, these days, novelists deliberately try for 'polysemic densities' and for whorls of ambiguities of the kind appreciated, taught and explained in university classes.

> The esoteric impulse in twentieth-century music, literature and the arts reflects calculation. It looks to the flattery of academic and hermeneutic notice. Reciprocally, the academy turns towards that which appears to require its exegetic, cryptographic skills . . .
>
> (Steiner 1989: 38)

That's the essential point. And those who find all this talk of poets and painters and musicians unsettling, and who feel the dunderhead's question coming on ('What's this got to do with anthropology?'), should relax. Steiner's point illuminates a much wider area than just the arts, than *beaux-arts* and *belles-lettres*. The esoteric impulse is enormously important in all areas of what are loosely called the social sciences, too, for precisely the reasons Steiner refers to. 'RE-search' (let's put the accent on the first syllable) is (1) keeping the business going, and (2) aping the conventions and expectations of science.

STYLE, STRUCTURALISM, AND POMO

As an illustration of what I mean by the bogus nature of obscurantist writing – the kind of writing that is actually accepted by the academy and given the status of serious work – I'll do a brief exercise of the kind done by Robert Graves and Alan Hodge in *The Reader over your Shoulder* (first published in 1943), where they took short extracts from all sorts of established writers – A. N. Whitehead, I. A. Richards, Bertrand Russell, George Santayana and so on – and rewrote them to show up the ragged edges.

My example is the translation of the opening lines of Pierre Bourdieu's *Outline of a Theory of Practice*. And incidentally, the problem is not inadequate translation – it's just as awful in the original French. The test is this . . . the wager is this: if you can demonstrate that I've left anything out, you (and Bourdieu) win. If not, he loses, and he loses

badly, since he claims elsewhere that his execrable writing is necessary
to deal with the supposedly ever-so difficult ideas he is dealing with.
So here goes:

> The practical privilege in which all scientific activity arises never
> more subtly governs that activity (insofar as science presupposes
> not only an epistemological break but also a *social* separation) than
> when, unrecognised as privilege, it leads to an implicit theory of
> practice which is the corollary of neglect of the social conditions in
> which science is possible.
>
> (Bourdieu 1977: 1)

I wrote:

> There are social conditions that give scientists privileges: money,
> resources, prestige, thus allowing them to work. Scientists often do
> not recognize that they are privileged in this way. Nevertheless, the
> nature of these privileges governs what scientists do. Indeed, these
> privileges, going unrecognized, have a subtle effect on the
> presuppositions that lie behind the activity.

Have I left anything out? Who wins? I'd suggest, further, that the
original paragraph is in even worse a state than at first appears. The last
two clauses are tautologous:

> Scientists (or anthropologists if you like) who are unaware of the
> social privileges within which they work are working within a
> theory which does not include an account of the social privileges
> within which they work.

Given the way this was originally written, my first question is: Why
didn't an editor have the gumption to have this sort of stuff sent back
to the author for a rewrite? But the more important question is: Why
do people, even for a moment, take this sort of appalling prose
seriously? Because the ideas at the back of them are original and
exciting? No, they're not.

You can move from blatantly incompetent prose like this to a more
controlled, although in my view equally vacuous, obscurity in Claude
Lévi-Strauss's work – another writer who has been given wide
attention as having something serious to say, as well as being described
as a master of style. Well, when you read in *The Savage Mind* that 'castes
naturalize a true culture falsely, [and] totemic groups culturalize a
false nature truly' (1966: 127), and when you read that the names of
birds, dogs, cattle and racehorses reveal these creatures to be

metaphorical human beings . . . metonymical inhuman beings . . . and so on (ibid.: 207) (fill in the rest for yourself), do you take this, as many commentators have done, as evidence of the 'elegance' of Lévi-Strauss's prose? I think it's buffoonery.

The tragedy of the Lévi-Straussian phenomenon – a fashion that spanned two decades in anthropology and elsewhere – was not so much the poor quality of what Lévi-Strauss wrote, although that in itself is a serious enough matter. It's *the collapse of critical response* to what he wrote that is so alarming. And it's the discipline of anthropology which has to pick up the tab for that lingering irresponsibility.

Lévi-Strauss's books are a particularly good example of obscure writing which masks banal ideas, and which is taken for profundity. It's a useful example nowadays, since there are few people left who would claim to be devotees. Lévi-Straussian structuralism is *passé*, and those who want to be fashionable must needs find something else. It shouldn't, therefore, be particularly controversial nowadays to say 'it was just some passing clouds' and it *is* now possible to take seriously the question: 'Why, then, did so many people get taken in? Why the collapse of critical response? Why all the posing: "I am a structuralist"? Why did this example of trivial obscurity get away with it?' I'll return to this shortly.

It *would* probably be controversial to make similar judgements about Jacques Derrida's writing, although, for what it's worth, what I've read of Derrida is just a concatenation of spurious oppositions and old-fashioned themes that have been better dealt with decades ago. I mean, for instance, that there is no *opposition* between speech and writing (that's just playing with nouns); that, for instance, no one with a serious interest in linguistics is going to take Saussure as anything more than a historical curiosity; that, for instance, the 'intentional fallacy' was a hot potato of the 1940s and 1950s, 'a poem should not mean but be' and all that jazz – and the issues were flogged to death then – in decent prose too. (Wimsatt and Beardsley's essay on 'The Intentional Fallacy' appeared in 1946.)

And what about the PoMo brigade in general? Again it's precisely the same point. At the back of all the bombast are such pedestrian, old-fashioned ideas – 'Cauld kail het again' in Hugh MacDiarmid's words – (cold cabbage heated up again). It's the same old stuff, put in whizz-bang language. For a start they have got their chronotypes (not their chrono*topes*, but their chrono*types*) in a terrible fankle. They apparently took the word *POST-modernism* from architecture, but didn't notice that the tag 'modernism' in architecture had very little chronological overlap with the tag 'modernism' in literature, art and music, never mind physics and psychoanalysis. Ivor Winters, for example, was writing anti-modernist tracts in the late 1930s and Harry Levin wrote his essay 'What was Modernism?' in 1960. So the Post-Modernist label leaves us with a rather uncomfortable chrono-typical vacuum between 1950 and, say, 1975. Did everyone just go to sleep for twenty or thirty years? Let's call the chronotype Post-Rip-van-Winkle-ism.

And again, let me duck the arguments with just one quick example from the 'zap-pow' vocab of PoMo. We're supposed to get awfully excited about 'heteroglossia' – a whizz-bang from Mikhail Bakhtin's dialogic imagination. It's supposed to be a post-modern concern. If we're going to tame a notion like that and get it down from Bakhtin's misty abstractions and make it work, we'd have to notice (a) that all Bakhtin's examples demonstrate that heteroglossia is as old as the hills. It's not post anything. And (b) we'd have to notice that the notion is really very simple. It's all around us. It's commonplace, like all *topoi*. Think of Robert Browning's *The Ring and the Book*, starting with what he called the 'pure crude fact' about a famous triple murder trial in Rome and worrying about getting at 'the truth' through what he called 'the plague of squint' – the result of variegated human perspectives. So he writes the story from *ten* different points of view, thereby resuscitating the inert facts and coming to the conclusion:

That art remains the one way possible
Of speaking truth, to mouths like mine at least.

It's simply fatuous to talk of heteroglossia as being 'post-modern' or as reflecting something new. When Sir Toby Belch shows how ridiculous Malvolio is, and when Malvolio in turn shows how sordid Toby Belch is: that's heteroglossia.

There's all the difference in the world between saying: 'Let's break with the past and call ourselves "modernist"' (which none of those classified as modernists did, by the way, except those in Brazil involved in putting on the stunning 'Week of Modern Art' events in São Paulo in February 1922), and saying: 'I can't be bothered finding out anything about the past: I'm so exquisitely post-everything'. That's what is so bogus. Surely, if you say we're all post-Freudian, for example, you mean that somehow Freud's work has touched us all, whether we like it or not. It does not mean that 'you must lie upon the daisies and discourse in novel phrases of your complicated state of mind' (that's Reginald Bunthorne in *Patience*) relieved of the bother of having to pay any attention to Freud. Post-modernist posing shows no appreciation whatever of what they're supposed to be *post*. What *do* they know of Stravinsky, or Picasso, or quantum theory? Have they *read Ulysses?*

RAW IDEAS AND COOKED BOOKS

So, what about responses to obscurity? How do we deal with obscurity? How do we start riddling out spurious obscurity from genuine difficulty? The question is: How far can we make the texts or the problems we're dealing with clear, getting them into the form of interesting lucidity, doing justice to what's there, without fracturing it into dull simplicities?

Back to the Lévi-Strauss example, then. In 1967 an editorial appeared in *The Times Literary Supplement* which commented rather tartly on Oxford University's choice of their Zaharoff lecturer for that year. André Maurois had been chosen, and the author of the editorial evidently felt that someone so clearly anti-structuralist couldn't be representative of 'what was going on' in Paris. Maurois had made some comments about the spurious avant-garde novelty offered by the whizz-bang words of 1967. The TLS piece commented:

> But a mysticism of exclusive techniques may be a guarantee of their being fruitfully mastered later on, and a much more damaging form of reassurance is that which comes from supposing that M. Lévi-Strauss, for example, is really out to mystify and not to make more intelligible. It is a gloomy possibility that French Structuralism may be quickly defused in England [sic], as Existentialism once was, by being interpreted in exclusively sociological terms. To guard against fashions is one thing, but to guard against the ideas exploited by fashions is quite another...
>
> (TLS 1967: 961)

I think we could now all agree that 'the ideas exploited by structuralism' didn't amount to a row of beans. (The idea [singular] exploited by structuralism was binary opposition.) So let's not get duped by the simplistic contrast in that editorial between dull, old-fashioned people who are not up to date with what's going on, and smart, intelligent people who are. Competent criticism means taking on a bit of prose and making sense of it, not joining up in a research industry. Why was it left to Noam Chomsky to say, specifically of *The Savage Mind*, that all that was being said was that 'humans classify, if they perform any mental acts at all' (1972: 74)? There were not many voices like that crying in the wilderness of those days.

To this day Lévi-Strauss is France's best known intellectual. A decade ago he came top of the *Lire* poll of six hundred intellectuals, students and politicians, beating Raymond Aron, Foucault, Lacan and Simone de Beauvoir (Pace 1983: 1). And *Le Figaro* produced a fanfaronade about his latest book in September 1991. The popularity is iconic, not substantial. Nobody bothers with structuralism, at least not any more. Structuralism is not the point, and never really was. Lévi-Strauss became a name, not because of the structuralism, but because of the publication of *Tristes Tropiques* in 1955. It became a bestseller – a classy bestseller, not like *The Naked Ape*, nor *The Joy of Sex*, nor Jane Fonda's *Work Out*. It was supposed to have been both scholarly and popular.

Tristes Tropiques is not generally thought of as an inconsequential piece of work. Susan Sontag speaks of:

> the incomparable *Tristes Tropiques* . . . *Tristes Tropiques* is one of the great books of our century. It is rigorous, subtle, and bold in thought. It is beautifully written. And like all great books, it bears an absolutely personal stamp; it speaks with a human voice.
>
> (Sontag 1970: 186)

That's from the person who also wrote that 'anthropology . . . is one of the rare intellectual vocations that does not demand a sacrifice of one's manhood' (ibid.: 189). George Steiner says Lévi-Strauss's prose is reminiscent of La Bruyère and Gide, and at times reveals a 'mannered Pascalian concision and syntax' (Steiner 1970: 171).

Tristes Tropiques is not a boring book, but I am puzzled about all the fuss. There are indeed a few passages of inspired writing: his regrets in Rio de Janeiro that he will never be able to see the Tupinamba villages that used to surround Guanabara Bay, together with the simultaneous realization that the yearning is unrealistic, since, had he come with the European invaders, he wouldn't have approached the Tupinamba with any kind of anthropological appreciation (Lévi-Strauss 1955: Chapter 4). The section on geology, psychoanalysis and Marxism is as good an introduction to structuralism as you could find anywhere (1955: Chapter 6). The section on crowds and beggars in India (1955: Chapters 15 and 16) stood on its own as an article in the *New Left Review* in the 1960s.

I can't find much more to recommend. The four ethnographic sections are too slight to be of much interest; and, alas, you can't teach the book to an Islamic audience because of the scandalous 'Taxila' chapter, the penultimate one (1955: Chapter 39). It was once suggested that the editorial decision to omit the chapters on India in the first translation (which appeared as *A World on the Wane*, 1961) was taken because the structure of the book was such a mess that it didn't matter anyway. (I've found one solitary commentator who tries on the suggestion that the organization of the book is 'subtle' – nice try, but not convincing – the structure of the book *is* a mess. Funny that, from the inventor of structuralism.) I wonder, though, about missing out those chapters. Was there a more serious reason? Did an editor spot those appalling statements about Islam at that time, and appreciate that they could cause offence? Perhaps not. Perhaps 'Islam' in those days had no more status than any other 'primitive people', and it didn't matter too much what you said, because in those days Islam didn't talk back. I just don't know. It's even more puzzling that there was no comment in Paris at the time, 1955 remember, given that Algeria would have been so much on people's minds.

If you're not involved with anthropology, and if you're not involved with academic discourse, (and if you're not Islamic), *Tristes Tropiques* will remain an interesting enough read. I'm not Islamic, but I do confront academic discourse and anthropological efforts. Knowing first hand about the disaster of structuralism, I find myself reading *Tristes Tropiques* in a different way. I find it a sinister book. It begins with an outburst of hate and ends exchanging glances, in a gesture of involuntary understanding, with a cat. In between are visits to Brazil and India, where all human encounters are like mime shows or silent movies. *Hauteur* is the tone: the condescending regard of the privileged outsider, who, having completed his observations, turns to apostrophize his elegant Parisian public.

Beggars in India, for example, by making objects out of themselves, make objects out of us, and the human gulf that opens up is impossible to cross (1955: Chapter 15). In Brazil, upstream from Pimenta Bueno in Rondônia he gets to the Mundé, and promptly leaves again with 'a feeling of emptiness', since he couldn't speak their 'jolly language' with its words ending in stressed syllables: *zip, zep, pep, zet, tap* and *kat*, which accentuate speech like a clashing of cymbals (1955: Chapter 31). And so on through the frozen vignettes of the four case studies: Caduveo, Bororo, Nambikwara and Tupi-Kawahib.

The ox-train goes plodding off through the Mato Grosso for a few weeks, and Lévi-Strauss writes about it as if it was the most oppressive spell of drudgery: 'We may endure six months of travelling, hardships and sickening boredom for the purpose of recording a hitherto unknown myth' (Lévi-Strauss 1974: 16). He did all that! He went through the Mato Grosso in the 1930s and all he got out of it was *a myth*, and a dose of sickening boredom? The emptiness of the response is breathtaking – a glum, lifeless, masochism. It's as if he'd been put through one of those cruel tricks played on apprentices, where they're told they must do something or another, in order to learn the trade, and are inveigled into absurd antics. Only in this case the victim never got the joke, even when it was all over. His own 'structuralism' should have taught him that you don't *have* to do it if you don't want to. If, as he emphasizes throughout his four volumes of *Mythologiques*, if a myth refers first of all to another myth, not to a social infrastructure; if, when you're dealing with a Bororo myth and you couldn't care less about Bororo infrastructure; then you can get your texts, as he did, from the Salesians or from Nimuendajú. You don't *have* to endure six months of the Mato Grosso if all you're going to get out of it is sickening boredom. And don't you pity the man who can travel from Dan to Beersheba, and cry "tis all barren'?

He *hates* travelling and exploring. In the 'Quest for Power' (Lévi-Strauss 1955: Chapter 4) it's argued that, while travellers and travel books are bound up in this quest, like some sort of Indian Braves going through their initiation ceremony, anthropology isn't bound up in this at all. Have you ever heard such nonsense? Academic writers in general and anthropological writers in particular are just as obsessed as anyone else with self-publicity, with their CVs and promotions and their little quests for power.

The picture we're presented with is a fake. The contrast we're supposed to assent to (that between the frivolous traveller and the serious anthropologist) is bogus. We're supposed to appreciate the sturdy integrity of a scholarly mission that takes on these privations and endures them in order to come through to a scholarly goal. It's all done for scholarship. It's all done for anthropology. Well, it doesn't convince me. Time and again the picture reveals that something has been lost. I don't know whether to say the centre's gone, or that the floor has dropped out of the enterprise. I've always been taught that the anthropological effort had something to do with an intelligent involvement with the lives of other peoples.

Without *Tristes Tropiques* becoming a bestseller there would have been no 'structuralism'. There would have been scant attention paid to the collection of essays called *Structural Anthropology* in 1958 had it not been written by the darlin' boy of Parisian intellectual life. Certainly there had been little attention paid to *Elementary Structures of Kinship* which had been on the go since 1948. Without *Tristes Tropiques*, no structuralism. And WITH *Tristes Tropiques*, curiously, structuralism didn't matter. It just had to be there – as the new fashion. It never managed to get outside the academy, but nobody cared.

David Lodge wrote that: 'Structuralism may be the first such movement to go through the complete life-cycle of innovation, orthodoxy and obsolescence, without ever touching the popular consciousness' (Lodge 1980). He was explaining that a very unhealthy gap had opened up by then – 1980 – between educated discourse inside and outside the academy. And he traced this malaise to Lévi-Straussian structuralism. Again this unsettling dislocation of sense and sensibility; this fracturing, this fissuring opening up.

The unhealthy gap has grown even wider. I'd want to remind those people involved with anthropology, who turn their backs with disdain on the baroque discourse of literary theory and PoMo, that the genealogy of ideas goes straight back to the Lévi-Straussian/Saussurian/structuralist package that appeared during the 1960s. The collapse of critical response to structuralism allowed it to thrive for nearly two decades, suffocating anthropology and setting the atmosphere that allowed deconstruction and PoMo to pop up. Hence it's misjudged to turn away from the present excesses and say: 'These matters have nothing to do with anthropology'. It has a great deal to do with anthropology.

With Derrida and PoMoChatter on the go, the whole thing is happening again: another collapse of critical response, another *trahison des clercs*. And I wonder if there are ways of addressing this sort of *nonsens* with a bit more responsibility. What strategies are there for dealing with obscurity?

THROUGH GLASSES DARKLY

I thought of contrasting Lévi-Strauss's output with that of Karl Marx. Marx was also an endless scribbler whose work involves massive obscurities. I'll suggest four directions that commentators can develop. First: can you make Marx accessible, at a simple level? Clearly yes. Mode of production, capital and labour, surplus value, alienation and so on; these are not impossible concepts to present in an immediately accessible way. Second: there's abundant scope for the commentary industry; for endless exegesis which can get as obscure as the writers wish. Third, and this is closely related to the previous line:

there's abundant scope for imitators to lose themselves in the obscure vocabulary and call themselves and their own writing 'Marxist'. Finally: there is enough in Marx, in the burning moral vision, in the views of the nature of capitalism and production, for writers to find an inspiring *vision* to follow, without being bound to the vocabulary. The best example I know is Eric Hobsbawm. I came across his books on the Long Century (1789 to 1914) and became a fan, knowing nothing about Hobsbawm's connection with the Communist Party or that he self-consciously referred to himself as Marxist.

It's a curious question. I still find myself asking of Hobsbawm's books: does it matter that he's supposed to be a Marxist? Is there any necessary connection between an interest in Marx's writing and the particular, peculiar and riveting way Hobsbawm wrote about the nineteenth century? Think about Chomsky's linguistics. I'll comfortably accept that Chomsky's particular transformational grammars could have been produced by all sorts of people who did not share his political views. There is no necessary connection between Chomsky's political/historical/social commentaries and what he says about the nature of language. You can't really have a Tory generative grammar as opposed to an Anarchist generative grammar. (Well, you could, but you wouldn't take either seriously.) You can't have Catholic mathematics and Protestant mathematics, even in Belfast. But you do accept a distinction between 'the Whig interpretation of history' and 'the Marxist interpretation of history'. You *would* expect an intimate connection between Hobsbawm's political intuitions and political concerns and his accounts of nineteenth-century history. You would certainly expect Norman Stone or Trevor-Roper writing about the same areas to produce different accounts. And indeed, that's what you get. But the important point about this fourth line is that the inspiration can be followed through without becoming caught up in the obscurities of the idiom.

I don't think anyone would describe Hobsbawm as a popular writer as if he belonged to a category appropriate to Jeffrey Archer, Barbara Cartland or Desmond Morris. But if anyone offered the opinion that his trilogy on the Long Century (*Age of Revolution*, *Age of Capital*, *Age of Empire*) is in some sense or another amateur, unscholarly, simplistic, partial, unsophisticated, you would seriously question the judgement. That trilogy is accessible to an enormously wide audience, to all sorts of readers outwith the academy. It is not esoteric, obscure, specialized, jargon-laden. It's a magnificent achievement. It's the result of scholarship at its best.

Let's compare this with Lévi-Strauss. In terms of quantity, in terms of a word count, Lévi-Strauss's output may well be approaching Karl Marx's, but it has nothing of the awesome aspect of Marx's. Whatever the personal ambitions that drove Marx to write, there was a clear moral/political/social concern driving him too. He was angry and passionately involved with the world. *En revanche*, there's not a shred of passion in Lévi-Strauss beyond the usual academic backbiting: snide comments about those he doesn't like and puffs for those he does. His moral concern is degree zero. As for the style, once you get used to the limited bag of tricks, you can see that it's a sort of automatic writing, a prose that reproduces itself endlessly. Where Marx's pen was driven by *saeva indignatio*, Lévi-Strauss's is propelled by *cacoethes scribendi*.

If Marx's most inspiring aspect is his passion, what's Lévi-Strauss's? I think it's those massive bundles of ethnographic facts that appear superficially exotic. But I'd like to compare the same four directions of commentary and see what happens. First, to make the basic ideas accessible at a simple level is ridiculously easy. It's binary opposition and that's that. And of course language *doesn't* work like that, and myth *doesn't* work like that, and the human mind *doesn't* work like that – or rather, to be as generous as possible, there's an awful lot more than binary oppositions going on. Second: is there scope for obscure comment and exegesis? Certainly. Piles of the stuff. Third: imitators? Yes, there are imitators, but you'll notice that most work that calls itself 'structuralist' or that claims some sort of inspiration from Lévi-Strauss's writing only uses the Lévi-Straussian style as a sort of embellishment. I can't think of any piece of work that you could say was thoroughly Lévi-Straussian discourse in the way you can point to all sorts of writing and accurately say that the language is thoroughly Marxist. Finally: is there a Lévi-Straussian vision that can be inspirational, without taking on the baggage of the structuralist jargon? I can't see it. The entire effort – to reduce everything to binary oppositions – is so thoroughly banal.

Marx is obscure. Lévi-Strauss is obscure. But it's not just an accident that, to this day, in Guatemala, for instance, or in Highland Peru, or in the Philippines, dispossessed peoples, many of whom would be speaking Quiché, or Quechua, or Tagalog, have found a voice for themselves through Marxist vocabulary, whatever you and I may think of what they say. It's frightening, for example, to hear the language used by Sendero Luminoso. What happens is that Marx's obscurity becomes refracted into a polyglossia: all sorts of different registers and intensities. Each one of these requires its own response in turn. I might find the language of Sendero Luminoso weird and threatening. I find the language of Eric Hobsbawm a delight. I find what Marvin Harris does with Marxism dull, and irritating in its naivety.

Looking at Lévi-Strauss in the same way, it's striking that there are no different registers of structuralism. There are no various and variegated interpretations and reinterpretations. It's no accident that structuralism never 'filtered through', in the TLS editorial's title phrase. The only questions to ask about structuralism are: how far, how often, and to what extent its devotees are prepared to imitate its bag of tricks before they get tired and move on to something else. There's nothing much to be done with Lévi-Straussian obscurity. It doesn't conceal a richness. It's a veil over an impoverished vision. The best response to this corpus is to let it be, as an antiquarian curiosity.

So, the question is more complicated than simply asking how to go about popularizing a scholarly discourse. A more useful image is that of how to allow for the creation and appearance of various interpretations and reinterpretations in different languages, different styles, different registers. This leads to two questions: (1) asking how far readers are capable of responding to a wide variety of voices and styles, taking each as it comes; and (2) asking how far can authors change registers effectively, writing and talking to different audiences. I'll illustrate the first point, then end with the second.

It doesn't matter in the slightest that *The Savage Mind* is classed as 'scholarly' while *Tristes Tropiques* is classed as 'popular'. What matters is how far we are capable of recreating something out of each, and I suggest that there's not a lot to be done with either. There's no point in saying that Bourdieu's writing is 'scholarly' and therefore reserved for specialists in the academy, whereas Hobsbawm's is more accessible and therefore can be safely let out on to a more popular market. The point is that Bourdieu's writing is hideous, and that Hobsbawm's breadth of vision, however popularly expressed, is anything but unscholarly. There's no point in saying that Marvin Harris's books are bad because they are written for a popular market. I find Marvin Harris quite entertaining. He writes rather well. But the fact that he's a popular writer is neither here nor there. What matters is that his vision can be properly criticized on account of its embarrassing simplicities – all these stupid little determinisms and *Just-So* stories.

PUBLICIZING THE YANOMAMO

Marvin Harris deliberately writes for a wide audience. Napoleon Chagnon has also done so in his book *The Fierce People* (1983). But Chagnon also does a lot of what might more strictly be called scholarly work. He would certainly like what he calls his 'scientific findings' to be taken seriously. Recently a fierce controversy raged round Chagnon's head which, although it implicated his popular book, centrally concerned the use made of his 'scientific findings' in the newspapers. What's in question here, then, is what might be called the 'popular' use of his 'scholarly' work.

In January 1989 a letter was published in the American Anthropological Association's *Anthropology Newsletter*, from the Brazilian Anthropological Association, specifically attacking an article Napoleon Chagnon had published in the journal *Science*, generally having a go at everything Chagnon has done, and even more generally making the point that Brazilian anthropologists *insist* that North American anthropologists (and all other First Worlders) should be aware of the 'political consequences of the academic images they build about the peoples they study'. Chagnon's article dealt with Yanomamo violence, as so much of his work does. The article was actually called 'Life Histories, Blood Revenge, and Warfare in a Tribal Population'.

The Yanomamo on the frontier between Brazil and Venezuela were and still are going through an appalling crisis. Twenty thousand gold prospectors were invading the lands of some nine thousand Yanomamo on the Brazilian side. The sheer numbers coming in were catastrophic. The public response of the government and government agencies was limp and *fainéant*. But that's a blind; a veil. Brazilian government policy in Amazonia was and still is the result of a vast military initiative, described in Suzanne Hecht and Alexander Cockburn's *The Fate of the Forest* (1990). And to let you see what we're up against, a journalist recently discovered a not-too-secret document, published by the Superior School of War (the Brazilian equivalent of Sandhurst), which stated: 'We, the military, declare ourselves in a state of war against anthropologists, ecologists, environmentalists, and all foreigners who concern themselves with Indian rights.' We're certainly into heavy manners here.

Chagnon's article was reported in the *Los Angeles Times* under the headline: 'Anthropologists Study Homicidal Yanomamo' and in the *Washington Post* under the title: 'Sexual Competition and Violence: Researcher Advances New Theory for Amazon Tribe's Homicide'.

Both these were translated and published in the principal Brazilian newspapers in 1988. It's also alleged that in the early 1980s Brazilian government officials used a *Time* magazine article called 'Beastly or Manly?' based on Chagnon's work as *part of* the justification for cutting up Yanomamo territory into twenty-one micro-reservations. This, it was said, would put an end to their aggressive practices. The new articles appeared just as the wave of gold prospector invasions was at its height, invasions that included a number of murderous incidents. The miners' lobby justified *their* violence by quoting the widely held view that the Yanomamo were themselves inveterately violent, and government officials referred to this 'known fact' and suggested that the Yanomamo 'deserved what they got'. Given that the Yanomamo are being wiped out in one of the nastiest disasters in Amazonia for many decades there's an enormous urgency to the question of anthropological involvement in the real world.

There's an academic squabble at the back of this. It concerns a Yanomamo category: *unokai*. In media terms the translation given is 'killer'. There are lots of Yanomamo men called *unokai* and the row between the anthropologists involved is that, according to two Brazilian anthropologists, most of these *unokai* men have only 'symbolically' killed. Yanomamo violence is, they say, exaggerated, and Chagnon is incapable of distinguishing between real practices and ideological elaborations. There's also a row about statistical data and there's the added twist that Chagnon's writings become overtly biosociological, where he says that *unokai* men have higher status, therefore get more women, therefore have better reproductive success, therefore murder is biologically advantageous for reproduction.

The main charges are, then, that Chagnon is falsifying and manipulating data; that he is describing the people he worked with in racist terms; and that in doing so he is fostering genocide. When you've finished reading the ABA letter you think: 'Well, that's that: old Chagnon's up the proverbial creek without a paddle.' But not quite. It's not as simple as that.

Chagnon's reply published in the same *Newsletter* was that the ABA letter is libellous. He says that academics can't control what journalists say about their work. Nor should we go around bad-mouthing 'the press' since the *Washington Post* and the *Los Angeles Times* in particular have done a great deal to alert the public to what's happening to indigenous minorities, tropical forests and so on. He stands by his statistics and says the Brazilian commentators show that they can't handle statistical procedures. There is a linguistic distinction made in

Yanomamo between 'true' and 'false' *unokai*, so the Yanomamo themselves distinguish between 'real' and 'symbolic'. He goes on to say that 'scientific understanding of human behavior requires an understanding of both biology and cultural anthropology'. He denies that he said as a general principle that murder is biologically advantageous. He said that 'there is a positive and statistically significant correlation between *unokai* status (the ritually purified killer of another real person) and marital and therefore reproductive success'. He says this is an important *scientific finding*.

The final point is this: he says indigenous minorities should be 'saved' no matter what their morality patterns may be. If anthropologists go around trying to conceal what's going on in order to make the indigenous people look 'nice' to help their survival, then that's even more dangerous for them. He also points out that Brazilian anthropologists giving lectures to US anthropologists is a reflection in academia of a more generalized xenophobia present in Brazilian society where you just blame the Yankee. He points out that *all* the Europeans who invaded the Americas have spent five hundred years exterminating native Americans in both the North and South continents, and that this has proceeded and will proceed, regardless of what anthropologists do or say, since it's driven by a gigantic economic process against which anthropologists can do very little, although all do their best.

I'd suggest a few short cuts in approaching this dispute. Let's leave aside the problem of Third World anthropologists and their alleged resentment of First World anthropologists. Let's also ignore any possibility that there might be personal animosity and rivalry among anthropologists who work in the same area.

I accept the point that Native Americans went and will go to their doom regardless of anthropological work. Generals, gold prospectors and land speculators will do what they want, and use any excuse that comes to hand. The forces at work involve such massive corruption and massive violence that academic debate is by the way. Besides, given the macho values of Brazilian frontier society, it's the supposed fierceness of some of the Gê peoples in the Xingu area that is said to make them respected by frontier Brazilians.

As far as Chagnon's 'popular' work goes, it's innocent enough. The descriptions in *The Fierce People* (1983), his arrival topos and so on, are standard. The writing is *a bit* sensationalistic, *a bit* playing for effect, and is certainly not in the Joseph Conrad league, or even the Malinowskian. But it's a lot more careful than most acceptable journalism would be in describing the behaviour of Yanomamo men. But notice the crux: it wasn't his 'popular' work that was either misused by the media or accused by the Association of Brazilian Anthropologists. It was the 'scholarly' stuff, the 'scientific findings'.

The squabble about statistics of mortality rates and sex ratios is neither here nor there. Counting *unokai* males is not the problem. A statistical correlation between *unokai* males and their 'reproductive success'? So what? That's just 'culture to biology in one easy step'. What kind of vision of the world is that? Biosocial anthropology, of course. And it's awful. Awful, not because it's unscholarly. The article in *Nature* is presented with all the required scholarly paraphernalia. Nor is it awful because of the use the newspapers made of it. It's awful because that biosocial vision is a dead end. There's nothing you can do with it. Be popular with it, in books about selfish genes or territorial imperatives, or be scholarly with it for an article in *Nature*, and it's still the same old stuff. It's devoid of significance. What went wrong was that the popular newspapers tried to invest the tedious correlations with a significance they didn't have. They tried to change registers but got the tune wrong. They tried to put a bit of life into it, when the matter was already inert. I don't think there's any honest charge that can be laid against Chagnon beyond that of the poverty of his biosocial vision. And that's not a matter of arguing about popular images. It's a matter of producing a competent response to the biosocial presuppositions underlying the 'scientific facts'.

THE ORIGIN OF *MAN'S* MANNERS

My first question was: 'Are we capable of responding to a wide variety of voices and styles?' My second was: 'Can we all learn to change registers ourselves?' An example that straddles both these questions is the convention of the 'introductory textbook' for students in anthropology. Contrast, for example, David Pocock's *Understanding Social Anthropology*, which appeared in 1975, and Edmund Leach's *Culture and Communication*, which appeared the following year. I'd judge them as follows: Pocock takes a broad view of nineteenth- and twentieth-century social anthropology and refracts the language, the vocabulary, the concerns, the ideas into an idiom accessible to sixth-formers and first-year undergraduates and other non-combatants. The result is exemplary. Leach takes a particular view, the cul-de-sac of Saussurian linguistics and Lévi-Straussian structuralism, ('my kind of anthropology' as he referred to it in his later Fontana *Masterguides* book, 1982: Chapter 4), and, also in an exemplary fashion, renders it accessible to students. Neither writer, in the process of translation from one register to the other, leaves readers with simplistic abstractions or misleading caricatures. And I couldn't be more convinced by the results. Pocock succeeds in suggesting that readers now get on with it themselves and do further worthwhile work. Leach successfully demonstrates that there's nothing more to this structuralism business outside the covers of his book. I'd seriously suggest that if you read *Culture and Communication* you need not bother reading any more Lévi-Strauss.

If it was *demanded* of academics that, to be taken seriously, every one had to produce a piece of work for the popular market, an introductory textbook, or something in that idiom, the exercise would generally be found enormously challenging, the difficulty being that many people who regard themselves as scholarly are locked in, in a sort of constipated way, to stuffy old conventions – like men in suits. That's all the initial distinction is trying to defend. It's not defending rigorous standards of writing, of presentation, of debate and scrutiny. 'Scholarly' over against 'popular' is nothing more than a prim vigilance about etiquette. And the main reason why 'scholars' don't write popular work is not that they have some sort of conscientious objection to it. It's that they can't do it. That's one of the answers to Mary Louise Pratt's question in her essay in the *Writing Culture* book:

> For the lay person, such as myself, the main evidence of a problem is the simple fact that ethnographic writing tends to be surprisingly boring. How, one asks constantly, could such interesting people doing such interesting things produce such dull books? What did they have to do to themselves?
>
> (Pratt 1986: 33)

What they had to do to themselves was to *conform* to the presentational etiquette of the discipline.

The question is not, then, scholarly as against popular. The question is how to dare being original without being eccentric; how to slip out of the conventions without kicking up an outrage that gets in the way; in other words, being prepared to take these risks.

I'd like to do examples of the vulgate of Social Anthropology, the Basic English that you collide with in any article in *Man*, the limited range of example and illustration that is referred to, the conventional postures. Watch, for instance, for the opening paragraph or section of an article or book containing a claim for novelty. 'No one has ever done what I'm about to do'. 'Things unattempted yet in prose or rhyme', as Milton ironically translated Ariosto's boast. This is the 'research' urge that Steiner referred to – the anxiety to be 'new' – revealing a confusion between novelty and originality. Having become aware of the convention, what about a vow not to indulge in it?

I'd like to query even the most minute manners: footnotes, for instance, that appalling tic – a dead give-away. A recent ASA volume even had a footnote attached to the *title* of an article. Where on earth did writers learn to abuse the linear medium with footnotes? (I don't mean references, I mean footnotes.) I'll end with an anxious statement that sums up the predicament of being struck rigid by conventions. (And look out for the footnotes.) It's someone discussing the recently fashionable abstraction 'advocacy':

> Once engaged in advocacy, we are likely to become saturated, however temporarily, in a communicative mode that is over-emotional, over-simplified, rhetorical, over-dramatic, exaggerated, single-minded, without footnotes: in short, the exact opposite of most of our academic writing
>
> (Van Esterik 1985: 81)

And the writer might have added: 'Just like Emile Zola's *J'Accuse*'.

'*Our* academic writing'? I hope I'm not included. Again, it's the simple binary contrast that's so limiting: either 'our academic writing' (most of it at any rate) or the other one (without the footnotes). A discipline that embraces the bewildering variety of world languages, that is founded on a thoroughgoing extroversion to cultural diversity, that willingly confronts a myriad of social forms, should be able to find a more generous vision of possible styles and registers and manners of expression and presentation.

REFERENCES

Anthropology Newsletter (1989) American Anthropological Association, January: 3–24.
Berlin, I. (1990) 'The State of Europe', in *Granta 30: New Europe!*, Harmondsworth: Penguin.
Bourdieu, P. (1977) *Outline of a Theory of Practice*, Cambridge: Cambridge University Press. (tr., by Richard Nice, of *Esquisse d'une théorie de la pratique, précédé de trois études d'ethnologie kabyle*, (1972) Switzerland: Libraire Droz).
—— (1980) 'Sartre', *London Review of Books* 2, 22: 11–12.

Chagnon, N. A. (1983) *Yanomamo: The Fierce People* (3rd edition), New York: Holt, Rinehart and Winston.

Chomsky, N. (1972) *Language and Mind* (Enlarged edition), New York: Harcourt Brace Jovanovich.

Graves, R. and Hodge, A. (1943) *The Reader over your Shoulder* (2nd edition abridged, 1947), London: Cape.

Hecht, S. and Cockburn, A. (1990) *The Fate of the Forest: Developers, Destroyers and Defenders of the Amazon*, Harmondsworth: Penguin.

Hollander, P. (1981) *Political Pilgrims*, New York: Harper and Row. (Quoted in Jerzy Szacki, 'Intellectuals between Politics and Culture', in B. Maclean, A. Montefiore and P. Winch (1990) *The Political Responsibility of Intellectuals*, Cambridge: Cambridge University Press, p. 229.)

Leach, E. (1976) *Culture and Communication: The Logic by which Symbols are Connected*, Cambridge: Cambridge University Press.

—— (1982) *Social Anthropology*, Glasgow: Fontana.

Lévi-Strauss, C. (1955) *Tristes Tropiques*, Paris: Plon.

—— (1961) *A World on the Wane*, tr., by J. Russell, of *Tristes Tropiques*, London: Hutchinson.

—— (1966) *The Savage Mind*, London: Weidenfeld and Nicolson.

—— (1974) *Tristes Tropiques*, tr. by J. and D. Weightman, New York: Atheneum.

Lodge, D. (1980) 'Structural Defects', *The Observer*, 23 March.

Pace, D. (1983) *Claude Lévi-Strauss: The Bearer of Ashes*, London: Routledge and Kegan Paul.

Pocock, D. (1975) *Understanding Social Anthropology*, London: Hodder and Stoughton.

Pratt, L. (1986) 'Fieldwork in Common Places', in J. Clifford and G. Marcus (eds) *Writing Culture*, Berkeley: University of California Press.

Sontag, S. (1970) 'The Anthropologist as Hero', in E. N. Hayes and T. Hayes (eds) *Claude Lévi-Strauss: The Anthropologist as Hero*, Cambridge: MIT Press.

Steiner, G. (1970) 'Orpheus with his Myths', in E. N. Hayes and T. Hayes (eds) *Claude Lévi-Strauss: The Anthropologist as Hero*, Cambridge: MIT Press.

—— (1989) *Real Presences*, London and Boston: Faber and Faber.

Times Literary Supplement (1967) 'Filtering Through', 12 October.

Van Esterik, P. (1985) 'Discussion 3: (2)', in R. Paine (ed.) *Advocacy and Anthropology, First Encounters*, Memorial University of Newfoundland: Institute of Social and Economic Research.

Williams, R. (1984) 'Afterword: *Nineteen Eighty-Four* in 1984', in *Orwell*, Flamingo Edition with Afterword, London: Fontana.

Chapter 3

Typecasting
Anthropology's *dramatis personae*

Wendy James

For the purposes of this essay, I take as my definition of 'popular anthropology' whatever has been written with a view to a large market. That implies that it is aimed (by definition) at a general readership beyond professional academia, though the target may often include school and university teaching courses. A 'popular' text may not necessarily get the large sales hoped for, of course, and there is always the odd counter-phenomenon of a professional text doing well commercially. Among those 'popular' texts aimed at the sales charts, we could distinguish three genres of writing: the personal tale of anthropological travel; the classroom teaching text (much more common in English than in French-language anthropology); and the grand new theory of human or social origins. One appealing quality of these three kinds of popular anthropology is a good strong story-line, as would also be true for popular history, or astronomy, or medicine. Is there an eye-catching start, a seductive unfolding of plot, a satisfying denouement? When Professor (later Sir Edward) Evans-Pritchard was once encouraging me to turn my thesis into a book, he tried to reassure me by saying it was just like writing a novel: all you needed was a story with a beginning, a middle and an end. Maybe a number of primary ethnographies could be compared to novels, though very few books of either category achieve the readability and memorable quality he was urging on me. While the analogy may be a reasonable one for a doctoral thesis or its immediate offspring, surely we can find a better one for the popular book. The novel is too logo-centric and parochial a form to find much response from a wide audience. The model offered by the playscript surely works better.

In addition to a sexy story-line, popular anthropology needs larger-than-life, translatable characters, as does a play or a masquerade. The play is an older form than the novel, and cross-culturally more portable; it does not usually depend on analytical or otherwise subtle language, and can flourish even without a written script; it is a little more like a ritual or a myth, a little more like a dance or a game. You can re-dress and re-arrange the characters, even putting yourself into it; its internal movement, visual display and differentiated parts lend themselves to the anthropological imagination. The linguistic scholar must pore over an old document, and of course it may illuminate (as does a novel) a language, a culture and a period; but it demands a close trained focus. The circumstantial details of a written novel-text are similarly of the essence, whereas a good drama, like a myth, does not depend for its power on this kind of contextual matrix. Everyone is free to act, translate, adapt, costume, film and choreograph the classical Greek or Shakespeare play in their own way. The play itself may well illuminate the specific cultural milieu or milieux which produced it, but it transcends those settings. Is *Julius Caesar* an 'ethnography' of some particular place and time? The action and performance of such a story can be recast to evoke other places and periods; a seventeenth-century playscript may contain within it a re-representation of the Roman or the Scottish medieval world, or a realm of the arcadian imagination, and those who re-enact it may transpose the story into further settings ad infinitum. But the counterpoint of roles and scenes, the juxtaposition of character and the choreography of human dilemma can rise above context and give the playscript a life of its own quite beyond its birthplace in Elizabethan England.

I think some of the best ethnographic monographs (though rarely articles) do approach an internal dramatic tension of abstracted situation and voice which could be compared to a playscript, and which, partly for this very reason, have secured enduring interest – even, through the inevitable accompanying simplification, classic status. But most remain little read in themselves, maybe 'boring' in their density and detail even for professionals, while other writers explain and introduce their contents for a wider audience, teasing out the most appealing elements to weave into a morality tale of 'us and them' – the 'popular anthropology' of a teacher, preacher, traveller or scholarly *enfant terrible*. The complexities of ethnographic presentation and sociological analysis are deftly merged to produce a 'character' out of 'a culture': too often, we must admit, one more 'caricature' to complement the growing set already coopted into the telling of the human story.

To recognize the dramatic potential of ethnography and anthropological presentation is nothing new. Victor Turner developed the notion of the social drama as an ethnographic technique and analytical tool, and some of his comparative writing articulates the choreography of social occasion; but his writing on the Ndembu remains dense, complex and difficult of access to most general readers (e.g. 1967; 1974). He rarely made easy concessions by offering the reader a role in the story as 'we moderns', 'we Europeans' or 'we Americans'. Such counterpointing self-reference certainly helps to boost the circulation, and to anchor the image of remote peoples in the popular consciousness, as Margaret Mead (1927) did for the Samoans (versus American educational theory), Malinowski (1927) for the matrilineal Trobrianders (versus Freudian psychology), Evans-Pritchard (1937) for the Azande (*contra* the rational European), or Colin Turnbull (1972) for the Ik (in order to question the reader's conscience and the fragility of all culture). The Ik did even more for Western self-reflection – not only did the ethnography of their suffering draw in the reader/audience as a point of reference, they were appropriated into the discourse of Western social concern as an indicator, a cipher for sociocultural pathology. Cast as a cultural type-character in themselves, their actor-impersonators literally walked the Western stage in a play made from the ethnography – in which mime played a dominant part; while the Ik themselves later attempted to sue their original ethnographer for defamation of character.[1] Could one imagine the same happening to the Samoans or the Trobrianders, coopted as part of our play or masque, to represent various forms of our quest for personal freedom, say, freedoms which could so easily turn to accusations of wanton sexuality? In a morality play, for example, their character might plausibly be developed on these lines, might come vividly through all the hedging about and difficulties of words – both their and ours – which tend to clog up scholarship. And their reception by a Western audience might well give them cause for offence.

But what about the Ndembu? Could a playwright or choreographer give them a 'popular' role? Their 'character' as a mnemonic *persona* is not so clear. The dramas which their ethnographer has given us are rigorously set within their world, between Ndembu 'characters' themselves; their predicaments seem transcendent only to the specialist scholar, who can see the vernacular differentiation of parts and hear the exchange of voices within their story. The Ndembu have not yet been individually merged and culturally typecast as a character in our play, coopted as a distinctive echoing chorus upon our dilemmas. Nor has there been much secondary simplification of their ethnography, which could yield the kind of typing that would make the Ndembu better known.

This rather cynical view of popular anthropology takes for granted that it is geared to address Western Everyperson's cosmic and worldly moral imagination, that it is writing which therefore finds an easy market, and that it tends to be self-reinforcing. It gets reviewed and discussed in newspapers, magazines and programmes, outside the narrow professional field – and here I would include weeklies, not only the Sundays but journals like the *Times Educational Supplement* and the *Higher*, whose eye is on the teaching use of a text or film. What makes a particular piece of anthropology appealing to the 'consumer' market in this kind of way is a concern, explicit or implicit, with some aspect of explaining or contextualizing *ourselves* rather than seriously being concerned with the imaginative or intellectual agency of anybody else living in another place or time. Other peoples, remote in time and space or both, are given a walk-on part in the story about one's own relation to the world, one's own origins, one's own history, one's own future. The drama itself is directed in this sense by the audience.

MEETING REAL-LIFE CHARACTERS

The three main kinds of popular anthropology sketched above all coopt tribal exemplars, turn them into masks and allocate them roles in our playscripts. 'Travel anthropology' sometimes seems to seek out difference in human character and role-playing for its own sake, and the author marches right on stage to confront these 'others'. Recent years have spawned a new generation of Waugh-clones, the smart youngsters who find Africa, say, rather disgusting, but a hilarious adventure at the same time. There are the concerned and serious travellers, too; but too much solemnity bestowed on those curiously empty phrases, 'alien culture', 'unique way of life' (or the nerve-grating 'lifestyle'), only plays into the hands of the tricksters and invites people like Nigel Barley to take the mickey. Barley is offered a calabash of beer by his Dowayo hosts, and raises it to his lips, proclaiming a toast:

Immediately, a deep and shocked silence descended upon the gathering. The boys stopped talking. Zuuldibo's smile froze upon his face. The very flies seemed hushed from their buzzing. I knew, as everyone knows who works in an alien culture, that I had made a serious mistake.

(Barley 1986: 58)

On circumcision variants: 'Anthropologists have continued to be fascinated by such practices as part of their awareness of the sheer "otherness" of alien peoples . . . It would seem that if anthropological theories can cope with the sex customs, they can cope with anything' (ibid.: 51). On ethnocentrism: 'In anthropology, enjoyment is often used as an approximate yardstick of understanding. The idea is that if an anthropologist does not like anything he encounters among an alien people, this is ethnocentrism. If he disapproves of anything, this is the result of bringing to bear the wrong standards. It is often ignored that very often the culture that the ethnographer enjoys least is his own, the one that he should know best' (ibid.: 102). 'A sound rule of thumb seems to be that when the alien culture you are studying begins to look normal, it is time to go home' (ibid.: 153).

On the other hand you can find, if not normality, deeply personal satisfactions, perhaps spiritual ones, in the course of your ethnographic journey. Listen to James Cowan on the spirituality of the native Australians:

> Aboriginal religion is largely ritual and myth-based in its expression, devoid as it is of any formal theology to flesh out the mysteries that we find in so much of its poetry and songs. The idea of such soul-stirring statements as *Sanctus Dominus Deus Sabaoth*, or 'Holy, Holy, Lord God Almighty', is entirely alien to the Aboriginal way of thinking . . . to unravel the spiritual subtlety of an Aboriginal creation-myth or an erotic song-cycle requires us to dispense with certain prejudices as to what constitutes holiness or sanctity. Sometimes we have to reproduce in ourselves what Maurice Aniane called the 'cosmogenic unfolding' – that is, 'the permanent creation of the world in the sense in which all creation, finally, is only a Divine Imagination.' In the process we begin to encounter what in Islamic esotericism is known as the *ta'wil*, a path by which we are 'lead [sic] back' via things, natural objects and sometimes scriptural exegesis from the outerness, or the letter, to their innerness or spirit . . .

(Cowan 1989: 71)

The chapter is entitled 'Nature as Numen'. Institutional Christianity may seem alien from the point of view of the Australian

Dreaming; but surely the latter's affinity with Islam is a fragile illusion produced by a peculiarly new Western brand of mystic Romanticism. Easy travel helps to foster such illusions; and airline magazines are among those popular publications which feature the tribal peoples of the world in their features on such Western concerns as healthy diets, natural childbirth, development of the inner self and divination of its needs, environmental harmony, gender relations and sexual fulfilment, and so on (the April 1993 issue of *Highlife*, the British Airways monthly, devoted several pages on these lines to the Yanomamo – their 'violent' image in the academic literature notwithstanding – illustrated with lovely pictures).

TRIBAL TYPES ARE GOOD TO TEACH WITH

After travel anthropology, we can comment on a second category of popular anthropology – the 'descriptive' teaching text. Simplified descriptions are increasingly being made available as self-contained booklets for course work. These are often presented as serious but easy-to-read field anthropology: for use as points of reference, sometimes reflexive points of reference, in a sort of literary cultural tourism – the varieties of man, peoples of the world and 'what we can learn from their traditional wisdom' type of coursework teaching or programme series. They are presented as representations of 'cultures', or of larger and longer accounts of 'cultures' (which is not the same thing); but either way, they can easily shift towards the style of cultural 'portraits' or 'types' as in an illustrated portfolio. The big multi-volume compendia, increasingly dependent on iconic photographs, are literally of this kind. Even the 'academic' text book relies to some extent on the repertoire of ethnographic cameos already established in the popular literature.

How do complicated primary ethnographies get simplified, and peoples get typed? It may even be a matter of straightforward shortening so that a long book can be used in course teaching; the process of shortening may, however, have an effect of impoverishing the significance of the study, cutting out a lot of the space for internal dialogue, and leaving the student with a sharpened view of the difference between 'home' and the world of the X or Y people. The editor engaged in this kind of pruning of a text, or selection from its various chapters, has to decide what is most relevant to the student reader at the time; what are the *main* points the student should grasp from this book? I was once in the interesting position of commenting on the way that the very long text of Evans-Pritchard's *Witchcraft Oracles and Magic among the Azande* was being shortened by the Oxford University Press for the purposes of bringing out a paperback, abridged version, mainly for the American college teaching market (Evans-Pritchard 1937; cf. 1975). You will remember how the pattern of the argument first sets forth a statement on what the Azande believe about witches or oracles or magic, and then spends several paragraphs or pages retreating from that statement, showing how it has to be modified, qualified, taken apart and contextualized, space even being allowed for its contradiction by the Azande themselves. The method, and the theory, of the analysis lies mainly in this mode of dialectic presentation, which depends as much upon the dozen pages of qualification as upon the original statement of belief. Abridging the book meant not only sacrificing a lot of detail, it meant sacrificing a good deal of the internal dialectic of interpretation, and in particular most of the discussion of magic as distinct from witchcraft (though the original analysis insisted on their interdependence). You are left with a nugget of existential *content* to witchcraft notions – and a more 'positivistic' treatment of 'belief' than in the original. Students who read only the abridged edition tend to write very standardized and stereotyped essays, and do not get as excited by the book's implications as those who make the effort – even cursorily – to go through the longer version.

My experience is, further, that when an anthropologist's ethnographic work on the 'so-and-so' has become officially a 'classic', it is rarely read in its original forms. Students come to know it through all the secondary comment, thumb-nail sketches, textbook cribs and so on; in fact it is this popularizing process which helps validate the 'classic' status of the work itself. And the less students tend to bother reading a (no doubt more difficult) primary text, the more bored and boring their own commentaries. I cannot politely convey the degree of frustration one feels after so many years of teaching social anthropology, to have to face yet more essays on the Nuer which assume (usually from secondary cameo accounts) that their 'kinship' system is based on expanding patrilineages constituted through the birth line, lineages which pay and receive bridewealth in marriage, and which automatically split and combine politically in a uniform manner from the domestic locality up to the macro-tribal level, and that all this is a part of 'Nuer culture'. If a student moved from the book on Nuer kinship and marriage to a careful reading of that on politics, he or she would see that Evans-Pritchard never said any of these things. It would be clear, on the contrary, that bridewealth defines the marriage contract according to the symmetrical bilateral principles of kinship categories; that agnatic descent groups are not the outcome of biological reproduction but socially and culturally constructed through claims to a kind of citizenship; that the discourse of descent is not congruent with that of kinship but is concerned rather with historical claims to territory and regional political identity on quite another level (Evans-Pritchard 1940; cf. 1991). Here, as in other examples, discourses and domains of action clearly distinguished in the original ethnography according to general sociological principle have been collapsed by popularizing writers into one local pattern, understood *sui generis* as a whole and distinctive system. Moreover, that 'whole system' is itself rarely understood by today's readers as a *society*, but rather as a disembodied essence of *culture*, inevitably sliding into the idea of a specific personality-type.

An inevitable result which follows from this kind of secondary typing is an exaggeration of cultural difference, for the sake of contrast and argument. The secondary literature shows how, even in serious theoretical discussion by sympathetic professionals, the decontextualizing of ethnographic accounts and their use as evidence can be a treacherous and tricky exercise. The proud and aggressive (and apparently mostly male) Nuer are a well-known case (cf. Johnson 1981), but even the Dinka (in spite of their subtler ethnography) are beginning to become psychologically typed, too. Godfrey Lienhardt analysed the way in which forces that we might in our 'theory of mind' attribute to an internal capacity are ascribed to external sources in the way Dinka speak about the world (Lienhardt 1961; 1985). But this has sometimes led to commentators suggesting that, because the Dinka do not have an elaborated theory of The Mind or The Self, they do not have any minds, or selves, or ways of speaking about them, on a less formal, or a differently formulated, level. Paul Heelas writes, for example, 'The Dinka of the southern Sudan provide a good illustration of what happens to the psychological when, as we might put it, the self is taken away from the human individual ... Not possessing our notion "mind", the Dinka have no firm basis for thinking of themselves as selves' (Heelas and Lock 1981: 9–10; cf., however, Heelas's discussion of the way 'the Powers function as surrogate minds', and of the arguments for the universality of the autonomous self in ibid.: 48). Charlotte Hardman goes even further, even allowing herself the following, surely overdone, reformulation: 'But although the Lohurung are not inward-looking nor oriented to the unique and individual, notions of "self" and "personality" *are not denied by the Lohurung to the same extent as they are by the Dinka*, for example, or Homeric Greeks' (ibid.: 161; my emphasis). Would it not require some sort of self in the first place to make such a denial? But then a 'character' without a Self, perhaps wearing a mask as do the archaic 'characters' of Mauss's essay (1985 [1938]), as a contrastive device, makes wonderful theatre.

My argument is in part an attack on the currently popular anthropological notion of 'culture' which opens itself to all these kinds of abuses; that is, the sense in which this notion constitutes a naive unity of typical socio-cultural characteristics and can in a quite unproblematic way take the plural form. In this sense, the term has acquired a particular contemporary colouring in undergraduate course texts and in the wider currency of lay anthropological imagery. I believe that the term was not widely used in this sense until fairly recently, at least in Britain (and I do not believe it has been absorbed into French-language ethnology/anthropology in the same way). It takes its bearings from that tradition of American anthropology which draws a primary distinction of psychological disposition as between one group and another, taken as a whole (for example Mead 1927; Benedict 1935) and its current use seems to fill a vacuum left by our conscious dissatisfaction over finding systematic terms of comparison in anthropology. It seems to promise some compensation for the status difference between us and them, in the sense of modern European versus remote non-literate peoples. By wishing to grant a kind of equality to all people, as individuals, one can try to speak of all cultures being equally worthy – postmodern and carefree Californian *jeunesse* studied for its chosen values alongside the survivors of some wretched Third World camp with their 'coping mechanisms'.

But in consciously doing away with older forms of the language of difference, I believe we have unconsciously fallen into a number of traps. Not least of these is a new and easy kind of relativism in popular ethnographic description, and in unthinking commentaries which are content to accept diversity as unproblematic. This can produce Punch and Judy versions of some of the classic texts on gender or politics, for example. The casual use of ethnography to illustrate 'contrasting' cultural types is partly responsible for generating some of the recent ambitiously theoretical literature on the problems of writing ethnography, because it now seems to be assumed that this has always equalled the idea of 'writing culture', rather than analysing social life (e.g. Clifford and Marcus 1986). The insidious effects of the new relativism have trickled down to, or quite possibly trickled up from, the language and enthusiasms of the people, and the people's media. There was a time when students joined a course in anthropology with an interest in, and a vocabulary from, economics or politics or philosophy. They now tend to arrive with the ready-made anthropological jargon of ephemeral magazines and TV. I have been told by brand-new undergraduates, when trying to illustrate similarities between the thinking and the historical experiences of Azande and British villagers, 'But that isn't anthropology, is it? Anthropology is the study of differences between their culture and ours.' But for Evans-Pritchard, I have to explain, the quest was rather one of testing the limits of a *common* capacity for empathy and reason. The same is true of Lévi-Strauss's life work. How is it that the broad generalizing and universalist vision of these two architects of postwar British anthropology has given way, in so much current popular writing and visual presentation, to a frequently more naive and impressionistic butterfly collecting than the inductive comparison of tribal social structures which Leach (1961) attacked over thirty years ago?

To illustrate the powerful popular notion of culture which I am criticizing, one need go no further than the series 'Case Studies in Cultural Anthropology' edited by George and Louise Spindler, and published by Holt, Rinehart and Winston. The publishers are listed in a 1972 volume as based in five US cities and two Canadian, together with London and Sydney. By 1983, Philadelphia has replaced Atlanta and Dallas, but the list extends to Tokyo, Mexico City, Rio and Madrid. The common Foreword to the volumes states that the case studies in the series are designed

> to bring to students in the social sciences insights into the richness and complexity of human life as it is lived in different ways and in different places... It is our belief that when an understanding of ways of life very different from one's own is gained, abstractions and generalizations about social structure, cultural values, subsistence techniques, and other universal categories of human social behavior become meaningful.

The establishment of *difference* here constitutes a starting point, and its emphasis runs through many of the individual Forewords by the Spindlers. Cultures exist in the plural, and it is quite remarkable how even the covers of this series constitute an iconic masquerade of types: the vast majority carry facial or full-length portraits of an individual man representing the community in question, very often in characteristic costume or pose. Very few show spontaneous, unposed action. Very few show groups of people, interacting among themselves. Very few show women or children (who are clearly not seen as standing, part for whole, in the same way).

The Dinka volume in the series does allow a girl's portrait on the cover; but then, the author (Francis Mading Deng) is himself a Dinka, and has his photo inside (incidentally, hardly disclaiming selfhood!). In this case the book as a whole stands for the cultural type. The fact that the author is the son of a Dinka chief (though he has served as his country's ambassador and a person whose adult life has been spent largely abroad)

> in itself suggests that the reader is in for an unusual experience ... There are many passages in this book where we are privileged to enter the cultural system with the insider's view ... Young men identify with their 'personality' oxen ... This identification with the cattle is a phenomenon quite alien to the Westerner ... From (Dinka) songs we can at least dimly sense the real qualitative differences between Western and Dinka patterns of thought and expression ...
>
> (Deng 1972: vii–viii)

In conclusion the editors express the hope that, in the future, the author's people will be able to find peaceful interaction with other elements of the Sudanese nation, 'at the same time preserving many of the characteristics of traditional Dinka culture that have made his people unique' (ibid.: ix).

A bestseller of the genre has proved to be *Yanomamo: The Fierce People* (Chagnon 1983, 3rd edition [1st edition 1968]), with a cover photo of an archer on a hunting trip. The editors note that, when it first appeared,

> it immediately became the most widely used study in the series of which it is a part ... Its popularity has continued. Instructors of anthropology and students alike are intrigued with the character of the Yanomamo, their conflicts and how they resolve them, and the fact that they yet retain their tribal sovereignty. Though no single people can be held to be representative of tribal life everywhere, before serious inroads have been made by the outside world, the Yanomamo are indisputably sovereign, indisputably tribal, and indisputably themselves.
>
> (ibid.: vi)

Threats from the outside world are mentioned; but it is pointed out that the focus is upon the Yanomamo as:

> a product of long-term sociocultural evolution without intervention from outside alien populations and life ways . . . [The book] is a particularly useful aid to instruction in anthropology because it is about a tribal people celebrating their own sovereign existence . . . In our extended experience as instructors of introductory anthropology at Stanford University, the combination of a challenging, exciting case study and well-executed ethnographic films is unbeatable. The behaviors and norms of people who are very different from us become, though shocking and disturbing at times, real and comprehensible when placed into anthropological perspective.
>
> (ibid.: vii)

A particular spice is added to this tale because of the focus on violence (which the editors admit is represented in some form in 'nearly all human societies'); and in the third edition by more detail on the author's own experiences, which are 'entertaining . . . and adventurous at times'. In conclusion, the editors commend this expanded version of a book which, on the evidence of earlier editions, 'made the Yanomamo one of the most important examples of tribal culture in the ethnographic literature' (ibid.: viii).

A very few quotations from the text itself (a critical reading of which could stand in place of the remarks running through this whole essay) indicate the construction of personal encounter and the processes of typecasting which help to make anthropology popular.

> It should be borne in mind, however, that each field situation is in many respects unique . . . There are a few problems, however, that seem to be nearly universal among anthropological fieldworkers, particularly those having to do with eating, bathing, sleeping, lack of privacy, loneliness, or discovering that primitive man is not always as noble as you originally thought – or you yourself not as culturally or emotionally 'flexible' as you assumed. This is not to state that primitive man everywhere is unpleasant.
>
> (ibid.)

Chagnon gives us, to illustrate this last point, an aside on his fieldwork among the Yanomamo's northern neighbours, the Carib-speaking Ye'kwana Indians.

> This group was very pleasant and charming, all of them anxious to help me and honor bound to show any visitor the numerous courtesies of their system of etiquette. In short, they approached the image of primitive man that I had conjured up, and it was sheer pleasure to work with them.
>
> (ibid.)

He elevates his own experience to a general principle:

> Other anthropologists have also noted sharp contrasts in the people they study from one field situation to another. One of the most startling examples is the work of Colin Turnbull, who first studied the Ituri Pygmies ... and found them delightful but then studied the Ik ... of the desolate outcroppings of the Kenya/Uganda/Sudan border region, a people he had difficulty coping with intellectually, emotionally, and physically. While it is possible that the anthropologist's reactions to a particular people are personal and idiosyncratic, it nevertheless remains that there *are* enormous differences between whole peoples, differences that affect the anthropologist in often dramatic ways.
>
> (ibid.: 8–9)

Even Turnbull, however, does not fail to put the drama of his encounter with the Ik in the context of a famine with partly political causes, rather than seeming to imply – as Chagnon does – that their nastiness is the result of socio-cultural evolution in 'desolate' scenery. But our ethnographer clearly relishes the sense of difference as such (his first day in the field illustrated what his teachers had meant by 'culture shock' [ibid.: 9]) and he indulges right away in a visual image of the Yanomamo character:

> I looked up and gasped when I saw a dozen burly, naked, sweaty, hideous men staring at us down the shafts of their drawn arrows! Immense wads of green tobacco were stuck between their lower teeth ... and strands of dark-green slime dripped or hung from their nostrils.
>
> (ibid.: 10)

The Yanomamo have become a standard character in the anthropological drama, and the 'cultural' cipher for a predisposition to violence in several broader debates. Harris, in his *Cows, Pigs, Wars and Witches*, refers to them frequently in the context of the argument that protein deficiency leads to violence, offering among others the following memorable comment, which must have found its way into numberless essays and examination answers: 'War is the ultimate expression of the Yanomamo lifestyle' (1975: 48, 68, 72). In a very different context, arguing for the need to take tolerance as far as one can in anthropology, Hatch uses the Yanomamo as an illustration of the dilemmas of the relativist who supposedly has to approve their behaviour (1973: 92–3).

It would be too easy to do a satirical piece on the Yanomamo, and the culturalist style of their anthropological advocates which makes them so appealing to the popular psychology magazines of the West. But 'psychological' themes in anthropology need not take this route. Consider by comparison other ethnographies of violence: say, Suzette Heald's study of the Gisu, their male circumcision rites and their high levels of homicide (Heald 1989); or the Rosaldos on the Ilongot and their headhunting (R. Rosaldo 1980; M. Z. Rosaldo 1980). In ethnography of this quality, you have an enquiry into events, personal lives and voices, into violent behaviour not merely as 'culture' but as intelligibly set in historical process and in vernacular interpretation. A playscript on the problem of human aggression could be produced, on the evidence of these complex texts, by the Gisu or the Ilongot themselves.

BIT PARTS ON THE HUMAN STAGE

My third kind of best-selling anthropology is represented by those ambitious works purporting to deal with the origins and nature of humanity, the bases of society and culture and religion – in fact, a resurgence of the concerns of nineteenth-century evolutionary literature. The modern progeny draw in a wide range of ethnographic reference, as their forebears did, regardless of provenance or quality or original context. Idiosyncratic points of reference are used to reconstruct and illustrate a fresh general theory or dramatic story-line about our common humanity, such as the Marvin Harris argument about material/nutritional causes of social behaviour (Harris 1975), or the Ardrey argument about territory and male dominance (Ardrey 1966), or the Dawkins argument which explains matriliny, among most other social institutions, in terms of selfish genes – and invents by analogy a totally impregnable theory about the success of cultural 'memes' (Dawkins 1976). Other general anthropologists have recently attempted broad syntheses: for example, Vernon Reynolds (1976) and Tim Ingold (1986), each, as I think they would admit, with a visionary myth of his own concerning the essence of our nature and our beginnings as cultural agents.

As with the other genres of popular anthropology (the travellers' tales and contrastive tribal-cultural exemplars), the ambitious synthetic vision of humanity entails a winnowing and a re-sorting of evidence, a bricolage of fragments drawn from existing literature. In this case, it is particularly clear how the original complexity, interpretive intention and internal ambivalences of the primary ethnographic work may be ruthlessly pruned out. So are, too, for the sake of the wider drama, the structured interplay of events and internal dialogue of parts which could perhaps have made a good playscript of the primary ethnography itself. Also gone from these new broad syntheses are the linguistic and stylistic character of the original – quite apart from any respect for the original author's research strategy – all are sacrificed for the sake of the relevant nuggets of ethnographic history. Even works in which theory, interpretation and evidence are closely knit together are thus mined for the sake of extracting factual fragments.

An example of the continuing vigour of this kind of popular 'scientific' anthropology is the recent book by Chris Knight, *Blood Relations: Menstruation and the Origins of Culture* (1991). Rather than building a model of early human society on dominant competitive males wheeling and dealing with each other over females, this new theory credits women with the initiative for making the essential transition to culture, through their Greenham Common-style collective resistance by sex-strike to male dominance. The central thesis of this fascinating, in fact startling, 581-page book, by a doctoral graduate of University College London, is that distinctively human society stems from that crucial point in evolution when women formed solidary alliances among themselves and forced their menfolk to go hunting by periodically withholding sex until more meat was provided. This is presented as realistic Upper Paleolithic history, which has survived through the transmission of cultural 'memes' (cf. Dawkins 1976) into a wide range of modern ethnographic contexts. The story is offered as a personal myth of the author's for our enjoyment, but also, at the same time, as a serious effort to synthesize structuralism, symbolic cultural analysis, Marxist political vision and feminist history (though the eye-catching title is obviously designed to attract more readers than can probably cope in practice with the biological, ethnographic and paleo-archaeological sources used). In a specific way a deliberate variant on the older origin myths of matriarchy, the model places late twentieth-century gender politics at the start of culture and the heart of human society. A partial summary of the explanatory model would include the following elements. Women ovulate at full moon, and menstruate at dark. As they tend to merge their cycles into a shared pattern signified by blood, this becomes the signal for withdrawing from sexual contact, to oblige the men to go hunting. Gender solidarity at this point of the monthly cycle overrides pair-bonding. By full moon the hunters must have been collectively successful in bringing home more meat, and women are again willing to prepare the cooking fires. A basic form of exchange, and of alternating time, is established; feasting and sexual activity are resumed.

As a student, Knight tells us he had read of the vicious battles between males over females and territory which dominated animal ethology; this reminded him of Lenin's accounts of inter-imperialist rivalries exploding at the expense of workers everywhere during the First World War.

> Becoming human, it seemed obvious to me, meant escaping all this via some kind of revolution. I took this idea literally. It meant the overthrow of Capital by the Proletariat – which I translated as the overthrow of Primate Male Dominance by Female Reproductive Labour. In what follows, I will refer to this as my 'mythical' version of the story central to this book. It was *Blood Relations* before I began worrying about what specialists in the field might have to say on such topics.
>
> (Knight 1991: 24)

'The Tyrant Male' had to go, he stood in between the solidary females who needed meat, and the males who had to work together to provide it because they needed sex. So he was overthrown. Hence ordered relations in society as a whole for the first time, for the fertility of the women of a group as a whole was in the collective interest.' The transition to culture was consummated in that revolutionary act' (ibid.: 25). Hence, also, a new insight into the proper interpretation of widespread rituals of blood-avoidance, hunting and the moon; the principles of food exchange, and the rules of exogamy and incest; and a way of rejuvenating the old anthropological categories of sacrifice and totemism, not to mention rain rituals and Rainbow Snakes (here evidence of gender solidarity).

Backed by each other and by their kin, women periodically reassert sufficient control over their own sexuality to clarify that men cannot take their availability for granted. In this way they make it clear that men as hunters must 'earn their keep' by regularly surrendering their kills.

Knight explains that this is the basic argument of his book.

> Women, from the beginning, have held the future in their hands. Their responsibilities for offspring have often compelled them to resist men's advances, subordinating short-term sexual to longer-term economic goals... We begin with female child-rearing and economic priorities, female ultimate determination of social structure and female sexual self-restraint in women's own direct material interests. From this, the incest taboo, food taboos and the other basic features of the human cultural configuration will be derived.
>
> (ibid.: 153)

It is interesting that Knight deplores the image of culture as a jumble, or as functionally explicable in terms of utility; he has more sympathy for the 'culture and personality' school (ibid.: 61). How do the various peoples who happen to have been mentioned in this essay so far (and who were not selected for this purpose) fare in Knight's story of the gender-based revolution at the heart of culture?

The Ik seem to get no mention, nor do the Samoans (perhaps more surprisingly). The Yanomami are adduced as an example of what Knight terms the 'own-kill' norm – that is that male hunters do not eat but give away their catch; he suggests that in this case 'generosity is an essential prerequisite of hunting success' and quotes Hanbury-Tenison's account of these people for Time-Life Books (Hanbury-Tenison 1982; no other reference is given to the Yanomami). Both the Azande and the Ndembu crop up briefly, too, as Knight selects 'a few interesting statements' from the African continent reflecting the 'own-kill' ban.

> Evans-Pritchard...cites a Central African (Azande) anecdote concerning a furious woman who complains of her husband: 'That man, that man, he is not a human being, he behaves just like a dog...he goes and kills a beast and keeps it entirely for himself.' Among the Zambian Ndembu, a hunter who eats his kills is likened to a cannibal, suspected of incest and believed to be quite

capable of killing his own human kin by sorcery to consume their 'meat' or 'flesh'.

(Knight 1991: 101)

The famous work of Turner on the matrilineal Ndembu and their ritual and symbolism might have lent itself to serious treatment in the context of Knight's enterprise, but all we get is a brief reference to their using red ochre. This occurs in the secondary context of an article by an upper Paleolithic archaeologist who 'freely uses ethnographic analogies in his speculations on the prehistoric significance of ochre' (ibid.: 437).

In Central African Ndembu rites of the river source, according to Wreschner, red clay represents the blood of the 'mother'... The relationship between ochre, blood and 'mothers'... is signified by the Greek *haema* ... and is related to the basic Indo-European root MA which means 'mother'. Citing the Africanist Victor Turner ... Wreschner observes that 'the womb is in many cultures equated with the tomb'.

(ibid.: 101)

Whatever happened to that multivocality and interpretive agility for which Turner made the Ndembu so much more importantly well known? Or even the contrariness and multiple voices of the Azande (who get no other mention in the whole book)?

The Nuer appear as part of an extension to the above argument, Knight using them to demonstrate that (*contra* Lévi-Strauss) sacrifice is closely similar to totemism, in that the meat or flesh of one own's kind should not be consumed but exchanged (with others, or with the gods). But both kinds of ritual form part of such a long spectrum (including atonement rituals, hunters' taboos, increase rites, blood avoidances, menstrual taboos, cooking rules, the couvade, male initiation rites) – 'and so on indefinitely' (ibid.: 115) – that the interest of the specific argument is lost. Knight's discriminations are finely wrought, but they refer only to his own ritual/mythical schema and lack any curiosity about the significance of other formulations. His theory depends upon our accepting the model of a former holistic ritual scheme of which a few elements only survive. Hence, perhaps, his coopting of the Dinka – at least at second hand, by quoting Mary Douglas who writes that their ritual, at the same time as being form, 'is inseparable from content ... It is appearance, but there is no other reality' (Douglas 1982: 36). Knight comments that 'for many people in non-Western cultures, ritual *is* culture' (Knight 1991: 80). This takes us, in my view, a long way from the manner in which Godfrey Lienhardt presented the tension between image, representation and experience in Dinka religion (Lienhardt1961). Neither Evans-Pritchard nor Lienhardt use the terms 'ritual' and 'culture' in the large and vapid way that this book does.

It is in the Trobriand Islands that Knight finds one of his most satisfactorily dramatic exemplars. The Trobrianders not only have the 'own-flesh rule', but men '"pay" for sex' (Knight 1991: 107–8; 186–7). And on moonlit nights, the primal myth of culture is enacted almost to the letter. Knight quotes Malinowski:

> Throughout the year there is a periodic increase in play and pleasure-seeking at full moon. When the two elements so desirable in the tropics, soft light and bracing freshness are combined, the natives fully respond . . . I have seen the whole population of a large village gathered on the central place . . . The close bodily contact, the influence of moonlight and shadow, the intoxication of rhythmic movement, the mirth and frivolity of play and ditty – all tend to relax constraint, and give opportunity for an exchange of declarations and for the arrangement of trysts.
>
> (ibid., quoting Malinowski 1927: 201–22)

Knight explains:

> Malinowski says nothing of menstrual synchrony, but clearly in a culture of this kind, it would not be adaptive for women to menstruate too frequently at full moon . . . Returning, now, to our model, we might say that if it is indeed the case that nocturnal light helps to stimulate ovulation . . . then all of this would make good biological sense. Celebrating out in the open late into the night would ensure maximum exposure to the moon's rays, and all-night dancing by the light of fires – as among the Cherokee – would enhance this effect.
>
> (Knight 1991: 348–9)

How can your average reader resist (on theoretical grounds) this entrancing scenario, of soft light, bracing air and sex *al fresco*, entirely in character with the passions we have come to expect of the Trobrianders and their ethnographer? Knight apparently does not see how Malinowski's use of the term 'tropics' gives the whole game away. How can the Trobrianders know they live in this suggestively seductive, soft and fresh part of the world? While it is quite true that moonlight has its uses, and that the lunar cycle is much better known to people who work the land and do not live in cities, not all 'cultures of this type' have placed the same emphasis on the symbolism of night-life or even lived under the requisite clear skies. The Upper Paleolithic was on the chilly and overcast side for considerable periods, surely, even in the currently warm tourist-trap of the Dordogne, where so much of the archaeological evidence comes from.

Compressed ethnographic evidence from contemporary peoples is thus adduced with splendid indiscrimination in the classic grand manner, in combination with a range of data from ancient prehistory, evolutionary biology and animal behavioural studies. But while the anthropology student should beware the book's heady drama and enticing story, it may well bewitch the general reader. It would also make a wonderful pantomime or film, even a ballet. The characters would be mnemonics, not of cultural types but of the archetypes of all culture, merged into a primitivity which in its own drama saw the beginnings of differentiation.

I have sometimes asked myself, how would I present the Uduk, the Sudanese people I know best, in the *dramatis personae* of a popular book, such as 'My Ethnographic Travels, Fieldwork Mistakes and Home Thoughts' or 'A Story of the World'? It could be done in so many ways; one could certainly write a *Mysteries of the Dream Time* on them, or a convincing variant of *The Territorial Imperative* or *The (Non-)Fierce People*. In particular one could draft 'Blood Relations: Confirmations from Archaic Africa', almost as if the research had been carried out for this purpose. What aspect of culture, what fragment of an ethno-grapher's notebook, is *not* a meme? Identify a meme and the Uduk can probably illustrate it. One could certainly have offered plenty as evidence for Knight's argument – the matriliny, the red ochre, the moonlit dancing, the periodic silence in the fields and sexual abstinence, the sharing of meat, the hunting rituals and even the Rainbow Snake. On the other hand, all ethnographers get letters from specialists in other fields wanting to confirm their ideas, and we are usually able to rummage through our notes and oblige – in my case, for example, confirming someone's pet theory of bird symbolism; some-one else's about sex and myth; someone else's about lizard vocabulary and Mithraic religion. More recently, since their multiple dislocation as refugees to Ethiopia, aid agencies and the media have helped put together a picture of the Uduk as a people with a remarkable 'inherited' stamina for survival through war and famine, in the face of the odds, and I have had to confirm to them that there is in some sense a truth in this (James 1979; 1988; 1993 film; 1994). Perhaps this is the role for which they can best be typecast in the contemporary world story; but it's a pity. They did not choose this role, and they could have played, and might still play, so many other parts.

NOTE

1 Peter Brook directed the stage production *The Ik* at the Round House, London, in 1976. For recent contributions to the continuing controversy surrounding Turnbull's study of the Ik, see, for example, Heine 1985, de Waal 1993, Knight 1994, Littlewood 1994.

REFERENCES

Ardrey, R. (1966) *The Territorial Imperative*, London: Collins.
Barley, N. (1986) *A Plague of Caterpillars: A Return to the African Bush*, Penguin Travel Library, London: Penguin.
Benedict, R. (1935) *Patterns of Culture*, London: Routledge and Kegan Paul.
Chagnon, N. (1983) *Yanomamo: The Fierce People* (3rd edition), Case Studies in Cultural Anthropology, G. and L. Spindler (eds), New York: Holt, Rinehart and Winston.
Clifford, J. and Marcus, G. E. (eds) (1986) *Writing Culture: The Poetics and Politics of Ethnography*, London: University of California Press.
Cowan, J. (1989) *Mysteries of the Dream-Time: The Spiritual Life of Australian Aborigines*, Bridport: Prism Press.
Dawkins, R. (1976) *The Selfish Gene*, Oxford: Oxford University Press.
Deng, F. M. (1972) *The Dinka of the Sudan*, Case Studies in Cultural Anthropology, G. and L. Spindler (eds), New York: Holt, Rinehart and Winston.
de Waal, A. (1993) 'In the Disaster Zone', *Times Literary Supplement*, 16 July.
Douglas, M. (1982) *In the Active Voice*, London: Routledge and Kegan Paul.
Evans-Pritchard, E. E. (1937) *Witchcraft, Oracles and Magic among the Azande*, Oxford: Clarendon Press.
—— (1940) *The Nuer: A Description of the Modes of Livelihood and Political Institutions of a Nilotic People*, Oxford: Clarendon Press.
—— (1975) *Witchcraft among the Azande* (paperback edition), Oxford: Clarendon Press.
—— (1991) *Kinship and Marriage among the Nuer* (paperback edition with a new introduction by W. James), Oxford: Clarendon Press.
Hanbury-Tenison, R. (1982) *Aborigines of the Amazon Rain Forest: The Yanomami*, Amsterdam: Time-Life Books.
Hatch, E. (1973) *Culture and Morality. The Relativity of Values in Anthropology*, New York: Columbia University Press.
Hardman, C. (1981) 'The Psychology of Conformity and Self-expression among the Lohurung Rai of East Nepal', in P. Heelas and A. Lock (eds) *Indigenous Psychologies*, London: Academic Press.

Harris, M. (1975) *Cows, Pigs, Wars and Witches: The Riddles of Culture*, London: Hutchinson.

Heald, S. (1989) *Controlling Anger: The Sociology of Gisu Violence*, Manchester: Manchester University Press.

Heelas, P. and Lock, A. (eds.) (1981) *Indigenous Psychologies: The Anthropology of the Self*, London: Academic Press.

Heine, B. (1985) '*The Mountain People*: some notes on the Ik of North-Eastern Uganda', *Africa* 5, 1: 3–16.

Highlife (1993) British Airways Magazine, April issue.

Ingold, T. (1986) *The Appropriation of Nature: Essays on Human Ecology and Social Relations*, Manchester: Manchester University Press.

James, W. (1979) *Kwanim Pa: The Making of the Uduk People. An Ethnographic Study of Survival in the Sudan–Ethiopian Borderlands*, Oxford: Clarendon Press.

——— (1988) *The Listening Ebony: Moral Knowledge, Religion and Power among the Uduk of Sudan*, Oxford: Clarendon Press.

——— (1993) 'Orphans of Passage' (film, directed by Bruce MacDonald), *Disappearing World: War*, Manchester: Granada TV.

——— (1994) 'Civil War and Ethnic Visibility: the Uduk on the Sudan–Ethiopia border', in K. Fukui and J. Markakis (eds) *Ethnicity and Conflict in the Horn of Africa*, London/Athens: James Currey/Ohio University Press.

——— (1995) 'The Bonga Scheme: Progress to 1994 and outlook for 1995. A report for UNHCR on assistance to Sudanese (Uduk) refugees in western Ethiopia', Addis Ababa: UNHCR.

Johnson, D. H. (1981) 'The Fighting Nuer: Primary sources and the origin of a stereotype', *Africa* 51, 1: 508–27.

Knight, C. (1991) *Blood Relations: Menstruation and the Origins of Culture*, New Haven and London: Yale University Press.

Knight, J. (1994) '"The Mountain People" as Tribal Mirror', *Anthropology Today* 10, 6, December: 1–3.

Leach, E. R. (1961) *Rethinking Anthropology*, London: Athlone Press.

Lienhardt, R. G. (1961) *Divinity and Experience: The Religion of the Dinka*, Oxford: Clarendon Press.

——— (1985) 'Self: Public, Private. Some African representations', in M. Carrithers, S. Collins and S. Lukes (eds) *The Category of the Person: Anthropology, Philosophy, History*, Cambridge: Cambridge University Press.

Littlewood, R. (1994) 'Lessons for Society', letter to *The Times*, 3 August.

Malinowski, B. (1927) *The Sexual Life of Savages in Northwest Melanesia*, London: Routledge.

Mauss, M. (1985) *The Gift. Forms and Functions of Exchange in Archaic Societies*, trans. I. Cunnison, London: Routledge; orig. published as *Essai sur le don*, Paris: Presses Universitaires de France, 1938.

Mead, M. (1927) *Coming of Age in Samoa*, New York: Mentor Books.

Reynolds, V. (1976) *The Biology of Human Action*, Oxford and San Francisco: Freeman and Co. Ltd.

Rosaldo, M. Z. (1980) *Knowledge and Passion: Ilongot Conceptions of Self and Social Life*, Cambridge: Cambridge University Press.

Rosaldo, R. (1980) *Ilongot Headhunting, 1883–1974: A Study in History and Society*, Stanford: Stanford University Press.

Turnbull, C. (1972) *The Mountain People*, New York: Simon and Schuster.
Turner, V. W. (1967) *The Forest of Symbols: Aspects of Ndembu Ritual*, Ithaca: Cornell University Press.
—— (1974) *Dramas, Fields, and Metaphors: Symbolic Action in Human Society*, Ithaca and London: Cornell University Press.

Chapter 4

The chrysanthemum continues to flower

Ruth Benedict and some perils of popular anthropology

Joy Hendry

Ruth Benedict and her work on Japan could be described in quite as paradoxical a manner as the way in which she set out to represent Japan. In a discipline which characterizes itself by the learning of language, and long-term participant observation in the field, Benedict produced, without the benefit of either of these research tools, a book which to this day epitomizes the anthropology of the Japanese people. Although carried out without even a visit to that country, the results of Benedict's inquiry are still cited as genuine source material, her work is regarded as a classic in the field (e.g. Saeki and Haga 1987: 187), and she must have sparked off as much, if not more, debate from the subjects of her study than any other ethnographer.

Benedict's book *The Chrysanthemum and the Sword* owes its title to the apparently contradictory way in which Japanese people had been perceived in the West. To use some of Benedict's phrases, they were 'unprecedentedly polite', 'but also insolent and overbearing'; they 'adapt themselves readily to extreme innovations' but are also 'incomparably rigid'; they are 'loyal and generous', but 'treacherous and spiteful'; and are 'a nation with a popular cult of aestheticism which lavishes art upon the cultivation of chrysanthemums', but are at the same time 'devoted to the cult of the sword' (Benedict 1977: 1–2).

Benedict wrote this book as an assignment from the United States Office of War Information. She was approached in June 1944 to 'use all the techniques I could as a cultural anthropologist to spell out what the Japanese were like' (ibid.: 2). Thus, while at this crucial point in the Second World War, other social scientists engaged in the same endeavour were scanning the library shelves for history and statistics, and analysing Japanese propaganda and responses to past events, Ruth Benedict set out to seek face-to-face contact with Japanese people interned in the US. She also read books written by Westerners and by

Japanese, and she went to see films, but she made a point of going over them afterwards with Japanese people who had seen them in Japan.

In the introduction to *The Chrysanthemum and the Sword*, Benedict explains the techniques she used to unravel the mysteries of Japanese behaviour and to make sense of the human commonplaces of Japanese life. 'The more baffled I was at some bit of behaviour, the more I therefore assumed that there existed somewhere in Japanese life some ordinary conditioning of such strangeness', she writes. 'If the search took me into trivial details of daily intercourse, so much the better. That was where people learned' (ibid.: 8). The book is about habits, 'habits that are expected and taken for granted', and the 'ideal authority for any statement in this book would be the proverbial man in the street', she wrote (ibid.: 11).

emp. on everyday life

Benedict's aim as a student who was 'trying to uncover the assumptions upon which Japan builds its way of life' was, according to her introduction, 'to report how these accepted practices and judgements become the lenses through which the Japanese see existence' (ibid.: 12). And you will not be surprised to hear that, once her task has been accomplished, 'many contradictions Westerners are accustomed to see in Japanese behaviour were no longer contradictions', they were part of 'a system consistent within itself', and her book 'can try to show why' (ibid.: 13). Or, as Geertz puts it in *Works and Lives*, 'the enemy who at the beginning of the book is the most alien we have ever fought is, by the end of it, the most reasonable we have ever conquered' (Geertz 1988: 121). All good anthropological stuff, despite the unconventional methods used in its acquisition.

In this paper, I would like to follow Benedict's lead, although rather than explain contradictory Japanese behaviour I would like to address the paradox of why Benedict's apparently unorthodox approach achieved such astounding success – or shall we say notoriety, for just as there are few clear benchmarks against which to measure the likes of *The Chrysanthemum and the Sword*, and this is one of the factors which underlies much of the debate about it, neither is there an agreed finishing line in measuring the success or otherwise of anthropological writing. The book is well known, and it could therefore be described as 'popular anthropology'. Whether this has been good or bad, and for whom, is the substance of the other question to be addressed.

The next section details some of the continuing success the book enjoys, in the US, Europe and Japan. The subsequent section examines criticisms which have been directed against it, in particular noting ways in which reactions to *The Chrysanthemum and the Sword* have negatively influenced views of anthropology, seen then as 'perils' of popularization. The nature of these so-called 'perils' is analysed in a further section, leading to a final evaluation of the book itself and some concluding general remarks about the popularization of anthropology.

THE CONTINUING IMPACT OF BENEDICT'S WORK ON JAPAN

Originally published in New York in 1946, *The Chrysanthemum and the Sword*, whose complete title continues: *Patterns of Japanese Culture* (reflecting Benedict's even better known work, *Patterns of Culture*), has been republished and reprinted several times. In Britain, it was, from 1967, kept in print for many years by Routledge and Kegan Paul, who also produced a paperback version in 1977. Although it is now on the lists of neither Routledge nor KPI International, it is still in print in the US and Japan in a series of classic books in English about Japan, published by Tuttle.

In 1988, Geertz (1988: 111) reported that it had sold 350,000 copies (*Patterns of Culture* has sold nearly two million copies in more than two dozen languages). In French, *Le Chrysanthème et le sabre* was published for the first time in 1987, and went into a second impression in 1991, currently having sold some 4,000 copies. More importantly, perhaps, in this world where even citations may be counted to support one's reason for existence, *The Chrysanthemum and the Sword* is still to be found cited for one reason or another in the bibliographies of many books coming out on Japan, anthropological and otherwise. A check through my own bookshelves revealed an entry in over half of the books on Japan.

For example, in the early work of Ronald Dore, the most prolific, scholarly, and probably the most highly regarded social commentator on matters Japanese, Benedict was cited frequently as genuine source material. Moreover, in *City Life in Japan* (Dore 1958), almost a whole chapter is devoted to defending her work in the face of an attack by the Japanese philosopher, Watsuji Tetsuro, where Dore tries to demonstrate that both writers have right on their side. In a much more recent book which has made considerable impact in the field of Japanese studies, *The Myth of Japanese Uniqueness* by Peter Dale (1986), a great deal of space is devoted to analysing and explaining the reactions of several Japanese writers to Benedict's work (see below), one aspect of this exercise again occupying a whole chapter of the book.

In an American–Japanese collaborative study of child development and education in Japan (one of Benedict's most often cited subjects of concern), she is referred to as having been the first to introduce anthropological discussion to Japanese concepts of duty and obligation, *on* and *giri*, 'which have been discussed at length in the anthropological literature on Japan since the writings of Benedict' (Befu 1986: 23); and also with having initiated 'psychological studies of Japanese personality [which] began during World War II through interviews with Japanese Americans' (Chen and Miyake 1986: 136).

Another interesting way in which the chrysanthemum continues to flower, with or without the sword, is in the inspiration the title has apparently sparked off. Further book titles are a good example. There is *The Thorn in the Chrysanthemum* (Iga 1986), a study of suicide in Japan; *The Chrysanthemum and the Bat* (Whiting 1977), a comparison of baseball in Japan and the US; and *Without the Chrysanthemum and the Sword: A Study of the Attitudes of Youth in Post-War Japan* (Stoetzel 1955). The sub-title of *The Chrysanthemum and the Sword, Patterns of Japanese Culture*, undoubtedly also influenced a subsequent anthropological study covering much of the same ground, called *Japanese Patterns of Behaviour*, by Takie Sugiyama Lebra (1976).

A further example of such influence is to be found in a quotation from Geertz (1983), cited more recently by Moeran (1989), where he notes that social scientists are in recent years 'looking less for the sort of thing that connects planets and pendulums and more for the sort that connects chrysanthemums and swords', thus marking a move to what he calls a 'cases and interpretations' approach. Benedict was not only influential in her title, then, but also apparently well ahead of her time in the explanatory device she adopted.

Actually, to use one of her own yardsticks to measure the success of her work, namely the degree to which it makes the people she describes predictable (Kroeber *et al.* 1949: 18), the book seems to have more than impressed her colleague, Clyde Kluckhohn. Sent to Japan in the wake of the war effort which lay behind the study, he writes 'I was astonished to discover the extent to which I knew what was coming in unformalised situations or contexts not covered by my reading . . . Before I went to Japan, my admiration for that book was great. When I left, my respect was enormous' (ibid.: 19). These were, however, words written in a memorial after Benedict's death. The Japanese reaction to Benedict's work was much more critical.

SOME PERILS OF POPULAR ANTHROPOLOGY

A book which becomes popular is, by definition, more easily available than a strictly academic tome which only runs to a limited edition. It is thus more likely to be read by the subjects of its study. This is fine, and all anthropological books would do well to be available to the people under study in this way, but it also potentially opens the work to misunderstanding, especially if the translation into the native tongue is not done carefully enough. In a situation of conflict, such as that which inspired the study under scrutiny, this kind of misunderstanding could indeed have perilous consequences, not only for the peoples concerned, but also for the discipline which supported such a study. The actual situation with Ruth Benedict's book has been less clear-cut than this, but it has not been without its sources of peril.

First of all, *The Chrysanthemum and the Sword* – it rolls even more easily off the tongue in Japanese, where it becomes an alliteration, *Kiku to Katana* – is extremely well known in Japan. The mere publication of such a study, written by a foreigner who had never stepped on Japanese shores, was, however, found to be quite alarming to Japanese people. It is a collective representation in Japan that no one but the Japanese can understand the Japanese, and this book definitely seemed to be setting out to do just that. Moreover, it actually seemed to get quite a few things right. Doi, a psychiatrist who later also achieved considerable acclaim in his attempts (legitimately as a Japanese) to explain the Japanese, wrote as follows:

> an American lady I got to know lent me Ruth Benedict's 'The Chrysanthemum and the Sword'. I read it immediately, and I still remember the vivid impression I had of seeing myself reflected in it. Time and again, as I turned the pages, I gave a nod of surprised recognition. At the same time the book stirred my intellectual curiosity as to why the Japanese and the Americans should be so different.
>
> (Doi 1973:13)

This last sentence is a telling one, in fact, because Doi and Benedict are now just two of a plethora of authors whose books, essays and articles attempt to explain differences between Japan and America, often described as Japan and the West, usually in efforts to establish and describe a Japanese identity. According to a survey of the Nomura Research Institute, some 700 titles were published on this theme in the thirty years between 1946 (when Benedict's book became available) and 1978 (Befu and Manabe 1990: 124; Dale 1986: 15). Indeed, the genre has become almost a national obsession, a subject for anthropological analysis in its own right.

In 1987, for example, the American anthropologists Harumi Befu and Kazufumi Manabe carried out a survey of 2,400 adults in central Japan which found Ruth Benedict still an author of whom, by extrapolation, some sixteen million Japanese had heard, and, more interesting perhaps, some twenty million (again by extrapolation) claimed to have read (Befu and Manabe 1990). This number, who had apparently read *Kiku to Katana*, though some may have forgotten the name of the author, was 33 percent of the sample, a proportion shared by Doi's book *Amae no Kôzo*, translated as *The Anatomy of Dependence*, and outstripped only by a book entitled *The Japanese and the Jews*, by one Isaiah Bendasan whose actual ethnic origins few people seem to be clear about.

The list of such studies includes work by other well-known anthropologists. Nakane Chie is a Japanese anthropologist whose *Tateshakai*, translated as *Japanese Society*, made a great impact, and Ezra Vogel, an American anthropologist, whose book *Japan as Number One* was a bestseller in Japan and the US. However, there have been many more contributions from academics in a variety of other fields and, as those familiar with the genre will know, some of them have been positively bizarre. The study by neurologist Tsunoda Tadanobu (1978), which argued for a kind of unique wiring of the Japanese brain (though morphologically identical to other brains) influenced irrevocably by the unique nature of the Japanese language, is perhaps the most often cited. Others include a study by a 'professor of English studies' who, in a book translated as *The Peasant Soul of Japan*, contrasts the fundamental agrarian nature of Japanese society with the equestrian nature, apparently of everyone else (Watanabe 1989).

The literature *en masse* has quite rightly been criticized on a number of counts, not least for over-generalizing about the Japanese, for describing them as though they were one homogeneous people, with very little to distinguish between them, and (less often perhaps, though with as much justification) for generalizing about everyone else in the Western world. Individual contributions have been criticized, again with some justification, for taking only one aspect of Japanese society and using it as *the* chief explanatory device for understanding this '*unique*' people. The notion of *amae* (dependence), described by Doi, and the notion of agrarianism, described by Watanabe, are two such cases.

Ruth Benedict is not held entirely responsible for the existence of this body of literature, but she did make a highly significant early contribution to it, and there has been a general tendency to blame anthropological approaches for the reductionism it is thought to exemplify, particularly by people who seem to have little understanding about what an anthropological approach is. A pair of Australian-based sociologists, Sugimoto and Mouer, have been particularly influential in this respect, as I have already pointed out in two previous publications (Hendry 1986, 1987). They describe the general problem as the result of a holistic approach, initiated by Ruth Benedict's experience with 'the small-scale societies which formed the more traditional subject matter' (Hendry 1986: 8) of her field.

In my opinion, Sugimoto and Mouer also have a fundamental misunderstanding of the meaning of holism, but their work is prolific and apparently widely read. In some ways it is a breath of fresh air in studies of Japanese society, but it has done nothing for the name of anthropology. In particular, after Benedict, Nakane Chie is probably the anthropologist who has been subjected to the most virulent criticism in this respect, for her model about the vertical nature of Japanese hierarchy, which has also been popular and immensely influential, is seen as another unique key, altogether too simple and all-embracing.[1]

In fact, most of the critical points made by Sugimoto and Mouer about Benedict had already been voiced by a group of Japanese scholars who published in 1949 a special issue of their journal of ethnological research, *Minzokugaku Kenkyû*, on Benedict's book. This was summarized in English, together with other Japanese comments, in an article in *American Anthropologist* in 1953 (Bennett and Nagai 1953). Benedict was criticized for writing about 'the Japanese' as if there were no differences between them, and for using data from the 'feudal' period, carried in the heads of people who left Japan long before Benedict met them, as if it could equally well apply years later.)

More technically she was criticized for assuming the importance of 'culture' as a determinant of change without establishing empirically its role (Yanagida), and for describing the 'ideal-typical Japanese', i.e. (failing to distinguish between what people say they do and what they actually do (Minami). As Bennett and Nagai point out at the end of their article, 'collectively, these Japanese appraisals of Benedict actually make up the most thorough and exhaustive critique of a particular specimen of the whole culture-patternist approach ever made, or at least printed' (ibid.: 410; cf., for example, Bohannan and Glazer 1973: 176).

This kind of exchange within the halls of academe is one thing, however; another aspect of the criticisms was much more perilous in the wider world. At a symposium on *The Chrysanthemum and the Sword*, the sociologist Tsurumi Kazuko noted that, in *Patterns of Culture*, Benedict had said primitive societies should be studied first by anthropologists, because the configurations were fairly simple compared with America where there were different classes. Tsurumi seems to have assumed Japan was seen by Benedict in this way, for she goes on to write 'yet she sees Japanese society as uncivilised, undifferentiated pre-modern society' (Tsurumi, quoted in Bennett and Nagai 1953: 408).

This is the crux of what really upset many Japanese commentators. It was the implication they read into Benedict's work that she was describing a society which was behind that of the United States in terms of a notion of social progress which the Japanese have held dear at least since they became acquainted with the work of Herbert Spencer. Benedict herself was unlikely to have held such a notion, anyway at the level of conscious awareness, for she wrote much in 'The Science of Custom', the first chapter of *Patterns of Culture*, about the basic equality of different peoples and, in particular, of their religions. Indeed, I can read no such implicit assumptions into *Kiku to Katana* myself.

Nevertheless, Mouer and Sugimoto describe in her work 'a tendency to underline the feudalistic, the socially backward or semi-barbaric aspects of Japanese society (Mouer and Sugimoto 1986: 45), and they refer to the writings of an American lecturer in Japan who was highly critical of the evaluative aspect he also perceived in her work which he saw as 'a retreat from her earlier commitment to cultural relativism' (ibid.: 62). I have not been able to find a first-hand example of the work of this American (Douglas Lummis), who started his life in Japan as a US Marine based in Okinawa, and wrote *A New Look at the Chrysanthemum and the Sword* some twenty years later. However, he is quoted by a Japanese writer for describing the book as 'nothing but political propaganda', 'well-written but poisonous misunderstanding', a 'tombstone for Japanese culture', and 'the work of a poet rather than a cultural anthropologist' (Ikeda 1984: 156, 160, 161, 166). Lummis apparently concluded that the book was a product of Japanese military ideology and Benedict's complexity of thought (ibid.: 169).

Also highly critical of the book was the philosopher, Watsuji

Tetsuro, who claimed that Benedict should have made clear she was speaking mostly of 'the military and fascist cliques during the last war', and that she should have sub-titled her book 'patterns of Japanese soldiers', or 'patterns of the ultra-nationalist group of Japanese soldiers'. I don't know enough about Lummis to relate his ire to his own circumstances after twenty years in Japan, but Watsuji's fierce objections were undoubtedly related to his self-image as being highly educated in Western systems of thought, a representative of the generation which had tasted the intoxication of Western freedom in the early part of the century before the build-up of oppression preceding the Second World War. He was thus particularly disturbed by Benedict's description of the Japanese as 'conditioned to a world where the smallest details of conduct are mapped and status is assigned' (Bennett and Nagai 1953: 409).[2]

A CLOSER LOOK AT THE PERILS

It is evident, then, that *The Chrysanthemum and the Sword* sparked off a great deal of debate in Japan, and that it has been heavily criticized. But just how perilous has this been, and for whom? The most specific area of Benedict's work to spark controversy and further debate was in fact her description of the difference between guilt cultures and shame cultures (1977: 156–7), and her perceived characterization of Japan as a shame culture, as opposed to America, which was more associated with guilt. This catchy distinction was oversimplified in representations of it elsewhere, and suffered much the same fate as labels in *Patterns of Culture* like 'paranoid' and 'megalomaniac' for Dobuan and Kwakiutl cultures respectively, and Apollonian and Dionysian as culture types – immediate, if misunderstood, appeal, and a barrage of criticism for explanatory and analytical limitations. It also seemed to imply again to Japanese readers that they were being described negatively in comparison with the US.

Doi, the psychiatrist, for example, writes:

> it is evident that when she states that the culture of guilt places emphasis on inner standards of conduct whereas the culture of shame places emphasis on outward standards of conduct she has the feeling that the former is superior to the latter...
>
> (1973: 48)

In fact, all that I could find in Benedict which could possibly be interpreted as expressing such a feeling is the following: 'Shame is an

increasingly heavy burden in the United States and guilt is less
extremely felt than in earlier generations. In the United States, this is
interpreted as a relaxation of morals.' However, she also notes
immediately that 'we do not harness the acute personal chagrin which
accompanies shame to our fundamental system of morality' (1977:
157) – unlike in Japan, as she goes on to explain.

Doi is actually inclined 'on the whole' to agree with Benedict's
distinction and launches into an attempt to refine her ideas with a
more detailed look at the distinction. Another Japanese commentator,
this time a sociologist, was inspired by what he saw as Benedict's
oversimplified representation of so-called shame-culture, to write a
whole book on the subject (Sakuda 1967). He felt that Benedict had
dealt only with 'public shame', neglecting to examine a notion of inner
shame which he argues is equally important (ibid.: 10). An implicit
assumption in the writings of these critics is that inner sanctions, such
as those described as guilt, represent greater depth, although this was
never, as far as I can tell, argued by Benedict. Hence the concern to
demonstrate the existence of inner sanctions in Japan too.

Peter Dale takes up the argument with a vengeance, first of all
citing a virulent attacker who prefaces his particular study, *Concepts of
the Carnivores* – ('an attempt to explain Western institutions, values
and intellectual history in terms of the effects of meat-eating and
pastoralism'), 'with a plea for studying the Occident in terms of
Japanese notions of culture to redress the balance for the fact that
Westerners like Ruth Benedict have taken the liberty to look on Japan
from a Western angle' (Dale 1986: 31). Dale immediately makes the
point that, while 'Ruth Benedict shows herself acutely aware of the
dangers of ethnocentric bias, and consciously attempted to avoid
making value judgements, Sabata [the author of *Concepts of the
Carnivores*] makes a conscious effort to ground his theories in
nationalistic perspectives'.

Doi, too, according to Dale, follows his criticism of Benedict's
apparent application of value judgements to her distinction between
guilt and shame culture by trying to turn the tables – in other words to
show how, on the contrary, the Japanese system is superior (ibid.: 179).
Dale cites several other people who became embroiled in the debate,
each concerned both to detect ethnocentric bias in Benedict's work,
and to turn it around into Japanese superiority. Dale argues that few of
these writers have understood Benedict properly, tending to associate
guilt with an internal dignity of Protestantism or early Christianity
contrasted with a Confucian emphasis on external dignity, whereas he

sees Benedict's notion of guilt much more in a post-Kantian, Freudian way. He also argues that all of them are caught in a 'linguistic snare', namely an unawareness that the concept of 'guilt' has been mistranslated into Japanese as *tsumi*, a notion much closer to 'sin'. These misunderstandings, he argues, help to account for the strange way in which they assail Benedict's thesis.

Dale also relates the Japanese reaction to Benedict's work to its timing. The translation of *The Chrysanthemum and the Sword* appeared just as Japan was remodelling itself on the West, and such profound differences implied damage to a status equated with identity with the West (ibid.: 185). Whereas Benedict's intentions in the book were to preempt facile moral judgements in terms of Western values about Japanese wartime behaviour, her thesis was in fact read as 'a vainglorious snub to a defeated country by one of the impudent victors' (ibid.) – quite a different point of view to that of Erik Erikson, the artist whose drawing appears in the Viking Fund Memorial publication. He wrote, 'In her book on Japan she fulfilled her function in this nation by adding thoughtful understanding to the very vigour of victory, adding the chrysanthemum to the sword' (Kroeber *et al.* 1949: 16).

It should also be noted that, of the fifteen Japanese scholars cited in the bibliography of Bennett and Nagai's article, all but two are described as presenting a 'generally favourable attitude towards the book', and the well known legal scholar, Kawashima Takeyoshi, approved of her attempt to 'grasp the total structure which is constructed out of reciprocal inter-relationships among various Japanese modes of behaviour and thought' (Bennett and Nagai 1953: 406). Colleagues in the social sciences, then, treated her work with respect, though they may have criticised her approach.

In a recent summary of the book in a collection of articles in Japanese about famous works on Japan by foreigners, she is credited with having influenced considerably the success of General MacArthur's Allied Occupation (Saeki and Haga 1987: 186), and for having broadened the study of cultural anthropology from its interest only in primitive society to work in the cities of highly developed societies. Some of the perils are at least offset by positive remarks such as these.

SO JUST WHAT IS THE VALUE OF 'POPULARITY'?

How, then, are we to evaluate Benedict's work? Is the fact that she has been widely read and quoted good or bad? Considering the perils we have noted, perhaps we should argue negatively, especially since it seems that she has also been much misunderstood. But my own gut reaction is rather positive. In this last section of the paper I would like to try to explain why this should be so, and at the same time complete the exercise I set myself at the beginning, namely to explain *why* she became so well known.

First of all, there are of course the general aspects of Benedict's writing. *The Chrysanthemum and the Sword* sold far fewer copies than *Patterns of Culture*, as mentioned above, but it displays many of the same features. The advantages of patterns, and in particular their labels, is that they can be easily and quickly assimilated, better still if they can be recognized as in some way appropriate. They then become 'characterizations', to borrow Chris McDonaugh's neat way of describing their effect. This is a feature of other works of the culture and personality school, and naturally come in for the same kind of criticism.

However, Benedict's work has been much discussed for its own special qualities. One of these was undoubtedly her eloquence and clarity of style. Alan Dundes, for example, wrote as long ago as 1968 (as you will soon see, pre-dating gender-aware linguistic alterations), 'Anthropology has been fortunate in having had its fair share of articulate spokesmen, and of these spokesmen none have been more eloquent than Ruth Benedict' (Dundes 1968: 180). Geertz was more specific when he described her as having developed 'a powerful expository style at once spare, assured, lapidary, and above all resolute: definite views, definitely expressed' (1988: 108).

He goes further, to describe the 'defining characteristics of virtually all her prose' as 'passion, distance, directness and relentlessness so complete as to very nearly match that of the giant who is here her model' (ibid.: 105). This is a reference to Swift, creator of Gulliver, whose influence is clear in her 'The Uses of Cannibalism', a research proposal unpublished until a posthumous collection of her writing was compiled by her student, friend and intimate, Margaret Mead (1959: 44–8). For, as Clifford has recently noted in *Writing Culture*, Benedict, Mead and their friend Edward Sapir, all saw themselves as literary artists as well as anthropologists, though they had at that time to hide the poetry they wrote from 'the scientific gaze of their teacher Franz Boas' (Clifford 1986: 3–4).

Mead and Benedict also had another common element in their approach which undoubtedly contributed to their popularity. They were both concerned to use their anthropological knowledge ultimately to respond to problems current in their own society. As Clifford writes, 'The ethnographic stories Mead and Benedict told were manifestly linked to the situation of a culture struggling with diverse values, with an apparent breakdown in established traditions, with utopian visions of human malleability and fears of disaggregation' (ibid.: 102).

Handler even describes Benedict as concerned with 'social engineering' (Handler 1986: 152). He wrote of her, 'She discovered her convincing sense of selfhood not simply in anthropology as scholarship, but in the role of the technical expert, the scientific creator who puts her individual talents at the service of the collectivity' (ibid.) Benedict herself is quoted in a memorial published shortly after her death as follows: 'We hope a little, that whereas change has hitherto been blind, at the mercy of unconscious patternings, it will be possible gradually, in so far as we have become genuinely culture-conscious, that it should be guided by intelligence' (Kroeber et al. 1949: 10).

Certainly, Benedict was entrusted with a mission, as she herself describes it, of great importance to the efforts of the United States at a crucial point in the course of the Second World War. She has also, as noted above, been seen as responsible for much of the success of General MacArthur in his dealings with the Japanese people during the Allied Occupation (Saeki and Haga 1987: 186), and in particular, for the retention of the Imperial System in Japan (Cobbi 1987: 6) when the first intention had been to remove it (Lévi-Strauss 1986: 39). Books have and are still being written about whether this was good or bad, but it is certainly unusual for an anthropologist to be asked to contribute to such momentous decisions.

In a lecture given in Tokyo in 1986, Lévi-Strauss commented precisely on this anthropological influence, suggesting that Benedict's advice could well have helped to avoid even more tragic circumstances than those which resulted from the military defeat. He explained that the removal of one part of a system which has developed over centuries could well risk destroying other parts, and although Benedict had never been to Japan, her anthropological methods, and inspiration, allowed her sufficient understanding of the system to offer such advice. This alone, he suggests, is enough to justify a more and more important place for anthropology among the sciences of man and of society (Lévi-Strauss 1986: 39).

Again, as noted by Japanese commentators, Benedict's work was also an early attempt to apply anthropological techniques of analysis to a complex society, and, despite the complaints, there is still much to learn from her book. Even if we looked only at the complaints, it can eventually surely only help intercultural understanding to have people examining the different possible notions of shame, guilt, sin and so forth. One Japanese commentator, who argued strongly for the external dimension of guilt, noting how Christians behave under the scrutiny of other Christians, also attributed the success of the book to its timing – 'when it was fashionable to badmouth Japan' (Aida Yûji, quoted in Dale 1986: 180–1). Perhaps this could explain the recent French translation, which coincided approximately with Edith Cresson's indiscretions, though I very much doubt it.

In this one study Benedict not only demonstrated the potential value of anthropological inquiry for the practical purposes of intercultural encounters – even having been credited with creating the climate necessary for the success of the Allied Occupation of Japan – she also illustrated the value of a concealed weapon for long, and far better, understood by the Japanese (and perhaps by many other people) than by their enemies in the West. This weapon was to be found in a knowledge of the thought processes of the other side. As she wrote in the introduction to the book, 'The question was how the Japanese would behave, not how we would behave if [we] were in their place' (1977: 3) – an obvious notion to anthropologists, maybe, but not always understood by others active in an international arena.

In the end, I think we can only evaluate positively a book which reaches out to the general public with a powerful point such as this. Some Japanese may have been upset or offended by their perception of the arguments of the book, but it also made them think about themselves and the differences between the Japanese and other peoples, notably Americans. The book may have become associated with works much less scholarly, it may have contributed to the bringing into disrepute of the very subject which it is supposed to exemplify, but it actually seems to be riding through all that. Perils or no perils, it looks as though the chrysanthemum will continue to flower for some time yet.

NOTES

1 It is actually a useful structural principle, which she originally contrasted with the horizontal form of hierarchy she observed in the Indian sub-continent, but this has been poorly understood.

2 His own work, *Fûdo*, relating Japanese thinking to the climatic conditions of the archipelago, also figures high in the list of theories of Japanese identity.

REFERENCES

Befu, H. (1986) 'The Social and Cultural Background of Child Development in Japan and the United States', in H. Stevenson *et al.* (eds) *Child Development and Education in Japan*, New York: W. H. Freeman and Company.

Befu, H. and Manabe, K. (1990) 'Empirical Status of *Nihonjinron*: How Real is the Myth?', in A. Boscaro *et al.* (eds) *Rethinking Japan*, Sandgate: Japan Library.

Benedict, R. (1935) *Patterns of Culture*, London: Routledge and Kegan Paul.

—— (1977) *The Chrysanthemum and the Sword*, London: Routledge and Kegan Paul.

Bennett, J. W. and Nagai, M. (1953) 'The Japanese Critique of the Methodology of Benedict's *Chrysanthemum and the Sword*', *American Anthropologist* 55: 404–11.

Bohannan, P. J. and Glazer, M. (1973) *High Points in Anthropology*, New York: Alfred A. Knopf.

Chen, S. and Miyake, K. (1986) 'Japanese Studies of Infant Development', in H. Stevenson *et al.* (eds) *Child Development and Education in Japan*, New York: W. H. Freeman and Company.

Clifford, J. (1986) 'Introduction' and 'On Ethnographic Allegory', in J. Clifford and G. E. Marcus (eds) *Writing Culture: The Poetics and Politics of Ethnography*, Berkeley: University of California Press.

Cobbi, J. (1987) 'Preface' to *Le Chrysanthème et le sabre*, Arles: Philippe Picquier.

Dale, Peter N. (1986) *The Myth of Japanese Uniqueness*, London: Croom Helm.

Doi, T. (1973) *The Anatomy of Dependence*, Tokyo: Kodansha International.

Dore, R. P. (1958) *City Life in Japan*, Berkeley: University of California Press.

Dundes, A. (1968) *Every Man his Way*, Englewood Cliffs, NJ: Prentice Hall.

Geertz, C. (1983) *Local Knowledge: Further Essays in Interpretive Anthropology*, New York: Basic Books.

—— (1988) *Works and Lives: The Anthropologist as Author*, Cambridge: Polity Press.

Handler, R. (1986) 'Vigorous Male and Aspiring Female', in G. W. Stocking Jr (ed.) *Malinowski, Rivers, Benedict and Others*, History of Anthropology 4, Madison: The University of Wisconsin Press.

Hendry, J. (1986) 'Introduction' to *Interpreting Japanese Society*, Oxford: Journal of the Anthropological Society of Oxford, Occasional Paper 5.

—— (1987) 'Review of Mouer and Sugimoto, *Images of Japanese Society*', *Journal of Japanese Studies*, 13, 2: 491–5.

Iga, M. (1986) *The Thorn in the Chrysanthemum: Suicide and Economic Success in Modern Japan*, Berkeley: University of California Press.

Ikeda M. (1984) '*Nihon Bunkaron no Genzai*', in *Hikaku Bunka no Susume*, Tokyo: Seibundo.

Kroeber, A. *et al.* (1949) *Ruth Fulton Benedict, A Memorial*, New York: Viking Fund.

Lebra, T. S. (1976) *Japanese Patterns of Behaviour*, Honolulu: University Press of Hawaii.

Lévi-Strauss, C. (1986) 'Eighth Ishizaka Lecture', April. Unpublished ms.

Mead, M. (1959) *An Anthropologist at Work: Writings of Ruth Benedict*, London: Secker and Warburg.

Moeran, B. (1989) *Language and Popular Culture in Japan*, Manchester: Manchester University Press.

Mouer, R. and Sugimoto, Y. (1986) *Images of Japanese Society*, London: Kegan Paul International.

Saeki, S. and Haga, T. (1987) *Gaikokujin ni yoru Nihonron no Meicho*, Tokyo: Chûkoshinsho.

Sakuda, K. (1967) *Haji no Bunka Saikô*, Tokyo: Chikuma Shobo.

Stevenson, H. *et al.* (eds) (1986) *Child Development and Education in Japan*, New York: W. H. Freeman and Company.

Stoetzel, J. (1955) *Without the Chrysanthemum and the Sword: A Study of the Attitudes of Youth in Post-War Japan*, London: Heinemann.

Sugimoto, Y. and Mouer, R. (1980) 'Reappraising Images of Japanese Society', *Social Analysis* 5/6: 5–19.

Tsunoda, T. (1978) *Nihonjin no nô*, Tokyo: Taishûkan Shoten.

Watanabe, S. (1989) *The Peasant Soul of Japan*, London: Macmillan.

Watsuji, T. (1949) 'Ruth Benedict "Kiku to Katana" no ataeru mono: kagakuteki kachi ni taisuru gimon', *Minzokugaku Kenkyû* xiv, 4.

Whiting, R. (1977) *The Chrysanthemum and the Bat: Baseball Samurai Style*, New York: Dodds, Mead and Co.

Yoshino K. (1992) *Cultural Nationalism in Contemporary Japan*, London: Routledge.

Chapter 5

Communicating culture
Margaret Mead and the practice of popular anthropology

William E. Mitchell

In 1901 Queen Victoria died and Margaret Mead was born. Each, in her way, was a remarkable woman and a definer of her times. While Victoria's name defined an age famous for its unabashed sexism and sentimental notions about family and marriage, Mead's career was dedicated to challenging these and other views she found outmoded, exploitative, or false. A ceaseless critic and commentator on her times, Mead was a leading figure in transforming the consciousness of twentieth-century Americans. As Marcus and Fischer (1986: 130) have observed, 'Margaret Mead . . . became *the* model of the anthropologist as cultural critic'.

After a long and brilliant career, Margaret Mead died of cancer in 1978 in New York City. The city was her home – more or less – since 1920 when she entered Barnard College where she had discovered anthropology in a course with Franz Boas during her senior year. Although Boas's lectures were factual and formal, it was his teaching assistant Ruth Benedict's informal and sometimes irreverent comments during class field-trips to the American Museum of Natural History that humanized the material for Mead (1972: 113). Nearing graduation, Mead lunched with Benedict and mused about whether to go into sociology, as Professor William Fielding Ogburn wished her to do, or into psychology as she already had planned. Benedict's response was that Professor Boas and she had 'nothing to offer but an opportunity to do work that matters'. Mead later wrote, 'That settled it for me. Anthropology had to be done *now*. Other things could wait' (1972: 114).

From then onward, Mead devoted her professional life to the practice of anthropology. In a career that lasted almost sixty years, she never wavered in her belief that anthropology mattered. As a scientist and a humanist with superlative communication skills, she convinced millions that anthropology not only provided a unique window on the 'otherness' of the world, but that this knowledge could bring insights to our own predicaments.

A tireless publicist for and popularizer of anthropology, she spread her messages throughout the world via public lectures, radio and television talks and interviews, newspaper and magazine articles, and books. (Once, asked what she did, she replied with a trace of annoyance, 'I write books!') Her style, whether speaking or writing, was emphatic, immensely caring, often witty, occasionally scolding, and usually surprising.

In time, Mead became a legendary public figure with a degree of fame unknown by any social scientist before or since. *Time* magazine heralded her in 1969 as 'Mother to the World,' a woman who was 'something more than an anthropologist and something less than a national oracle' (*Time* 1969: 74).[2] How did Mead succeed in teaching so many people that anthropology mattered? How was she able to extend her influence toward so many? How *did* she popularize anthropology?

The term 'popularize' is sometimes used in a pejorative sense; that is not my intent and it certainly was not Mead's. The dictionary says what I have in mind, namely, 'to cause to be liked or esteemed', and 'to present in generally understandable or interesting form'. Mead worked to enhance the esteem of anthropology and to make its findings understandable and relevant to the layperson. Unlike some academicians, she had great respect for her fellow citizens, a respect reflected in the time and energy she gave to them. Her colleague in Columbia University's Department of Anthropology, Robert Murphy, commented that some of their colleagues felt that Mead's interest in undergraduate students, as well as the anthropologically naive general public, was misplaced. 'The academy,' Murphy added, 'was invaded by horrible hubris, of which Margaret Mead had no part whatever' (Howard 1984: 335–6).

It was Mead's conviction that almost any idea could be stated simply enough to be intelligible to laypeople. With characteristic no-nonsense rhetoric she declared that if one cannot state a matter clearly enough so that even an intelligent twelve-year-old can understand it, one should remain within the cloistered walls of the university and laboratory until one gets a better grasp of one's subject matter' (Metraux 1979: 252–3).[3] And her thumb-stick might punctuate her remark with a thud on the floor as she threw a look of mock fierceness toward her audience.

Mead was an enthusiastic public lecturer, sometimes speaking a hundred or more times a year (Chassler 1979: 280) to audiences extraordinarily diverse in terms of class, culture and special interests. Although most of her audiences were Americans of one kind or another, she sometimes lectured abroad. In 1943, for example, she made a lecture tour in Britain which included talks on the BBC, while trying to clarify some of the culturally related communication problems generated by wartime romances between British women and American servicemen whose conflicting expectations about dating and courtship had created a serious problem. The result was a short but insightful analysis of the problem (Mead 1944) and, exactly fifty years after the GIs first arrived in the United Kingdom, the *Guardian Weekly* remembered with approval her advice (Gardiner 1992: 22). Following her dictum that everything was anthropology, Mead's curriculum vitae lists the trip among her major field expeditions (Fox 1979: 7).

All speaking engagements for Mead were a form of fieldwork, as she hoped to learn as much from her audiences as they did from her. After a lecture she took questions from the audience to learn what was on *their* minds, not only as feed back as to what was on hers, but to identify the emergence of new attitudes and problems. As her colleague Rhoda Metraux (1979: 9) notes, Mead 'made a point of answering each query thoughtfully and concisely – sometimes with a single word, sometimes sharply and most often with humor'. Aware that she could not answer all her questioners, Mead often asked the members of her audience to write out their questions, and later reviewed the unanswered ones. Many of these questions were the basis for her monthly *Redbook* column, written in collaboration with Metraux, that appeared for a sixteen-year period from 1963 to January 1979.[4]

As a lecturer, Mead was as comfortable and compelling when talking to several thousand people as she was to a handful of seminar students. She rarely used notes in the classroom or public lecture hall, and she said that she never gave the same lecture twice. Although the central themes of a lecture might be similar to a previous one, the talk itself was influenced by her last audience's questions, her profuse reading, new thoughts and experiences, and local information gleaned from her lecture hosts, any of which could send her talk into new and surprising directions.[5]

An important factor in Mead's success as a popularizer of anthropology was that, as a lecturer, she also was a lively and passionate *performer* – not an actress, for she was always assertively herself – but a performer who delighted in provoking others to think unconventional thoughts about conventional things. She spoke with a strong sense of conviction that seemed, at times, to border on infallibility. Her supreme self-confidence and optimism made it difficult for those who flatly disagreed with her to convince her that she was wrong.[6] While the public usually related positively to her no-nonsense approach, it did not endear her to those of her colleagues who preferred a voice less stubbornly sure.

In the earlier part of her career, her lecture attire was forgettably conventional. Later she deliberately decided to assume a distinctive persona to make herself more easily identifiable (Dana Raphael, pers. comm.). Her new attire consisted of a brocaded cape and a shoulder-high forked staff of British cherry wood that also steadied a chronically weak ankle. Typically, she rejected the use of a cane as symbolically wrong.[7] Striding purposively across the stage to the lectern in her cape and preceded by the impressive thumb-stick, she had a trademark as famous in her time as Susan B. Anthony's red silk shawl was in hers. She was both amused and pleased with her new, more theatrical, persona, prompting Winthrop Sargeant (1961), writing in the *New Yorker*, to describe her as a 'middle-aged and extraordinarily intelligent Valkyrie'.

Mead's love for lecturing was actually a culmination of an interest in public communication that began in her childhood when she wrote and directed pageants and skits for her family and friends. At that time she was more the 'behind-the-stage' producer than a performer, but in her maturity, she was centre stage. "'I'm so exhausted," she once complained, "If only I could give a lecture!'" (Howard 1984: 375).

Lecturing to an appreciative audience energized Mead, as did a lively discussion or argument with a friend or colleague. She seemed compelled to interact with others and found little interest in animals or nature except in their relationship to human activities. When a New Zealand host arranged for her small plane to land briefly to see a famous glacier, she was puzzled. "'Glacier!" she said, "Why should I want to get out of a plane just to look at a glacier? Who'll be there to *talk* to?'" (Howard 1984: 401).

Mead was a charismatic speaker in a long line of spirited American women public lecturers that harkens back to the likes of Anne Hutchinson, Susan B. Anthony and Jane Addams. Like them, she too was a 'social reformer' (Webb 1972). Unlike them, she had impeccable academic credentials – a curatorship at the American Museum of Natural History and a professorship at Columbia University – that gave her pronouncements, however controversial, a cachet of scientific validity.

As a communicator of ideas, Mead was most successful in her hands-on, face-to-face, public appearances where the group was *always* regionally defined and frequently also defined in terms of a common occupation or social interest. In social and cultural terms, she 'knew' her audiences and her talk took their specific concerns into consideration, just as she similarly would modulate her conversation among her amazingly diverse network of family, friends, students, colleagues and acquaintances.

Such sensitive attention to differences obviously is not possible on national television where one is addressing both everybody and nobody. Consequently, her television appearances, as those on film, often lack the zestful and focused immediacy of those on the lecture platform. She was, I think, very aware of this problem. When I was a student she asked me if I would be her interviewer for a nationally distributed NBC television show called 'Wisdom', that featured internationally distinguished men and women. As I was planning fieldwork in the South Pacific, where she already had studied six cultures, she felt that by talking about cultural anthropology directly with me she could give a more convincing interview. Nevertheless, there was a somewhat stilted quality in our prepared performances. I already knew the answers to the questions I was asking, and we both knew it.[8] Her on-camera performance in the film *Four Families* is similarly marred. Even as a guest on Johnny Carson's late night talk show, she sometimes displayed a kind of smiling primness while explaining a point; the way one smiles when trying to do the right thing.

Although Mead was the most casual of television viewers, she appreciated its power and place in contemporary society and used the medium to get her messages out. On one visit to my Vermont farmhouse when she was lecturing nearby and my children were still small, she chided me for not having a television set. The children, she said, would be different enough in this rural community; television would at least give them something in common with their peers.

As important as Mead's public lectures and television appearances were for publicizing anthropology, the primary basis for her reputation as a social scientist and a popularizer was her writing. But in 1925, when Mead docked in Pago Pago for her first fieldwork on a problem regarding adolescence designated by Boas, she was as unknown as any other new PhD. *Coming of Age in Samoa*, the celebrated and controversial result of her study, appeared in 1928 and catapulted her into instant fame. Unadorned with social science jargon, it was written in a fluid literary style with a rich vernacular vocabulary, at that time an anthropological novelty. Having found an effective and influential authorial voice that could be heard beyond a college campus, she sustained and nurtured it throughout her life.

While Mead was writing *Coming of Age in Samoa*, she began to lecture locally on the educational implications of her Samoan fieldwork for American society. At the suggestion of her publisher, she added the two famous final chapters, 'Our Educational Problems in the Light of Samoan Contrasts,' and 'Education for Choice'. As one of her biographers has noted, 'these concluding chapters set the pattern for all of Mead's future work by relating her experience among primitive cultures to the problems of contemporary American society' (Cassidy 1982: 29).

More than any anthropologist I know, she was exquisitely careful in her choice of words and their phrasing, always keeping in mind their power to direct and influence sentiment. New Englanders, she would say, aren't 'stingy' but 'thrifty'. When there was a public furore over her proposing the legalization of marijuana (she once laughingly recalled how on this occasion the governor of Florida had referred to her as 'a dirty old woman'), she blamed herself for not thinking the problem through more carefully, realizing that this issue, as with abortion, was one of 'decriminalization', not legalization (Bateson 1984: 202).

Much of her originality, especially concerning issues of social policy, resided in her genius for finding new ways to rephrase old problems. By finding fresh language, an intractable problem could be viewed from a novel perspective, offering hope for an acceptable solution. For Mead, language – the quintessential requirement for the creation of culture – was to be used in imaginative and positive ways to improve the human condition. This remarkable skill to use language effectively earned her the respect of those outside anthropology, especially those who spend their careers wrestling with difficult and/ or volatile social problems.

Although Mead was fully familiar with current anthropological jargon and used it when necessary, she favoured grace and clarity of expression in both her anthropological and popular writing. Consequently, the distinction between her anthropological and popular writing is often difficult to establish. This 'postmodern' blurring of genres was annoying to some anthropologists; they couldn't be sure what was 'anthropology' and what wasn't. One of the techniques Mead used to give scholarly credibility to her graceful anthropological manuscripts and to fend off criticism, was to include copious informative notes and a nearly exhaustive bibliography, as well as detailed appendices larded with supportive factual information on her methods and the people studied. Although this helped to keep her detractors at bay, it certainly didn't quell them.

As prolific as Mead was as a writer, she was outdone by the journalists who reported on her lectures and other public appearances in the local press and national magazines. Even those individuals who never had seen her or read her work were often aware of her presence as a critical force in American life from the media's reporting on her diverse activities. When she spoke in Oak Ridge, Tennessee, home to a large community of nuclear scientists, anyone who read the local paper knew she had chastised her audience for doing so little to bridge the gap between themselves and their disadvantaged Appalachian neighbours (Howard 1984: 376).

Another factor in Mead's public success with so many professionals and laypersons was that she always appeared to be on the cutting edge of what was happening in American society, and had something cogent to say about it while others were still fumbling to understand. This ability to be both 'out-front' in terms of current social issues and 'up-front' with a critical commentary brought her both praise and criticism. Her remarkable talent to know so much about the socially and intellectually critical areas of American society was, to an unappreciated extent, influenced by the time she spent with leaders in other disciplines at small interdisciplinary conferences.

She was introduced to her first such conference by Lawrence K. Frank in 1934, when the idea of bringing together accomplished specialists from different fields to work on a common problem was still new (Mead 1964: iii). Her first – the Hanover Seminar of Human Relations – was composed of a variety of specialists who worked for a month on issues of adolescent human development. Mead immediately became an enthusiastic convert to the small conference format. For the rest of her life when not at a conference, she was usually in the process of planning one or arranging to attend one. The small conference – she also co-authored a book about its process (Mead and Byers 1968) – provided Mead with an excellent opportunity to extend her expert knowledge on a host of problems, as well as a forum to express her own findings and insights.

The men and women she met at these highly selective conferences became part of her increasingly large and complex network; a network she relied on for advice and information and, in turn, gratefully reciprocated. I first met Mead in the spring of 1954 when, having recently discovered anthropology and the liberating concept of cultural relativism while doing research for a master's essay in philosophy, I climbed to her tower office at the Museum for a ten-minute interview about the possibility of a career in anthropology. When our brief time was finished, she invited me to stay, that is, if I didn't object to our being interrupted by telephone calls. During the next hour or so, I was astonished at the number of calls she made and received from people in different parts of the world, the variety of subjects she spoke about, and the diversity of her telephone partners, one of whom was a United States senator.

The generosity she had extended to me, an unknown student, was typical of Mead. Clifford Geertz (1989: 340) records a similar incident when he and Hildred Geertz, also young students and strangers to Mead, visited her office in 1950. A woman generous with both her friendship and her ideas, she left the latter lying around like pencils, she said, in the hope they would be stolen (Howard 1984: 231). She was equally non-exclusive in her friendships, as willing to share her friends as her ideas. Without this vast network of friendly contacts spanning continents, cultures, professions and ages, it is doubtful Mead could have accomplished so much, so effectively, so swiftly.

On the telephone she would come right to the point, as if it were the next sentence in a conversation already under way, although you may not have spoken with her for months. She might need the name of a Vermonter who was experimenting with wind power or ask you to do a protocol in New Hampshire on the birth of a foal. Whatever it was, you mostly said yes and found yourself suddenly involved – sometimes more than you planned to be – in one of her fascinating problems. Because of her superior facility in networking, she knew most of the movers and shakers on the problems that interested her and, as her colleague Eliot Chapple observed, 'which three or four people in any group would, when you got down to it, provide the clout' (Howard 1984: 231).

Mead herself had considerable 'clout' and did not hesitate to use it to further a cause. She was not, however, an agitator; she did not join demonstrations, even peaceful ones. She felt that demonstrations, sit-ins and similar activities by academicians should not be 'substitutes for the search for new knowledge and ways of applying it to the living world' (Metraux 1979: 92). For Mead, contested social divisiveness was harmful. Instead, she sought the middle ground that would bring people together. To maintain her significant influence, she was more cautious than many politicians in keeping her public reputation acceptable to as large a constituency as possible. Although Mead's personal life, as her daughter (Bateson 1984) has disclosed, was far from conventional, she succeeded in keeping her love affairs private during her lifetime and did not even publicly acknowledge in biographies her first of three divorces until 1972, when her autobiography (Mead 1972) appeared.

It was the unusual combination of Mead's ability to speak and write interestingly and clearly, and her ability to apply anthropological knowledge and insights to contemporary social problems, that probably contributed the most to making her a popular public figure. In her lifetime, there was no social issue which concerned the American public that she did not address, if not once, then many times. The fact that she openly – and sometimes very courageously – addressed pressing social problems contributed greatly to her popularity as a thinker and a doer. The family, sex, marriage, abortion, feminism, adolescence, urban blight, overpopulation, pollution, civil rights, crime, alcoholism, drugs, atomic energy, education, student uprisings, space exploration, racism, religion, warfare, madness, technology, hunger, civil disobedience, and euthanasia, are but some of the contentious topics on which she spoke out.[9] There were those who criticized the oracular nature of her opinions. Mead ran the risk, as do all Americans who are unusually well informed and articulate, of being dubbed a 'know-it-all', an egregious status in American life.

Almost any educated American over 40 knows Margaret Mead's name. For many, she is the only anthropologist they can identify. Mary Catherine Bateson, Mead's and Gregory Bateson's daughter, recalls camping trips with her father when fellow campers, on learning that her father was an anthropologist, might innocently launch into a discussion of her mother, as often 'with hostility as with admiration' (Bateson 1984: 52). During her life, Mead was, as she continues to be, a controversial figure. One of my colleagues remembers as an undergraduate the excitement she experienced on learning that Mead was to speak at her college. But her anthropology professors did not attend. 'That's not anthropology!' they huffed. Another colleague who spent eight years at Cambridge said that Mead's name was never mentioned.[10]

Anyone willing to be an adventuresome pioneer in a young discipline and to share freely her opinions with the world – especially as unhesitatingly and forthrightly as Mead did – will not please everyone. I imagine it is this one quality – that of speaking out publicly with confident authority on a myriad of subjects – more than any other which irritated some of her anthropological colleagues. What could be rhetorically characterized as an attention-getting emphasis might be interpreted by others as an unsubstantiated sweeping pronouncement. Ironically, it was just this quality – the ability to get the layperson's attention by speaking emphatically and imaginatively from an anthropological perspective on a relevant problem – that made people pay attention to what she had to say.

Mead knew that her ready opinions, her success with the general public, and her ability to be heard in Washington and other corridors of American power, made her an ambivalent figure for many in her discipline. But she rarely looked at the hole in the doughnut. Only once do I remember her alluding to her colleagues' perception of her. In 1960, after a party in my hotel room following her presidential address to the American Anthropological Association, I walked her to the elevator. As we chatted about the evening, she mused rather ruefully how very long it had taken for her own discipline to acknowledge her work with an important honour.

It would be a mistake to characterize Mead as a person who saw a schism between her professional responsibilities at the Museum and Columbia University, and her role as a communicator of anthropological knowledge to a wider audience. Indeed, her original appointment to the Museum in 1926 by the Curator of Ethnology, Pliny Earle Goddard, was granted with the hope that she would 'help Americans understand cultural anthropology as well as they understood archaeology' (Howard 1984: 66), thus making possible her career as a public lecturer from the Museum. Skilfully utilizing her extensive personal gifts and her training under Boas, Mead spent her adult life dedicated to demonstrating the importance and relevance of anthropology to contemporary life, especially as lived in America. Because she saw this as a major responsibility, she never thought of her lecturing or writing for lay audiences as anything but a serious and important commitment. Although she sometimes could be impatient or scolding, she was not patronizing;[11] rather, it was the urgency of her concern for the shared problem at hand that contributed to her success with the public. That, and her wit and ease of laughter – even at herself.[12] Although she took anthropology seriously, she seldom was solemn about it.[13]

I have suggested and discussed some of the factors that contributed to Margaret Mead's extraordinary success in popularizing the field of anthropology. Almost single-handedly, she both demonstrated and guaranteed its public relevance. Simultaneously celebrated by some and castigated by others, she was not a legend to me, but an intensely human woman of high energy, acute intelligence, abundant imagination, immense generosity, with a delightful sense of play, a deep and abiding concern for humanity on a global scale, and a passionate devotion to anthropology.

When Mead was dying in New York Hospital, I visited her briefly while *en route* to the American anthropology meetings in Los Angeles. Frail and tiny, she sat wrapped in a quilt and, drugged against pain, her eyes were closed. I took her hands and, when she opened her eyes, she spoke my name in her emphatic way and gave me a radiant smile. When I told her where I was going, she pressed my hands and said, 'Have fun!'

ACKNOWLEDGEMENTS

I am grateful to my Oxford hosts, Drs Jeremy MacClancy and Christian McDonaugh, for their invitation and the kindnesses they extended to me during my stay. For a critical reading of the paper, I am indebted to Drs Rhoda Metraux and Dana Raphael and to Professor Annette B. Weiner.

NOTES

1 In Marcus and Fischer's (1986: 158) pioneering study of cultural criticism in contemporary anthropology, this technique is called 'cross-cultural juxtaposition', and 'is synonymous with the career and writing of Margaret Mead'.
2 The article also described Mead as 'looking like a cross between a stern schoolmarm and an impish witch'.
3 But Mead also said that 'the ability to present material in a simple fashion improves as one gets further from the textbooks and has more experience in the real world' (Metraux 1979: 253).
4 *Redbook* is an American magazine for young women that also, at the time, had a wide audience of both women and men. Several collections of the *Redbook* articles have been published. See Mead and Metraux (1970; 1980) and Metraux (1979).
5 Mary Catherine Bateson (1984: 203), reflecting on her mother's lectures, writes, 'She almost always spoke extemporaneously but wove together old materials like the "singer of tales" who weaves and reweaves

familiar materials and phrasings of folk epic into new extemporaneous renderings, or the jazz musician engaged in practised and familiar improvisation, moving by organic connections and associations from one comment to another to cover the rough outline she had blocked out in advance, touching on a few new points of unfolding thought and curiosity.'

6 Her editor and friend at *Redbook*, Sey Chassler, remembers that 'She could be outrageous. I have heard her get into arguments concerning subject matter relative to publishing in which she was absolutely wrong and misinformed. I heard her once defend her position for twenty minutes before settling for a draw' (Mead and Metraux 1980: 6).

7 Befitting a person of her fame, the American Museum of Natural History has prominently displayed Mead's cape and thumb-stick with other information about her career at the entrance of the Oceania ethnographic exhibit whose artifacts were her responsibility as Curator.

8 The interview appears in Nelson (1961: 65–75).

9 To grasp more completely the vast scale of Mead's interests, see her bibliography (Gordan 1976).

10 Even today, when the importance of publicly communicating the relevance of anthropology to practical human affairs is widely recognized within the discipline, George Stocking (1992: 400), in a recent review of the British 'Strangers Abroad' film series on historically significant anthropologists, notes that Mead is 'somewhat patronized as a popularizer'.

11 As Bateson (1984: 97) observed, much of her mother's 'popularity with ordinary people has been based on the fact that she affirmed and respected their ways of doing things, their decencies and aspirations, even when she did not herself conform'.

12 See Bateson (1953: 21) for a funny story that Mead tells on herself when she unintentionally made a sexually suggestive double entendre before 'a conference of dreadfully solemn people on family life'.

13 I do recall, however, a conversation with her in the mid-1970s when she spoke about anthropology as a 'fragile' discipline and voiced her concern that it must not be destroyed from within.

REFERENCES

Bateson, G. (1953) 'The position of humor in human communication', in H. von Foerster (ed.) *Cybernetics* (Transactions of the 9th Conference), New York: Josiah Macy, Jr. Foundation.

Bateson, M. C. (1984) *With a daughter's eye: A memoir of Margaret Mead and Gregory Bateson*, New York: William Morrow.

Cassidy, R. (1982) *Margaret Mead: A voice for the century*, New York: Universe Books.

Chassler, S. (1979) 'Afterword: Margaret Mead 1901–1978', in R. Metraux (ed.) *Margaret Mead: Some personal views*, New York: Walker.

Fox, R. C. (1979) *Margaret Mead*, New York: Institute for Intercultural Studies.

Gardiner, M. (1992) 'Guys and dolls', *Guardian Weekly*, 2 February.

Geertz, C. (1989) 'Margaret Mead, 1901–1978', *Biographical Notes* (National Academy of Sciences) 58: 329–41.

Gordan, J. (ed.) (1976) *Margaret Mead: The complete bibliography 1925–1975*, The Hague: Mouton.

Howard, J. (1984) *Margaret Mead: A life*, New York: Simon and Schuster.

Marcus, G. E. and Fischer, M. M. J. (1986) *Anthropology as cultural critique: An experimental moment in the human sciences*, Chicago: University of Chicago Press.

Mead, M. (1944) *The American troops and the British community: An examination of the relationship between the American troops and the British*, London: Hutchinson.

—— (1947) 'The application of anthropological techniques to cross-national communication', *Transactions of the New York Academy of Sciences* 9: 133–52

—— (1964) *Anthropology: A human science*, New York: D. Van Nostrand.

—— (1972) *Blackberry winter: My earlier years*, New York: William Morrow.

Mead, M. and Byers, P. (1968) *The small conference: An innovation in communication*, The Hague: Mouton.

Mead, M. and Metraux, R. (1970) *A way of seeing*, New York: McCall.

—— (1980) *Aspects of the present*, New York: William Morrow.

Metraux, R. (ed.) (1979) *Margaret Mead: Some personal views*, New York: Walker.

Nelson, J. (ed.) (1961) 'Margaret Mead', in *Wisdom for our time*, New York: W. W. Norton.

Sargeant, W. (1961) 'It's all anthropology', *New Yorker*, December 30: 31–4.

Stocking, G. (1992) 'From Spencer to E-P: Eyewitnessing the progress of fieldwork', *American Anthropologist* 94: 398–400.

Time (1969) 'Margaret Mead today: Mother to the world', March 21: 74–5.

Webb, M. (1972) 'Margaret Mead: Anthropologist and social reformer', in *Britannic Yearbook of Science and the Future*, Chicago: Benton.

Chapter 6

Enlarging the context of anthropology
The case of *Anthropology Today*

Jonathan Benthall

Anthropology Today is a bimonthly which was launched in 1985 after eleven years' pre-existence under the title *RAIN*. This name, composed of the initials of *Royal Anthropological Institute News*, had been meant to evoke ideas of fertility and grace. I have been editor of both titles since I was appointed Director of the Institute in 1974.

RAIN began as a modest newsletter, but, from its first appearance, it tried to take part in the diffusion of anthropological insight to a public outside the discipline, and to underline the wider importance of anthropology, with an emphasis on images as well as words. The look and contents of *Anthropology Today* are now, probably, seen as part of the landscape of anthropology journals: not so far from the recently revamped (though quarterly and larger) *American Anthropologist*, while there are now also two well-established journals of visual anthropology. However, *AT* and its predecessor were earlier, more on their own, and occasionally a source of controversy. I hope that the following essay in institutional history may have some resonances to interest a wider circle than the members of a long-established, but relatively small, association.

In 1974 the Royal Anthropological Institute was a London-based 'learned society' in the old style, oriented around its great Library, although it had just been obliged to leave its headquarters in a leafy London square because of a rent increase. The Library had been moved to the premises of the Museum of Mankind (the Ethnography department of the British Museum) in the West End – and in 1976 the legal title was transferred, although Fellows' borrowing rights were retained by the RAI. In 1974 the remnant of the Institute was to be found in a cramped office in a back street. Other than the library, which was a financial millstone, the Institute's main academic asset was the journal *Man* (now reverted to a previous title, *Journal of the*

RAI) which has also proved to be its only activity which is at present financially profitable. As a non-anthropologist (my university degree is in English Literature) I was chosen to try to develop a new role for the Institute.

I must admit that, at that time, some of us had a dream of recruiting thousands of supporters for the Institute. Alas, this was not be realized (cf. Houtman and Knight 1995). Although some aspects of anthropology appeal to various sectors of the public, the fact is that a large part of what anthropologists have to say requires intellectual effort, and moreover is often rather disturbing to people's peace of mind. If the Institute had had as its Director a more flamboyant personality than myself, that person might have been able to attract the massive support which anthropology certainly deserves. But a temperament of that kind would probably have alienated the numerous anthropologists who expect that *their* Institute – it is supported by them, receiving no direct State subsidy, apart from tax concessions – should serve them and the discipline, rather than legitimating some cult of personality. The membership of the Institute is a consortium of interests, and its internal politics resemble those of the Lebanese constitution in its peaceful heyday, rather than a substantive democracy.

Following my interview with the Selection Committee at the end of 1973, it was expected that the Institute would publish a second periodical as a complement to *Man*. It was to be more an organ of popularization than *Man*. At the same time that I was appointed Director, the Institute chose an honorary editor for the proposed new journal. She was a fairly well-known and very agreeable social anthropologist, now deceased, who had once been a headmistress, and, from the start, I was convinced that the proposed formula was going to be dull and didactic. For instance, the editor was planning to publish a regular feature of 'student howlers'. I came to the conclusion that a new Director must take charge of the general tone of all publications emanating from the Institute and aimed at the wider public, and I acted (I hope, uncharacteristically) ruthlessly. The Council, the Institute's governing body, gave permission for a newsletter called *RAIN* to be published, an excellent graphic designer prepared a masthead, very 'sixties' in style, with drops of water falling inside the capital letters RAIN. The launch of the new journal was fixed for Autumn 1974, but it never saw the light of day, and I am afraid that the editor-that-never-was never forgave me.

The RAI Council supported *RAIN*. The first few years were notable for some lively controversies in the letters columns (on topics such as ethnographic film, ethnocide and race relations), and for a special number in 1976 on Ancient Egypt, in which all news and reviews were held over to accommodate a collection of articles guest-edited by John Baines, Professor of Egyptology at Oxford.

Some British anthropologists were reserved about the new newsletter. Others were openly hostile to it. Fortunately, the late Lucy Mair, well known for the severity and rigour of her thought, had been appointed the Institute's Honorary Secretary, charged with maintaining its intellectual standards. She was our 'watchdog', and she protected me from the risk of only listening to favourable comment, keeping me fully informed of the defects of the journal as she and her close colleagues saw them. In several cases, her advice on particular proposals saved *RAIN* from grave blunders, and I owe her a considerable debt.

In 1980, one distinguished critic reproached *RAIN* with being too preoccupied with what he called:

the juicier bits of anthropology: primitive art, the supposed role of anthropologists in development, sex, ethnographic films . . . The final product . . . seems to fall uncomfortably between two stools, manifesting a false and embarrassing trendiness like that of vicars who have services of blessing for motorbikes.

(Bloch 1980)

The commitment of the journal to the 'anthropology of development' and the serious study of ethnographic films were in fact constant, and are not a matter for regret, for the progress of both fields has since been highly constructive. Tribal art should have been given more space. As for sex, there was really very little of it in our pages. But I do admit that, like many of my contemporaries, I had been more or less influenced by the liberalism which prevailed on this subject during the 1960s and the early 1970s. Indeed, the appeal of anthropology does depend in part on its openness on such matters. I continue to believe that one of the great merits of anthropology is that it can help Westerners to free themselves from the blinkers of ethnocentrism, some of which are to do with our sexual anxieties and fears. However, since *RAIN*, and later *AT*, acquired a more international perspective, I came to realize that pictorial images in particular are 'read' in very different ways in different societies. Thus, for example, a photograph of a naked woman can be read by an educated Western reader as an extension of the classical tradition of painting of the nude, or frankly appreciated for its erotic qualities. For a reader brought up in, say, an Islamic tradition, such an image can seem deliberately provocative or degrading to women, which would also be more or less the point of view of some Western feminists. Furthermore, in certain cultures, such as the Maori, a visual image can be troubling because of its evocation of the almost physical presence of a dead ancestor, and that too has to be remembered.

The critic quoted above did not mention some notable successes achieved by *RAIN* during this early period, such as an article by John Sharp on Afrikaner ethnology in South Africa, cited in all later studies of the subject, or an exchange between Leach and Francis Hsu on the question of racism in Malinowski's *Diary*.

In the mid-1980s, one or two Council Members attempted to cut *RAIN* down to size, proposing that its format should be relegated to that of a humble stencilled newssheet. An inquiry was launched by the Council into the role of *RAIN*, and the decision was taken not to reduce it, but to expand it into *Anthropology Today*. A new design and layout were commissioned, and gradually the journal began, as it were, to put on weight.

One constant problem has been to know whether the journal should be addressed principally to anthropologists or to non-specialists. The policy has been to aim at both professional anthropologists and people working in neighbouring disciplines: the other social sciences, development, refugee and relief aid, health, education, community services and so on. However, the Institute has not yet elected to aim for a much wider circulation through sale in bookshops and newsstands, which would necessitate a large capital investment. There is a sharp division between trade and scholarly journal publishing which the Institute is not financially strong enough to try to overcome.

A yet more serious problem is that the Institute represents the whole field of anthropology as it was defined in the late nineteenth century (cf. Leach 1974). While a number of anthropology departments in old universities, as well as major institutions such as the American Anthropological Association and the Wenner-Gren Foundation for Anthropological Research, share this inclusive definition, it is to some extent a convenient fiction – or a utopian ideal. Only a minority of socio-cultural anthropologists are actively involved in the studies of ecological co-adaptation, energetics, parental investment, risk assessment and so forth, which are currently being undertaken by biological anthropologists. I think the overarching commitment of the RAI and these other institutions can be justified if one accepts the proposition that Darwinism is one big idea of the last two centuries which has not been conclusively disproved, and to which almost all anthropologists of whatever specialty give their assent. Much of the controversy between cultural anthropologists and human biologists may be due, as Adam Kuper argues, to confusion about time-scales. If we imagine human evolution as a clock, the hour hand measures our biological evolution as a species (in the course of which, natural selection operates anarchically on the genes); the minute hand represents long-term cultural adaptations which take place over dozens of generations, as a result of countless choices by individuals; and the second hand represents the history of wars and revolutions (Kuper 1994: 92–93). *Anthropology Today*, while assenting to the broad definition of anthropology, has tended to concentrate on the time-scale where seconds turn into minutes.

Another difficulty has been persuading authors to write for us simply and clearly. It may well be easier to write an article of 10,000 words for a learned journal, fortified by a rampart of notes and references, than an article for *Anthropology Today* of say 2,000 words. This is not a difficulty peculiar to anthropologists. It derives from a sectarianism or intellectual clannishness which pervades much of the academic world and which I have tried to analyse elsewhere (Benthall 1995).

Many of the most important socio-cultural anthropologists – Frazer, Malinowski, Evans-Pritchard, Leach, Firth, Lévi-Strauss, Godfrey Lienhardt, Needham, Geertz, Sahlins – have been not only scholars, but also, in different ways, accomplished writers; and this is one reason why the subject is still held in high esteem among well-informed non-anthropologists. Modern anthropology certainly requires close attention to method and details, but it is the conclusions which a writer reaches and the conviction with which they are expressed which make the extra-academic life of a subject. We do not have many individual anthropologists today who, as writers, are at ease with a wider intellectual public: Mary Douglas, Ernest Gellner, David Maybury-Lewis, Adam Kuper, Alex de Waal and Nancy Scheper-Hughes are exceptions – and some of these are rather specialized in their interests: de Waal in his passionate critique of the orthodoxies of official humanitarianism, Scheper-Hughes in her evocations of the lives of very poor and oppressed people. *Anthropology Today* makes a contribution to compensating for this deficiency, by encouraging lucidity and concision of thought. As a reward to its editors and writers, we find that its articles are now extensively used for teaching and some, such as Philippe Bourgois's study of the crack economy in Spanish Harlem or John M. Coggeshall's article on homosexuality in men's prisons, have found their way into student 'readers'.

I hope *AT* will one day develop into a journal with a much wider circulation, addressing all manner of public and topical issues from anthropological points of view. It probably needs the resources to print in colour, and eventually to pay its contributors.

However, an extensively popularized anthropology would probably cease to be recognizable as anthropology; for anthropology is so frequently counter-intuitive. To give one example, take what is often called 'gut-reaction': that split-second scanning upon which we all rely in our daily transactions. A compelling tradition in our literary civilization (represented in this century by W. B. Yeats and D. H. Lawrence) encourages us to trust in gut-reaction as the accumulated wisdom of pre-rational nature. Then Mary Douglas (1972) told us that gut-reaction, far from being irrational, corresponds to characteristics in a total system of classification. Hence the *more* our knowledge seems instinctive and 'natural', the more purely it may reflect culturally generated systems of classification. When a citizen recoils from a piece of excrement, and when he or she turns away from a homeless person begging in the Underground, a gut-reaction is being exercised in which the corporal and the social are fused. Anthropology should teach us to attempt to distinguish sharply the predicament, rights and dignity of the human being from the symbolism of rejected matter.

The comparative perspective offered by anthropology can pander to a predisposition to elitism. I have known a few anthropologists (of the older generation) who have elected to play God with human society, i.e. they have observed and commented as if they were somehow above the fray, not susceptible to self-delusion. Most anthropologists are much more modest. But the implications of an insight like Mary Douglas's are thoroughly demanding to the intellect. This is not to say that they cannot in principle be communicated to wider audiences. But they cannot be easily packaged and marketed. Though *Anthropology Today* does indeed fall between two stools – as the critic of *RAIN* noticed in 1980 – the middle ground it aims at may be near to the best that anthropology can do in seeking a popular market without becoming bland and flat, like poor wine bearing a fancy label.

ACKNOWLEDGEMENTS

Anthropology Today would probably never have seen the light of day in 1985 without the constant encouragement of the late Sir Edmund Leach, who founded the Esperanza Trust which still subsidizes the journal. Burton Benedict, Rosemary Firth, Stephen Gudeman, Jean La Fontaine, the late Michael Sallnow and Jonathan Webber were also especially helpful during the earlier years. I am also very grateful to two outstanding colleagues, Gustaaf Houtman, who has been assistant editor since the last year of *RAIN*, and John Knight, who became an assistant editor more recently.

An earlier version of this article appeared in French under the title 'Élargir le contexte de l'anthropologie: comment a commencé *Anthropology Today*' in a festschrift, *Pour Jean Malaurie* (1990, Paris: Plon).

Since this article went to press, we have lost with the death of Ernest Gellner a great advocate for the public role of anthropology.

REFERENCES

Benthall, J. (1995) 'From self-applause through self-criticism to self-confidence', Preface to A. Ahmed and C. Shore (eds) *The Future of Anthropology*, London: Athlone.

Bloch, M. (1980) 'Conforming with tradition' (review of anthropology journals), *Times Higher Education Supplement*, 17 October.

Douglas, M. (1972) 'Self-evidence', *Proceedings of the Royal Anthropological Institute*.

Houtman, G. and Knight, J. (1995) 'The Royal Anthropological Institute and the popularization of anthropology', *Practicing Anthropology* 17, 1–2: 37–41.

Kuper, A. (1994) *The Chosen Primate: Human Nature and Cultural Diversity*, Cambridge, Mass.: Harvard University Press.

Leach, E. (1974) 'Rain-making: the future of the RAI', Presidential Address, *RAIN* 4, September–October.

Chapter 7

Claude Lévi-Strauss and Louis Dumont
Media portraits

Dominique Casajus

In my contribution to the seminar series on which this book is based, I evoked the image of ethnology portrayed in the major French newspapers over the last few years. In fact the topic is immense and cannot be covered in the limited space of a single article. It was possible to be somewhat superficial and allusive in an oral presentation, especially one delivered to a sympathetic audience, but I cannot allow myself such latitude in a written paper destined for publication. This is why I shall restrict myself here to the media images of two anthropologists, Claude Lévi-Strauss and Louis Dumont.

The main French daily and weekly newspapers regularly publish ethnology book reviews, interviews with well-known ethnologists and articles on the current situation of the human sciences. It is on materials of this kind that this article is based. Not all of this published material is of equal value. *Le Magazine littéraire*, *Esprit* or *Les Temps modernes*, for example, publish articles written mainly by academics and which could equally well belong in our academic journals;[1] here, then, we have not really left the world of the university. More interesting for our purposes is what is published in *Le Monde*, *Le Nouvel Observateur*, *Libération* or *Le Figaro*, since it is without doubt that these papers reach a wider audience. Claude Lévi-Strauss is by far the most often mentioned author, followed quite far behind by Louis Dumont. This is the reason why it seemed to me legitimate to concentrate on these two scholars.[2] My paper is devoted in the main to articles by non-specialists, whose work comprises the bulk of the available literature.[3] It goes without saying that, in general, we do not hold with the — sometimes very odd — statements that we shall need to reproduce here.

Let us begin with what has been said about Claude Lévi-Strauss. As a tribute to him, from 18 October 1989 to 24 April 1990 the Musée de l'Homme mounted an exhibition entitled 'Les Amériques de Claude Lévi-Strauss'. He commented with humour on the exhibition in an interview with Didier Eribon[4] in the *Nouvel Observateur*, published under the heading 'When a great ethnologist acts as guide' (19–25 October 1989: 162–3). *Le Monde*, on 18 October, published an article on the same topic by Yvonne Ribeyrol (p. 22).[5] It was illustrated with photographs, taken in 1936 by the author of *Tristes tropiques* himself, of a young Caduveo girl 'her face painted with a web of arabesques'. This article goes on to tell us that the exhibits include a Nambikwara shelter in which model figures are arranged in a scene delousing each other, Bororo funerals 'for which the participants wear enormous and superb crowns of feathers indispensable for the ritual dances', and, finally, Caduveo objects. As we can see, what is going on here is the staging of passages from *Tristes tropiques*, which we can all remember, and we are even told in *Le Nouvel Observateur* that the positions of the models were copied from the author's own photographs. Under no illusion as to the ethnological education of her readers, Yvonne Ribeyrol felt it necessary to justify the inclusion of objects originating from the north-west coast, and she recalled that 'Claude Lévi-Strauss . . . had drawn parallels between the masks and the myths of the Indians of British Columbia'. She also mentioned the presence of copper plaques used in potlatches (a term whose meaning she gives in a footnote). The masterpiece of the exhibition was a Haida canoe in which a delegation of Indians from British Columbia had come up the Seine from Rouen to Paris between 27 September and 2 October. When it reached Paris, Claude Lévi-Strauss and his wife joined the canoe and, as Didier Eberon tells us, the final stretch from the bridge of Iéna to the Hôtel de Ville was covered 'to the rhythm of paddles and the ritual chanting of a score of Haida Indians'.

As much as the exhibition itself, the triumphal and imperial procession that accompanied it give a good idea of the status of Claude Lévi-Strauss in France. In the first place he is seen essentially as the author of *Tristes tropiques*. For the rest, as Yvonne Ribeyrol tells us, he is the 'first Frenchman to bring scientific rigour into ethnological research'. This statement could lend itself to many different interpretations. Are we to understand that other traditions (no doubt Anglo-Saxon ones) had already attained scientific rigour at a time when French ethnology was still floundering in literary self-indulgence, from which Lévi-Strauss was at last to lead the way forward?

Obviously all the mystery and terror aroused by the word 'structuralism' is implied in this simple statement which, indeed, some of Yvonne Ribeyrol's readers might still have been able to recall on 8 October 1991. One can well imagine their perplexity on reading *Le Monde* of that day. In an interview with Roger Pol-Droit (*Le Monde*: 2 ff.), Lévi-Strauss remarks with some annoyance, it seems to me, that 'the "human sciences" can only be considered sciences under the guise of a flattering deception'. Further on, he adds, with annoyance giving way to weariness, 'When we endeavour – and it is here that we have the meaning of the structuralist project – to substitute for the illusory knowledge of impenetrable realities, the knowledge – possible in this instance – of the relations which link them, we are reduced to clumsy endeavours and to mumblings.' These are banal statements right enough, and ones to which we all subscribe, but their appearance in a major daily newspaper makes us aware of the abyss separating this man from his flatterers.

In the introduction to an interview published in *Le Figaro* (22 August 1990: 23), Bruno de Cressole credits 'this mind, among the most fertile of the twentieth century', with having 'begotten structuralism', and he celebrates him as 'the greatest living French thinker, the only one who is held in respect and for whom we are envied in countries abroad'. The journalist does not forget to recall that his interviewee has been elected to the Académie française 'to the chair previously held by Montherlant',[6] but, while praising Lévi-Strauss for being careful to avoid taking a position on anything and everything, proceeds to ask his opinion on just about anything, even including as a conclusion his views on stoicism. The article is embellished with a suitable photograph of this successor to Montherlant, in the library of the Laboratory of Social Anthropology, which he founded and then headed. In this photograph he appears against the background of an archway which surrounds him like a halo on which are depicted the words: 'For country, the sciences and glory' ('Pour la patrie, les sciences et la gloire'). The centring of the image is too well done for this proud device to have happened by chance: Lévi-Strauss's face is exactly in the centre of the arc of the circle formed by the archway. Did the photographer know that this archway has nothing to do with the author of *Tristes tropiques* and that it in fact belonged to the École polytechnique, the military school which previously was housed in the same building?

Only one expression is missing from this interview, that of Lévi-Strauss as '*maître à penser*' (intellectual mentor). We need not have worried, however. An article in *Le Monde* presenting a series of television programmes on Lévi-Strauss is entitled 'One of the last *"maîtres à penser"*' (Sunday 30 to Monday 31 October 1988, radio-television supplement: 7). The headline tells us 'in contrast to Sartre or Foucault, Claude Lévi-Strauss refuses to become involved politically, but his work continues to exercise a powerful influence'. In these programmes, Luc de Heusch, Jean-Pierre Vernant, Jaques Le Goff, Pierre Bourdieu, as well as the essayist André Comte-Sponville and the novelist Michel Tournier, were invited in turn to describe the influence that Lévi-Strauss had had on them. Less crudely eulogistic and better informed than his colleague on the *Figaro*, the author of the article expressed regret that no real opponent had been invited to take part and that those invited had chosen to remain silent about their possible areas of disagreement with Lévi-Strauss. For my part I believe I remember that, unsurprisingly, Bourdieu had made some respectful criticisms, but with such a degree of understatement, and expressed in such a confused way, that they must have escaped most of the audience.

If we rely on these scattered pieces of evidence, to which much more could be added,[7] we must come to the conclusion that anthropology, or at least the most famous French anthropologist, is very popular in France today.

In fact, the situation is not that simple. To begin with, I strongly suspect that Yvonne Ribeyrol was not far wrong in thinking that the wider educated public hardly read him.[8] And there is more. Jacques Meunier, who frequently writes reviews of ethnology books for *Le Monde*, concludes his review of *Histoire de lynx* (Lévi-Strauss 1991) with these words:

> That said, let us not hide our disappointment. Beyond *Tristes tropiques* and *L'Homme nu* (1971) and after *la Potière jalouse* (1985), we have been awaiting a wider discourse. Something more outstanding. We were expecting that Lévi-Strauss, who had begun the dialogue with other ways of being and of thinking about the world, would put forward a new form of understanding and would introduce us to a 'new humanism', bringing together biology, mathematics and the human sciences. Like Marcel Mauss reverting too late to his earlier good ideas, or like Henri Poincaré encumbered by a certain 'conservatism' and narrowly missing the discovery of relativity, Lévi-Strauss has not achieved this. This is a shame.
>
> The praise of Montaigne (chapter XVIII), the philosophy of anti-philosophy, and the acerbic critique of comparative

mythology are not enough: unquestionably this book addresses itself to the closed world of anthropology.

(*Le Monde*, 6 September 1991: 30)

These harsh words appear on the same page as a very respectful and rather academic review of the same book, by Marc Augé.[9] One could smile, but it would be wiser to ask oneself what has led these authors to write these reviews. Perhaps, after all, Meunier's naive expectation, which seems to have been let down here, was itself aroused by the Promethean ambition which drove the author of *La Pensée sauvage* (Lévi-Strauss 1962a) or *Anthropologie structurale* (Lévi-Strauss 1958). The author of the review recalls, moreover, that in order to reinforce his approach Lévi-Strauss has never ceased to refer to other sciences besides ethnology – he cites cybernetics and communication theory – and he remarks 'the introduction of graphs and of algorithms into his articles has gained widespread acceptance'. Lévi-Strauss remains undoubtedly the person who has brought science into ethnology.

We find the same disappointment with the essayist Alain Finkielkraut. In 1987 he published *La Défaite de la pensée*, a pamphlet which, judging by the frequent references made to it in the major press, has sold quite well in the bookstores. The aim of the book is very confused but, with regard to ethnology, one can note the following claims: with the certainly laudable intention of defending the dignity of distant cultures, ethnologists, and Lévi-Strauss in particular,[10] have contributed to undermining the idea of a universal human mode of thinking (*communauté de conscience entre les hommes*); in these times of the resurgence of the idea of the nation as rooted in a common ethnic identity, ethnologists share some of the responsibility for discrediting the universalistic values that our societies have inherited from the Enlightenment. Some quotations from *Le Totémisme aujourd'hui* (Lévi-Strauss 1962b) or *Le Regard éloigné* (Lévi-Strauss 1983) are included in the evidence of the case for the prosecution. All this, without doubt, gives academics considerable influence, though they may be little read. But this accusation is not, after all, very different from that of Jacques Meunier. For him, the anthropologists – or at least one of them – have nothing more to say to their co-citizens, while for Finkielkraut, they have come to discredit the fundamental values, so threatened today, that are espoused by their co-citizens.

In actual fact, as Jeanne Favret-Saada says to Finkielkraut in an interview published in *Terrain* (Favret-Saada and Lenclud, 1991), his comments apply less to 'ethnology as a discipline than to . . . a moral relativism based on ethnological arguments and the assertion that all cultures are of equivalent value'. In fact, though it is doubtful that ethnologists share this assertion in their lives as ordinary citizens, it has to be recognised that this view is sometimes in evidence on the fringes of, or outside, the profession, as the scattered quotations in Finkielkraut's book show.[11]

In the rest of the interview, in the course of an exchange with Favret-Saada, Finkielkraut expresses a more precise viewpoint, which adds a different nuance to his hostility towards ethnology. Favret-Saada makes this remark (ibid.: 73):

> for it [ethnology] has lost what made the reading of L'Afrique fantôme (Leiris 1934) so fascinating for us: the giving of an account of an encounter (rapport) with "the other", and the knowledge that ethnology is nothing other than that – the experience of an encounter (rapport).

Finkielkraut replies, approvingly:

> This, perhaps, has to do with its being blinded by its scientific nature and with its falling victim to the thoroughgoing compartmentalization of knowledge. It is becoming a more and more specialized area of knowledge, based on the model of science and forgetting what gave it its own driving force.

This, at any rate, is less silly than seeing Lévi-Strauss as 'the person who brought scientific rigour' into our discipline. In fact, it is not silly to consider that ethnology is suffering from a routinizing professionalism. We are not far here from Meunier's accusations, which suddenly seem a lot less naive than before.

More perfidiously, perhaps, Mathieu Lindon cites some recollections of Brazilian academics in a long article published to mark the occasion of Lévi-Strauss's eightieth birthday (Libération, 1 September 1988, Literary Supplement: I–IV). The journalist smugly reports the remarks of Luis de Castro Faria who, under orders from the then Brazilian government, accompanied Lévi-Strauss on his fieldwork trips. The latter is depicted as a mediocre ethnologist who saw his expeditions among the Indians as no more than the price that had to be paid 'to be recognized as a true ethnologist'. The very pettiness of the accusation, however, amounts to a tribute: it is necessary to elevate the stature of this scholar, who has always admitted to being more of an armchair anthropologist than a fieldworker, in order to take such obvious enjoyment in discrediting him.

Unlike Lévi-Strauss, Louis Dumont is hardly known to the wider public. Nevertheless, following the publication of *Essais sur l'individualisme* (Dumont 1983) and of *Homo æqualis II* (Dumont 1991), reviews or interviews appeared in *Le Monde*, *Le Nouvel Observateur*, *Le Magazine littéraire* and *Libération*. Previously, *Esprit* had published a collection of articles on him in its February 1978 issue. This collection included an article by the Indianist Henri Stern, as well as an article by Dumont himself which had already appeared in English in 'Contributions to Indian sociology' and was to become the second chapter of his *Essais sur l'individualisme*. The then director of *Esprit*, Paul Thibaud, prefaced these two papers by a short editorial. As a whole, the collection gave a complete enough overview of Dumont's ideas at that time. He appears, however, especially in Thibaud's piece, as above all a moral figure, a man preoccupied with the obstacles on the path to fulfilling the ideal of democracy. This aspect of his thinking is undeniably present in his work in which, as in Durkheim's, moral and political concerns are not kept separate from more purely academic issues. Thibaud writes:

> What is the good, one will ask, of this detour through history that leads us back to the disappearance of the values underpinning social cohesion and to the agonizing vacuum that follows? In the first place this historical trajectory demonstrates the profundity of the problem and that it is consubstantial with this history of the West, which Dumont's comparative approach enables us to see in a different way. At the least this analysis brings home to us a demanding lesson and the knowledge that strong words and exhortations will do nothing to alter our situation. All this brings to mind the well known title of Mounier's first article in *Esprit*: 'Refaire la Renaissance'.
>
> (Thibaud 1978: 5)

The term 'anomie' has not been used, but the start of this passage could equally well apply to Durkheim. The evocative reference to Emmanuel Mounier requires further comment. Of all the aspects of Dumont's work that could serve to reflect Mounier's 'Personnalisme',[12] I single out the following: Dumont has often repeated that our modern societies value the relations between people and things as against the relations between people themselves, whereas the opposite was true of traditional societies.[13] In *Homo æqualis* (1976: 134) Dumont has expressed this assessment of our situation even more pessimistically in a sentence which Thibaud also quotes in his article:

'It is our lot to be left with the choice between the accumulation of wealth as a goal and the pathological forces of oppression' (Thibaud 1978). As Marcel Gauchet (1979)[14] has clearly seen, such remarks constitute as much a moral judgement as a scientific statement and, as such, remain highly debatable. One can understand how this pessimism, with its strong moral overtones, attracted the attention of the followers of Mounier, who himself made an opposition between the individual (for him a pejorative notion) and the person, who would only achieve fulfilment by living in community with others.

As for Henri Stern, he sees a need to defend Dumont against 'reactionary' interpretations of his ideas. Certain neo-fascist ideologues have actually drawn inspiration from Dumont. One can understand the reason for this misunderstanding if one considers an article by a certain Pierre Bérard (1982) which appeared shortly afterwards in a magazine published by people with links to the extreme right. In the first place, where Dumont only asserts the epistemological insufficiency of methodological individualism, this author sees instead a condemnation of the values of modern individualism. Furthermore, Dumont's pessimism, which the editors of *Esprit* (whom we certainly do not include with the ideologues of the extreme right!) take as a 'demanding and challenging lesson' and an incitement to work without complacency for the difficult realization of the ideal of democracy, becomes for Bérard an argument for condemning this very ideal, and for asserting on the contrary the eminent dignity of hierarchy and holism. In a general way, all the features that Dumont uses to draw a contrast between hierarchy and egalitarianism are turned round and used against egalitarianism. Let us give an example. In a comparison of the Indian trilogy of the goals of human life (*dharma*, *artha* and *kama*) with our opposition between good and evil, Dumont writes: 'Where we condemn and exclude, India hierarchizes and includes' (1966: appendix B, end of fn. 14). Bérard, forgetting that it is only a question of the exclusion of 'evil', uses this sentence as authority to assert that 'hierarchy sustains tolerance' (Bérard 1982: 106) and that 'western egalitarianism is what makes for exclusion'. This in turn allows him to launch into the following tirade:

> To accept the organic nature of society at the same time as recognizing the dead end to which individualism leads, means that we must view things from a hierarchical perspective.

Intolerance grows on the charnel house of difference. It sustains itself from the presuppositions that underlie egalitarianism.

(ibid.: 108)[15]

He goes on with yet more fetid observations when he contrasts a hierarchy linked to 'the Indo–European heritage' with an egalitarianism liked to 'the Judeo–Christian heritage'; one can easily imagine what the latter is worth to him, in the light of his final condemnation of the egalitarian ideal.

Following the appearance of *Homo æqualis II*, in two interviews published in *Le Magazine littéraire* (October 1991: 114–19) and *Le Nouvel Observateur* (2–8 January 1992: 68–70), Dumont recalls the broad stages in the development of his thinking. He outlines what caused him to study the caste system and then to return, with a partially Indian perspective, to the study of our societies. There is little room in this kind of text for journalists' own interpretations, but it is interesting to see what they make of it. The journalist from *Le Nouvel Observateur* describes Dumont in the introduction as a 'true *maître à penser*'. As for the interview in *Le Magazine littéraire*, it is illustrated with three photographs. Two of these are very small and are placed in the body of the text. One shows Dumont standing in a pleasantly furnished sitting room with walls decorated with paintings and Indonesian puppets; the other shows him in his garden in the company of his wife. In a word, these are everyday photographs of a senior academic in his home. The third photograph, which covers the whole page facing the first page of the article, is completely different. In it he is seated on a camp bed in a bare room, and he is wearing sandals which are made to appear disproportionately large by the camera's angle of vision. To the left one can see a piece of furniture which could be his desk. It is highly improbable that this cliché has been used here by chance; as several people have told me, it conveys a monastic impression. We are, in any case, very far here from the patriotic and, accidentally, military glory with which *Le Figaro* clothes Lévi-Strauss. Certainly no readers will have thought of juxtaposing these two photographs, which appeared several years apart and in newspapers that are hardly, if ever, compared in such detail by their readers. However, the economist Pierre Rosanvallon, in a review of *Essais sur l'individualisme* entitled 'Louis Dumont: the consecration of the individual' (*Libération*, 17 November 1983: 30), draws a parallel between these two authors that could almost have been illustrated by these clichés. Commenting at length on the discrepancy in fame accorded to these two scholars, he sees one as the leader of a school (*chef d'école*) and the other as a *maître à penser* in whose work 'the trial and error of intuition' has opened out 'belatedly into a great vision'. With the former comes the 'media hullabaloo' but also the 'imitators' and 'ingenious disciples', in a word the epigones, while with the latter comes the adherence of 'free pupils'.[16]

To give a fuller picture of Dumont's place on the French intellectual scene, we have to mention another article which appeared in *Le Monde* at the start of the Rocard government. Let us recall that, from 1986 to 1988, the French government was run by a right-wing prime minister, Jacques Chirac. In the spring of 1988, François Mitterand was re-elected President of the Republic, and the elections resulted in a narrow left-wing majority in the Chamber of Deputies. The first task of the new prime minister, Michel Rocard, was to remedy the disastrous situation in New Caledonia, for which the government of Chirac carried a heavy responsibility. Under his guidance, Kanak and French representatives from New Caledonia reached an agreement that was to be ratified by a national vote. Dumont wrote a vehement article for *Le Monde* (5 November 1988), which was republished later in *Esprit* (December 1988: 5–6). In this article he accused the right of muddying the debate 'for partisan interests . . . to cover up the obvious failure of its stupidly reactionary politics', and he argued strongly for a 'yes' vote in the referendum on ratification of the agreement. The firmness of tone and the vocabulary used are striking in a man not usually given to intervene in public matters,[17] especially in a time when human science professionals hardly dare to do so (incidentally, the article also shows how wrong the extremists are when they think they can count him as one of their own). Without doubt we have to go back to the editorial by Raymond Aron in *L'Express*, on the eve of the Presidential elections of 1981, before we can find another academic taking such a strong position on the eve of a national vote.

Although Dumont's article is about a particular situation, we can find in it some of the core themes of his thinking. In the first place, the article put forward some propositions in the context of a specific instance in which the practical application of democratic ideals was seen to be particularly difficult. This was because the situation involved balancing an affirmation of universal human rights with a defence of the integrity of a particular culture, the Kanak culture. Furthermore, one can see here the beginnings of a text later published in *Le Débat*, and which was to become the final chapter of *Homo æqualis II*. One knows that, in this paper, Dumont is seeking to interpret the right–left opposition in France in terms of his own analytical categories. The left, at least at a certain point in the recent history of France, is seen to represent the universalist ideals of the Enlightenment, while the right represents national identity; and the left and right are opposed as the 'encompassing' to the 'encompassed'. It is not the place here to decide if this analysis is convincing or not, and I have not seen it commented upon in the reviews of *Homo æqualis II*;[18] but it does seem that the book, taken as a whole, has been received quite favourably by the critics in the major newspapers. Evidently the main reason for this is that Dumont, and for this we are grateful to him, has given his co-citizens food for thought, something which some commentators have occasionally criticized Lévi-Strauss for failing to do.

This sketch is not complete, and cannot be so. I believe it is striking how the outside world fixes its attention on the men rather than the ideas of our discipline. Magazines and newspapers speak easily of Lévi-Strauss, depicting him sometimes as the nation's glory and sometimes as the bogey-man of structuralism, but structuralism only ever remains as a word about which the journalists never say anything. As for Dumont, who is at times enlisted in dubious debates, we have shown how bizarre the articles on his work can sometimes be. When one speaks on his subject of individualism one cannot be sure of avoiding misunderstandings. The concerns of our contemporaries readily lead journalists to place their microphones before the best of our colleagues, but curiously they hardly seem to hear what they then tell them.

NOTES

1 For *Le Magazine littéraire* we have found a collection entitled 'Ethnologie. Littérature. Sociétés' (no. 167, December 1980), including contributions from Jean Duvignaud, François Châtelet, Claude Gaignebet, as well as an interview with Edmund Leach by Jacques Meunier; a collection devoted to Claude Lévi-Strauss (no. 223, October 1985), including, besides an interview with Claude Lévi-Strauss himself, papers by Michel Izard, Jean Pouillon, Paul Jorion, Simone de Beauvoir, Marie Mauzé, Emmanuel Terray, Dan Sperber, Marshall Sahlins; a review of *Histoire de lynx*, as well as an interview with Louis Dumont followed by a bibliography of his main works (no. 292, October 1991). As one can see, the authors are mostly ethnologists. We shall discuss *Esprit* in connection with Louis Dumont. As for publications like *Les*

Temps modernes, not to mention *Débats* or *Critique*, they belong more closely to the academic world.

2   It should be pointed out, however, that the names of Marc Augé, Françoise Héritier, Maurice Godelier and Pierre Clastres also all appear quite frequently. Moreover, we are keen to point out that, at the very time the final version of this paper was finished, we heard of the appearance in *Libération* (8 April 1993: 19–21) of a long and excellent article on Jean Pouillon by Robert Maggiori and Philippe Roussin (regular contributors to the sociology or philosophy pages of *Libération*). The article, published on the occasion of the release of *Le Cru et le su* (Jean Pouillon, Le Seuil) is wittily entitled '*L'Homme des Temps modernes*' ('A man of modern times'); the title is given on the first page, where there is also a photograph of Jean Pouillon with the caption '*Pouillon tout cru*' ('Pouillon in the raw').

3   We must add that some academics like Georges Balandier or Marc Abélès regularly publish careful book reviews in *Le Monde*. This daily also mentions, sometimes with a brief comment, the appearance of books which it does not otherwise review. Most anthropology books of any importance are thus noted.

4   In recent years, this young, competent and enthusiastic essayist has produced respectable work of the popularizing kind.

5   This person usually writes for *Le Monde* on the subject of prehistory. Maybe she was given this assignment because it was about an exhibition in a museum.

6   Montherlant (1896–1972) was a French writer whose work was inspired by a proud ideal of personal fulfilment. For a journalist on *Le Figaro*, he certainly represents a figure of considerable merit in French literature.

7   Lack of space prevents us from mentioning the radio and television programmes in which Lévi-Strauss was invited to appear. Let us simply recall that, in the 1980s, one could have seen him on the literary programmes *Apostrophes* and *Caractères*, both very popular in their day, and one could have heard him on the radio programme *Radioscopie*. In 1988 Eribon published a book of interviews with him, *De près et de loin* (Odile Jacob), which was reviewed in *Le Monde* on the 2 September 1988. More recently, a long interview of Lévi-Strauss by Roger Pol-Droit appeared in *Le Monde* (8 October 1991); this was referred to above.

8   The reading of a book with academic pretensions but intended for a wider public (François Dosse, 1991–1992; see especially Vol. 1: 38 ff.) shows that, on the face of it, the author has scarcely understood *Les Structures élémentaires de la parenté*.

9   It is fair to say that the reviews of *Histoire de lynx* published in the press have, on the whole, been positive. Besides the one by Marc Augé, one can mention a piece by Pol-Droit in the same issue; a long interview with the author, done by Antoine de Gaudemard, appeared in *Libération* (special book supplement, special issue, March 1992: 68–9). *Le Nouvel Observateur* published a review of the book by Eribon as well as an interview with Lévi-Strauss (5–11 September 1991: 91–3). Another review is cited above in note 1.

10   Ethnologists are not the only people blamed for this process. The author puts in the same camp all those he calls the adherents of contemporary anti-humanism, among whom are included Foucault and Bourdieu.

11   There is particular and justifiable criticism of Régis Debray, the essayist and sometime adviser to the last President of the Republic. We should also note here that, in issues 1 to 4 (1988 and 1989), the *Revue du MAUSS (Movement Anti-Utilitaire des Sciences Sociales)* echoed a controversy which, *a posteriori*, proves Finkielkraut partly right. On the subject of female circumcision, the contributors to this journal have taken positions of unqualified relativism, providing good examples of the kind of attitudes that rightly make Finkielkraut bristle. In no. 3 of the *Revue* they go as far as to circulate an appeal urging the decriminalization of the excisions carried out on their young daughters by African parents living in France. It should be noted that this is a rather marginal publication and the relativism it displayed on this occasion, as far as I can judge, shocked many professional ethnologists. Recognizing, but without admitting, the untenable nature of its stance, in its fourth issue this journal produced a 'slightly modified' (*Revue* 4: 151) version of its petition. In reality this amounted to a text of a completely different philosophical nature, written by the researchers of ORSTOM (Office de la Recherche Scientifique et Technique d'Outre-Mer). In it the authors contented themselves with 'rejecting the temptation towards severe criminalization of those who manifest their humanity differently'. Included in this issue (ibid.: 155–6) was a list of signatories, among whom, it is true, are some ethnologists, but the editors of the *Revue* take care not to tell us whether these signatories had signed the first or the second versions of the petition, which are not at all the same.

12   'Personnalisme' is the term given to the synthesis of Christianity and socialism developed by Mounier (1905–1950), the founder of the review *Esprit*.

13   This remark is already present in the introduction of *Homo æqualis* (p. 13 of the French edition) and one finds it again in several passages in *Essais sur l'individualisme* (see the references under the heading 'relations' in the book's index).

14   I am grateful to Serge Tcherkezoff, one of the best of the French commentators on Dumont, for having drawn my attention to this paper as well as to that by Pierre Bérard discussed in this chapter.

15   It is undeniable that Dumont's pessimism renders his thinking very vulnerable to a whole range of misunderstandings and interpretations. We may cite an article by Philippe Gottraux, published in 1987 in the *Bulletin de MAUSS* (the previous form of *La Revue du MAUSS* mentioned above in note 10), in which the author appears to attribute conservative political views to Dumont. Gottraux's arguments are somewhat naive, but they recall the much less naive ones used by C. Wright Mills in a famous book (1959: 48, note 19) in order to establish the 'conservatism' of Talcott Parsons. Without doubt, Mills might have found Dumont's thought rather conservative.

16   When one knows the true nature of the circles that surround these two men, this description would make one smile.

17 In an interview published in *Le Nouvel Observateur* on 6 January 1984, entitled 'Dumont the untouchable', he explicitly refuses to do this, rejecting repeated requests from his interviewer.

18 We must note, however, that Tcherkezoff has used this idea to comment on the political situation in France after the legislative elections in March 1993, in an article entitled 'Left, Right: the historical logic of "cohabitation"' (*Libération*, 6 April 1993: 4). (The term 'cohabitation' designates a situation where the President and the Prime Minister belong to different ends of the political spectrum.) We shall not here enter into the question of how far this paper is intelligible to those who are not already familiar with the twists and turns of Dumontian thinking.

REFERENCES

Bérard, P. (1982) 'Louis Dumont: anthropologie et modernité', *La Nouvelle École*, 39, November: 95–114.

Dosse, F. (1991–1992) *Histoire du structuralisme*, 2 vols, Paris: Éditions La Découverte.

Dumont, L. (1966) *Homo hierarchicus. Essai sur le système des castes*, Paris: Gallimard. English, revised edition (1980) *Homo Hierarchicus. The Caste System and its Implications*, trans. M. Sainsbury, Chicago and London: University of Chicago Press.

—— (1976) *Homo æqualis. Genèse et épanouissement de l'idéologie économique*, Paris: Gallimard. English translation (1977) *From Mandeville to Marx: the genesis and triumph of economic ideology*, Chicago: University of Chicago Press.

—— (1983) *Essais sur l'individualisme. Une perspective anthropologique sur l'idéologie moderne*, Paris: Editions du Seuil. English translation (1986) *Essays on Individualism. Modern Ideology in Anthropological Perspective*, Chicago: University of Chicago Press.

—— (1991) *Homo æqualis II. L'idéologie allemande. France–Allemagne et retour*, Paris: Gallimard.

Favret-Saada, J. and Lenclud, G. (1991) '"Un clip vaut Shakespeare". Entretien avec Alain Finkielkraut', *Terrain*, 17, October: 71–8.

Finkielkraut, A. (1987) *La Défaite de la pensée*, Paris: Gallimard, Collections 'Folio Essais'.

Gauchet, M. (1979) 'De l'avènement de l'individu à la découverte de la société', *Annales (E.S.C.)*, 34, 3: 451–63.

Gotraux, P. (1987) 'Louis Dumont: sociologie du tout social ou pensée de l'ordre', *Bulletin de MAUSS*, 22: 393–425; 23: 153–76.

Leiris, M. (1934) *L'Afrique fantôme*, Paris: Gallimard.

Lévi-Strauss, C. (1955) *Tristes tropiques*, Paris: Plon. English translation (1973) *Tristes Tropiques*, trans. J. and D. Weightman, London: Cape.

—— (1958) *Anthropologie structurale*, Paris: Plon. English translation (1963) *Structural Anthropology*, trans. C. Jackobson and B. G. Schoep, New York: Basic Books.

—— (1962a) *La Pensée sauvage*, Paris: Plon. English translation (1966) *The Savage Mind*, London: Weidenfeld and Nicolson.

—— (1962b) *Totémisme aujourd'hui*, Paris: Presses Universitaires de France. English translation (1963) *Totemism*, trans. R. Needham, Boston: Beacon Press.

—— (1971) *Mythologiques IV, L'Homme nu*, Paris: Plon. English translation (1981) *The Naked Man. Introduction to a Science of Mythology, vol. 4*, trans. J. and D. Weightman, London: Cape.

—— (1983) *Le Regard éloigné*, Paris: Plon. English translation (1985) *The View from Afar*, trans. J. Neugroschel and P. Hoss, Oxford: Blackwell.

—— (1985) *La Potière jalouse*, Paris: Plon. English translation (1988) *The Jealous Potter*, trans. B. Chorier, Chicago: University of Chicago Press.

—— (1991) *Histoire de lynx*, Paris: Plon.

Pouillon, J. (1993) *Le Cru et le su*, Paris: Editions de Seuil.

Wright Mills, C. (1959) *The Sociological Imagination*, Oxford: Oxford University Press.

Chapter 8

Proximity and distance
Representations of Aboriginal society in the writings of Bill Harney and Bruce Chatwin

Howard Morphy

INTRODUCTION

My aim in this chapter is to compare the work of two popular writers who have written about the Australian Aborigines: Bill Harney, a Queenslander who spent his lifetime working among the Aborigines in Northern Australia; and Bruce Chatwin, the English author who visited Central Australia as part of his quest to seek out the nomadic psyche of the human race. In Harney's case, I will focus on two of his books *Life Among the Aborigines* (1957) and *Grief, Gaiety and the Aborigines* (1961), but bring in other works where relevant to my argument. In Chatwin's case I consider a single book, *The Songlines* (1987).

It may seem that I have set myself a difficult task, comparing the incomparable: on the one hand is a book that became a bestseller, written by one of the leading writers of his generation; on the other hand a set of books, in a somewhat folksy outback genre, that were dated almost before they were written. However, it is not my primary aim to compare them as literature (though I do feel that Harney has been considerably underrated as a writer), but rather to compare them as representations of Aboriginal society. Harney's books and Chatwin's book were both, in their own time, the most popular books written on Aborigines. My initial aims in this paper are very simple ones: to consider how their writings on Aborigines compare with anthropological knowledge about Aboriginal society, and to consider whether the contexts in which Aborigines are embedded in their work reflects any gaps in this anthropological knowledge.

The original idea for the paper sprang from a review that I wrote of *The Songlines* for *Anthropology Today* (Morphy 1988). I approached the task with some trepidation since, not only had Chatwin's book received a scathing review from Adam Kuper in *New Society* (July 1987), but rumours emanating from Australia suggested that almost the entire anthropological community had been outraged by it. On reading the book, I could find little explanation for the commotion it had caused. It seemed to me to be, on the one hand, a fairly unremarkable account of the concept of an ancestral track, a key concept in the analysis of Aboriginal religion; and on the other hand, an impressionistic account of the position of Aborigines in Central Australian society in the 1980s. While the concept of the Songline is, as we shall see, somewhat oversimplified, it accords reasonably well with most other popular accounts of the same concept, and the description of life on the edge of Aboriginal society in the Northern Territory seems as accurate as any available. One of the most interesting things about the book is that, although we can compare what he writes on Aboriginal religion with accounts by anthropologists of the same phenomena, we cannot find equivalent anthropological writings on the interface between Aboriginal and white society that Chatwin portrays so well – and yet it is precisely at that interface that the majority of anthropological work in Central Australia takes place today. Chatwin writes about familiar ground; about matters that are the topic of most anthropologists' gossip, and provide the context for much anthropological research, but that are almost entirely absent from anthropologists' writings. I will return to Chatwin towards the end of this paper, but before doing so, I will turn to Harney's books and see whether it is possible to identify an equivalent gap.

Bill Harney was born in 1895 in Charters Towers in Central Queensland. He had a varied career as a drover, cattle man, lugger captain and, eventually, government employee. His entire life involved working with or among the Aborigines. As a drover he rode with Aboriginal stockmen; as captain of a lugger he employed an Aboriginal crew; and in government employment he worked first as the superintendent of an Aboriginal settlement, and later on as a patrol officer and protector of Aborigines in the Northern Territory. He began writing towards the latter part of his career, stimulated in part by his friendship with the anthropologist A. P. Elkin. He did, in fact, establish a close relationship with a number of anthropologists, co-authoring two books with Elkin and acting as a guide on Charles Mountford's Australian–American expeditions to Arnhem Land, and Melville and Bathurst Islands (see Mountford 1956, 1958). Thus, although he prided himself on having only two years of primary school education, he achieved widespread recognition for his expertise on Aborigines. However, whereas Chatwin clearly makes use of anthropological knowledge in his writing about Aborigines, citing Strehlow as a major source, Harney writes from the viewpoint of his own experience, unmediated by anthropological discourse, though undoubtedly influenced by anthropologists and experts in native affairs. This position with regard to Harney's writings is supported by Elkin in his foreword to *Life Among the Aborigines*.

There was a time in the 1940s and 1950s when it seemed as though Elkin wrote a foreword to almost every book written on the Aborigines, and in most cases it consisted of a contextualizing 'put down'. He would provide the missionary's text with a pat on the head and a note about kinship and social organization (e.g. Chaseling 1957), and the anthropological protégé would be damned with faint praise. In Harney's case the praise was unqualified:

> To read W. E. Harney's book is not so much to learn about the Northern Territory of Australia and its Peoples, as to experience life in that Territory. Anthropologists and historians, by their observations and analyses, help us to understand aboriginal tribal organization and religion, and also the problems arising out of our contact with the aborigines. But Mr. Harney is history and is contact ... His factual data is reliable, and his interpretations, arising out of his own experience, deserve our respect. The general reader can be assured that in this book he is brought face to face with aspects of Northern Territory life during the past three-and-a-half decades as they really have been ... For the historian Mr. Harney's book contains significant source material, and for the anthropologist it will make alive the dry bones of social structure and the requirements of ritual duty. It certainly does this for me.
>
> (Elkin 1957: 6)

Of course, this says as much about Elkin as it does about Harney's book, but as a contemporaneous view by an anthropologist on Harney's writing it has some significance. In his day, Harney was viewed as positively by some Australian anthropologists as Chatwin, thirty years on, appears to be viewed negatively. Yet I think it fair to say that both writers were equally in keeping with the spirit of many of the anthropologists of their time, though in Elkin's case that time was rapidly passing. Elkin wrote books on Aborigines and 'how to understand them'. He was clearly deeply moved by the mysteries of Aboriginal religion, yet was an advocate of assimilation – the view that eventually, through education, Aborigines would have to adjust to the new world that was in the process of enveloping them. While in no sense a supporter of discrimination and violence against Aborigines, he viewed their absorption into mainstream Australian society as inevitable. At the time he would have viewed landrights as totally unrealistic and perhaps even as a regressive step (see Morphy 1983 for a relevant discussion), and his position was one which Harney shared. Chatwin, too, is clearly in the same camp as the anthropologists he is writing about, only now it is as an advocate of Aboriginal rights, and no supporter of assimilation.

Harney's writing is detailed, descriptive and non-analytical, presented largely as raw data stories of events, with few synthetic statements. His books are somewhat analogous to an anthropologist's diary, written years and possibly decades after the events he describes. The question thus arises: how would these books compare with an anthropologist's diary, written over the same decades? Do they show the same potential understandings of Aboriginal culture and society that we would expect from the informal writings of an anthropologist? Are they reliable as ethnographic anecdote? Clearly Elkin thought so, but inevitably we are dealing with subjective impression.

As an anthropologist writing some forty years on, I, too, find many of Harney's anecdotes convincing. The best way to demonstrate this is to select excerpts from his writings upon topics that I myself have written about, and assess their validity. I will look at three such topics: the concept of an ancestral track, the spiritual cycle, and trade and exchange. Harney never pulled together his data to write about a particular topic, as an anthropologist would and as Chatwin to an extent does. References to particular topics are scattered throughout his work, often amounting to no more than a line or two at a time, sandwiched between descriptions of events that have nothing to do with the topic concerned. I will be highly selective in my task, simply giving apposite examples, though I do believe that a detailed analysis of the texts would confirm what I have to say.

ANCESTRAL TRACKS, SPIRITUAL CYCLES, AND EXCHANGE

In Chapter XXX of *Life Among the Aborigines*, 'Out Catfish Way', Harney writes:

At one place on our travels we had passed by the nearly obliterated

Tanami Road that led from Wave Hill to the goldfield, and just as Bill was giving us a rather harrowing story about some travellers who had died of thirst upon the iron grill overlaying the well of water beside it, Smiler pointed to the red bluffs on our right and told us they were the 'Jumba', 'Jungala' and 'Warri' Dreamstone places of the Nginin mythology.

'Twas here, he told us, that the tribesmen of the Dreamtime gathered to await the 'old woman' who was coming from 'sunrise way'. Long they waited and chanted until the man of the Budgerega totem came in with the terrible news that the 'Dog-men of Wurangun' (a rain place West of Powell's Creek) had pulled her down in a savage running fight, and her bones were now scattered and transformed into the hills and mounds of that area.

And that night as we camped near 'Wundunga' (water goanna conception place) in Maggie Creek, Smiler told us how the enraged tribesmen marched north-east to wipe out the insult, but were persuaded not to by the Mudbra people of the Pelican totem who were camped at 'Pularowa', those basalt hills where we had passed by the natives clearing the road as we came in to this land.

As a part of that long legend, Smiler chanted a 'song cycle' and, translated, it told how one 'Kumberri' of the 'Jabariou' totem killed all in his path as he strode along as a Dream-time Ajax, and as he slew his enemies they arose again as totemic birds; the black crows from the burnt grass on which he slew them, the native-companions from the colour of the grey earth, the pelican who received his colour from the grey and black earth on which he rolled in his death agony, and the budgerigar from the green leaves on which he fell and died.

Kumberri continued on his march of death until he was slain by 'Judung the eagle' who, knowing that he was protected by magic, crept upon him as the killer fought at 'Pitjangun' (near Longreach water-hole) and, under a mantle of invisibility, he stabbed him through the heart so that he was transformed into the Dreamtime stone that still stands beside the Victoria River.

Noting our interest in his chants, Smiler lowered his voice and told us about 'Jundargul', the powerful serpent with the greenish-brown body and white-tipped nose. He came, so Smiler informed us, from salt-water country, and moving over the land he introduced his powerful cult.

The legend of how 'Jandarkul' came through the country of the Victoria River, then up the Armstrong Creek to the Muranji, where he left some of the hairs of his head, as Bullwaddie trees, at 'Muralanjilunga' (the ear of Muranji). Then he and his band went across the plains of Anthony's Lagoon to come finally to rest at 'Jeringyerree' on the Gregory River, over one thousand miles from the original starting place beside the Timor Sea...Strange, is it not, that on this patrolling of native reserves we have somehow broken away from factual things; for our aboriginal guides have transformed this place of waterholes, stones and trees into a land that is alive with people of legend and song. Hills of stone have been changed into chanting tribesmen, and small creeks are but the trails of Culture Heroes who once marched over this land.

(Harney 1957: 190–1)

This account of Harney's has the appearance of a very standard account of a Dreamtime creation myth, locating myth firmly in the transformation of landscape and the political relations among groups. It reminds me strongly of a passage in Strehlow's *Aranda Traditions* in which he recounts how landscape provides the context for the transmission of myth (Strehlow 1948: 1–5). Chatwin (1987: 68) uses Strehlow as his main source, but in some respects he could just as easily have used Harney.

One of the problems of Harney's work is that he is writing about Aboriginal groups from throughout the Northern Territory of Australia, an area of immense cultural diversity; and although it is usually possible to identify the particular group he is referring to in each case, there is a tendency for him to generalize his statements as if they were applicable to Aborigines as a general category. This tendency to overgeneralize, however, is one that he shares with many anthropologists. The problem is an understandable one for, although there is considerable variation across Australia, there are also underlying cultural structures that in many cases transcend regional difference, and make the ethnography of one area recognizable in terms of the cultural structures, categories and processes of another (Morphy 1993). This is borne out in the second example I will pull from the text for, although it concerns beliefs that differ in detail from those of the Yolngu people of Northeast Arnhem Land, with which I am most familiar, it nevertheless occupies a similar cultural space (see Morphy 1984: 19ff). This second example concerns the spiritual cycle of the Wadaman peoples of the Victoria River region:

In the 'Dreaming' (Boaradja) their spirit shades came with the Earth Mother 'Kunappipi' from the westward...she danced at certain places, and as she did so the 'spirit children' came from her body to people the earth.

(Harney 1957: 33)

[The spirit] was colourless and sexless, and when conceived as a spirit child into its mother through a dream of its father shall remain in that 'camp' until born into the world as a 'shade spirit' covered with a 'skin' (flesh) and thus become a living form once more.

At the birth of a child the grandmother is notified, and, thoroughly examining the child, she can tell by its 'marbun' (birthmark) which person in another life had that mark. Once this is established, the child becomes the reincarnated person, and as such will be given the dead one's name, marry the same reincarnated wife, and travel the same 'Djarp' (dream-time path) as the other.

And when death comes . . . the burial ritual is full of meaning, but the main idea is to get everything clear, so that the 'shade spirit' can wander once more on to the 'Djarp' finally to enter the abode of all the 'shade spirits' of the dead . . . and return renewed once more along the path of life, to be reborn.

And as this spirit child wanders about seeking its mother to be reborn, it may enter an animal . . . for protection, and should a native vomit from eating food when out hunting he will know it was 'spirit children food'.

(ibid.: 35)

The description here has as much validity as most of the anthropological contributions to the Virgin Birth controversy, and accords well with anthropological accounts of the spiritual cycle. However, in some ways Harney's writing on religion is not as interesting as his writing on trade and exchange, partly because the literature on exchange, both popular and anthropological, in Australia is generally thin. Harney sees exchange as a central element of Aboriginal society, and he even writes one of his rare synthetic statements about it: 'With the aborigines of many northern tribes, sex, marriage and trade are similar, and all sprang from the same idea – equality of barter [exchange]' (ibid.: 134). Here Harney voices an idea of some standing in anthropology! He also saw the links between trade and the transmission of myth and ritual, as can be seen by the continuation of his passage on Jundargul:

And as Jundargul marched in the past, so arose a great culture trading route over the land, and to its rituals each year the tribal elders came to escort it across their country. There they would also trade and exchange the knowledge they had acquired since the last one, and when they reached their tribal boundary another group of elders carried it on. Thus did each tribe add its quota to the sum of human experience, and by this the tribes were bound together in this council of old men, the dim beginnings of our modern science congress.

(ibid.: 191)

In *Life Among the Aborigines*, Harney writes in some detail about the role of trade with the Macassans as a component of the dynamic of Northeast Arnhem Land society:

It was the Macassans and their trade who first gave them the power to rule rough shod over the natives from the inland, who came to trade with those who were the medium of exchange [with the Macassans]... As a result of contact and trade, tribal ideas were exchanged and new terms travelled inland for considerable distances, and today we find many Malayan words in the interior that have been passed along the trade routes.

(ibid.: 135–6)

Harney links the development of trade with the structure of the moiety system in Arnhem Land; speculatively, it is true, but no more speculatively than do the anthropologists Berndt and Berndt (1954) and Thomson (1949). Harney concludes this particular section by considering the consequences of the forced ending of trade with the Macassans:

In 1907 the Macassan traders were debarred from these shores, and they left behind a complex trading system that had grown up over the years between the aborigines of Arnhem Land and the interior. This loss was a very great blow to the prestige of the head traders among the aborigines, and out of it came the flare-up of racial hatred between whites and the natives... The trouble was obviously brought about by a breakdown in the aborigines' local economy.

(Harney 1957: 137)

Harney's analysis is not an unreasonable one, since the secession of Macassan trade was one of the adverse consequences of colonialism in

Northern Australia, and the first to have an impact on the people of Northeast Arnhem Land. Certainly Yolngu oral history confirms Harney's feelings that it was the desire for trade goods, rather than trouble over sexual relations, that motivated Aboriginal attacks upon outsiders in coastal Arnhem Land in the 1920s and 1930s. However, the main point to make here is not whether the detailed arguments are correct, but rather the fact that Harney saw exchange and trade as important components of the politics and religion of Aboriginal society. His perspective is certainly one that fits in with contemporary anthropological perspectives.

HARNEY AND THE HIDDEN HISTORY OF THE NORTHERN TERRITORY

In many respects, however, it is not so much those areas where Harney fits in with anthropological writings that is so interesting, as the topics which he covers that are absent from anthropologists' texts. Part of the reason that his works do reflect anthropological knowledge is that he spent much of the last two decades of his life as a guide and confidant of anthropologists, in particular of Elkin and Mountford, but also of more contemporary figures such as Jane Goodale. Yet most of his books consist of a world about which these anthropologists did not themselves write, even if they were familiar with it, and it is this aspect of Harney's writings that I would like to pursue now. Elkin was right about the historical importance of Harney's work. Harney as a stockman and boundary rider, patrol officer and luggerman, represents the kind of person who had a significant role in the history of the Northern Territory. While colonialism may have been fuelled by capitalist enterprise and Government policy, Harney represented actual agency on the ground. Harney positions himself, in his writings, in the time following the initial colonial invasion of Aboriginal land in Northern Australia. He writes of the period of stability that followed the initial holocaust, the period often referred to in the past, by Aborigines and whites, as the Golden Age of the cattle station way of life, where Aborigines and colonists had established a *modus vivendi* of mutual dependence and relative harmony. The killings were over and Aboriginal land was occupied, but conditions were such that Aborigines continued to share occupancy of the land and live a relatively autonomous existence as long as they accepted certain conditions. In order to survive, however, they had to establish relationships of exchange and dependency with the European colonists (Morphy and Morphy 1984). In particular, Aborigines provided labour for the cattle stations and sexual partners for the European men.

The social and cultural significance of sexual relations between white men and Aboriginal women on the frontier is part of the hidden history of the Northern Territory. It is a history whose evidence is continually disappearing through the sensitivities of people in the present to a past from which they wish to disassociate themselves. But it is a history about which Bill Harney writes. The position he adopts varies from book to book. Sometimes he writes as if he were a participant observer of Rabelaisian comedy, where the liberal sexual mores of the Aborigines and the white working class subverts the controlling strategies of the managers and government officials. The sexual relations appear to have been established on a mutual basis and the stories are humorous and often literally lavatorial. He writes about the battle over Aboriginal women between the 'gin shepherds' (white men who control Aboriginal women for their own sexual access or on moral grounds) and 'gin burglars' (white men who attempt to have sexual relations with those women):

> Of all the men I ever met, Bullwaddie had the best system of watching over the women. Scorning the old idea of ever trying to watch a woman who wanted a sweetheart he would watch the stranger. Great would be the welcome when you arrived at his place; your packs would be taken off and your swag placed in the guest room, a stone place with heavy bark roof and a grill over the window to keep out thieves – well, that's what he told me.
>
> Ye Gods! could Edmond Dantes, of Monte Christi fame, ever have escaped from this jail, this torturing hell? Bullwaddie's bunk is across the door, as he likes company and is the perfect host. The bushman writhes in his bed as the old man talks, while outside can be heard the tinkling laughter of the girls of the woods. You try a new move and lie still as one asleep; then when he is breathing heavily, you rise to go out. But the damned bed jingles and jangles and creaks on its wobbly legs. He wakes – for he is a light sleeper – and tells you another yarn, so, in despair, you give up hope and pass into slumber.
>
> Nevertheless one man broke through this iron, or I should say stone wall and lived to tell the tale – and like all feats of 'derring do' the ruse was simple. The victim became ill by poking a finger down his throat after a big meal, and, vomiting violently, he sped past his

jailer into the bush where the lass was awaiting him. A drastic thing to do I will admit, but stranger things than this have been done for love.

(Harney n.d.: 239)

Many passages in Harney's books are written from the point of view of what he refers to as the 'combo'; a white man who has sexual relations with Aboriginal women. The combo is seen as an anarchic, egalitarian figure whose enjoyment of life largely comes through his pursuit of Aboriginal women. The books are full of poems about this aspect of frontier life, and are punctuated with an extraordinary variety of descriptive terms for Aboriginal women that appear today as thoroughly offensive: 'Black lilies', 'spinifex bride', 'spinifex fairy', 'young heifers' and, somewhat more obscurely, 'sleeping dictionaries'. As an example of traditional outback verse I can do no better than quote from the Combo's anthem. Harney writes that it is sung to the Irish tune 'O'Brien O'Lynn had no trousers to wear':

When stock panels slam on the last gnarled beast,
And the smoke signals rise, we will ride to the feast
Where the pandanus fairies are singing their songs,
And the wild ducks are mating by quiet bilabongs.

'Neath black velvet banners we'll carve our way through
As we march to the drone of a didgeredu.
We love and we laugh as pale introverts sigh,
We sneer at protectors, whose laws we defy...

They are comely and dark, and the glint of their eyes
Are as dew-drops that gleam on a wintry sun-rise.
And the firm rounded breasts that seductively tease
Are like seed-pods that sway from squat baobab trees.

(Harney 1957: 172)

Writing as a combo, Harney presents a positive, if one-sided, view of sexual relations between white men and Aboriginal women. He does not refer to such relations as the negative outcome of colonial power relations, as an instrument of colonialism and as a sign of the domination of Aborigines by Europeans. He does not write about them as if they were rape, but as the logical outcome of an absence of white women and an extension of Aboriginal attitudes on sexuality and exchange to include the colonists. He writes about the Aborigines and the itinerant white working-class population of the Northern Territory between the wars as if they jointly formed an underclass, albeit one with its own hierarchy, that existed in opposition to an establishment of cattle barons, police and government officials. It is in relation to what he sees as the hypocrisy and double standards of this establishment that the negative side of Aboriginal–white relations begins to appear explicitly in his writings:

> Bush hospitality is a phrase used mainly by those who do not require it; to the down-and-outs such as travellers like ourselves it was sparsely given and then, grudgingly.
>
> Thinking back on those strange times, I often wonder if I was as much to blame as the others. In that society of men without white women, whose place was taken by the female Aborigines, where black men were despised by the white men because they were rivals for the females of their own race, it was only natural that the white bushmen, who were proud in the glory of a harem, should frown on those such as I who married and thus moved into the camps of the Blacks.
>
> As their complexes developed, so did mine. The slightest hesitation from my host would have me crawling, as a hermit crab, into a protective covering of reticence with a desire to be away from it all.
>
> (Harney 1961: 67)

The position that Harney adopts shifts radically between his earlier and later books. In the earliest books he seems to identify more with the combos, and the books are littered with ribald stories of sexual encounters, though always told by others than himself. In the later books, more negative images tend to predominate, focusing on the hypocrisy of the majority of whites and the exploitative nature of most of the relationships. The libertarian combo clearly reflected an aspect of Harney's behaviour and of the values that he held: 'that there was nothing wrong with sexual relations with Aboriginal women', 'that they reflected shared humanity and common emotions' and even 'that they were a sign of equality and respect between people'. However, it is just as clear in retrospect that those values were not meanings that could easily be attached to any relationship between Aborigines and whites in the Northern Territory, and that this applied as much to sexual relations as to any other. Sexual relations were constrained by the colonial situation of the Northern Territory: if sex fitted in with the structure of colonial domination then it was permissible and understood; if it didn't, it was threatening and often proscribed. Harney, by marrying an Aboriginal woman, had crossed the boundaries and it almost seems from his writing that he did so without knowing what the consequences would be. In an extremely poignant passage in *Grief, Gaiety and the Aborigines* he described his first realization of the consequences arising from his change of status, from legitimate 'gin burglar' to social outcast:

> Next day we were off, and driving along I was full of thoughts about the good time we were going to have at the next stop . . . I am afraid I was inflated with ego as I told them about the hospitality of my friends . . . I went over and made myself known . . . Bill came out to stare, and thinking he had forgotten me I told him who I was. I saw him cast an understanding look at some of his mates, then he gave a quick glance at Linda [Harney's Aboriginal wife] . . . 'Oh yes, I know yer now. Yer the bloke who gave me a hand-out at Newcastle Waters . . . now look, come here, and I'll show yer a good camp.'
>
> I walked with him to a cleared place outside his crude home and, stopping, he pointed out to me a patch of mulga trees about four hundred yards away. 'That's a good camp' he said . . . 'If yer got traps there's boggins of rabbits about . . .'
>
> I could see he was embarrassed and that we were not wanted around, so I sheepishly returned to my family and friend . . . Over and over again Linda kept telling Andy about the many friends that I had scattered around the bush. 'They give him everything with their mouth . . . not like blacks,' sarcastically, 'who are mean and never give anything to their friends.'
>
> Andy could see how great was the blow to my pride. It was as though the world of mateship had gone up with a bang, and he also sensed it was a stab in Linda's heart, aimed by whites who were then keeping black concubines.
>
> (ibid.: 44–5)

The underlying themes of *Grief, Gaiety and the Aborigines* are in fact twofold: the structural position of Aborigines in the Northern Territory in the 1930s and 1940s; and the author's attempt to understand his own position in the world as someone who has tried to occupy a space in between. As a white man married to an Aboriginal woman, and as the father of her children, Harney continually found himself rejected by others. He was neither accepted wholly by white society or by Aboriginal society, but he found the latter far more sympathetic to his predicament and much more supportive of his family. Harney's writing is at its finest when descriptions of Aboriginal society and beliefs are interwoven with accounts of his personal predicament and its origins in the colonial situation. In one passage (see below), Harney movingly integrates the Aboriginal spiritual cycle within the destructive process of colonialism.

Grief, Gaiety and the Aborigines is set in the depression of the 1920s. Harney travelled the Northern Territory with his wife, who was seriously ill with tuberculosis, and his two children. He moved from one short-term contract to another, but for much of the time he was unemployed. His wife's condition deteriorated and he decided to return to Katherine, where she could receive medical treatment. On the way, he camped beneath some shady trees beside the Negri River, just below an outstation of the Orde River cattle property. He went up to the outstation to ask for some fresh tomatoes for his dying wife and was refused them. In the evening, Aboriginal women came down from the station bringing fresh vegetables and ripe tomatoes. I continue with Harney's description:

'We come look-look sick one ... poor fellow my sister.'

I pointed to where Linda and the children sat upon the swag ... they all trooped over to lay their gifts ... beside her. Linda placed her hand upon each gift in turn as a sort of tribal blessing.

No-one spoke during the giving and receiving of the gifts. There was a slight pause, then Linda's tribal sister began to rub the sweat from her own body with both hands, then passed these solemnly over Linda's ailing form ... 'changing sweat' ... was a communion of spirits in tribal sorrow. [Then] I heard the plaintive voices of our native friends chanting out one of their simple songs that custom demands shall be sung as a magic medicine for the aged and sick ones ...

Looking upon that scene, then, I became aware of how fixed were Aboriginal ties regarding kinship and ritual. To the Aborigines, the original soul was begat by the Earth-Mother from the first fruits grown on tree and plant life in the early gardens of the cultural food spirits. Each soul or shade was eternal and was passed from mortal mother to re-incarnated mother in an unbroken chain down the ages. It was this eternal soul that gave Linda, Beattie, and Billy a common heritage with the black people around our camp.

It is this law of fixed continuity in the soul that prevents a white person from becoming a blood brother; their soul is of another

people, another land ... I was just 'nothing' to the women who sat
and chanted their life-giving songs to my ailing wife.

(ibid.: 69)

Harney asked them later how they had come by the tomatoes:

'We been steal them from garden' one woman said proudly. 'That
white-fellow cook just rubbish ... all day him cry ... cry for black
girl ... [but] he can't give a tomato to our sick friend, so we steal
em ... that right, ain't it?' As she spoke the last words I could sense
that she regarded me as one of the hated conquerors, as indeed I was.
She stood there and awaited my reply, but the tenseness was broken
with a feeble 'good night' from Linda. In a flash the magic around
me was dispelled and those people, who were ritually conceived
from the food of Gods, became, in the fire-light's glow, the tattered
and conquered people of a dying tribe.

(ibid.: 70)

I find the passage a moving and revealing one. It juxtaposes
Aboriginal metaphysics and values with instances of colonial domination to simultaneously lay bare the politics and tragedy of the
frontier and the ambivalence of Harney's own position. It shows
Harney himself as being doubly an outsider: someone who, because of
his marriage to an Aboriginal woman, must remain in many situations
apart from both societies. Hardest of all must have been the
unconscious disregard for his emotions by those who implicitly
assumed he shared their values, in particular in times of anxiety about
his family and in times of grief. The book begins with an account of his
wife's admission to a hospital in Darwin, and ends with the death of his
son, his last surviving child, in Alice Springs some fifteen years later:

'I am afraid Mrs Harney is a very sick woman. She has a lung
complaint, and,' the local doctor looked at me with understanding,
'you know how it is with these coloured people, they just cannot
stand up to the diseases of our civilisation ... We are fortunate to
have just built a small segregation ward in the hospital, otherwise –
well you should know how it is with the white people and blacks –
they are very touchy.'

(ibid.: 13)

And, fifteen years on:

Billy ... had dived into the cold pool to save another lad ... The lad
was saved, but Billy was drowned ... His College in Adelaide

forwarded me his belongings and these I took to a deserving church home for children. The lady in charge . . . was full of sympathy for me . . . accepted the parcels and gave me her condolences . . .

'I am very sorry about your sad loss . . . it is sad, but not so sad when one realises that he was young and is now in the arms of his Maker . . . Perhaps it was best he went now. This is a hard World and, as you know, he was coloured.'

The superior white, I thought – not principle, but colour. What a strange damn World! I may have thanked her, I do not remember, but I did go away wondering why such genuine sympathy could at the same time be so cruel. Then I remembered that at Linda's first illness also, the doctor had informed me that her colour could deter her from getting well. Now, at the end of the road, the same argument was being used in sympathy to show that my son was better off dead than alive.

(ibid.: 190)

THE SONGLINES

In contrast to Harney, Chatwin wrote only a single book on the Australian Aborigines, and that a relatively short one; yet in world terms, Harney's works have made no impact whatsoever, whereas Chatwin's *The Songlines* has achieved considerable renown. Chatwin's book achieved so much partly because it was published at the right time (1987), when Aborigines had, through their art and through their continued resistance to colonialism, already become fashionable. Yet Chatwin, in turn, contributed significantly to the process. He coined a word, 'Songlines', that seems likely to enter the English language as a key characteristic of Aboriginal society; a word that has doubtless cropped up before in anthropologists' notebooks and in discourse about landrights in Central Australian legal process, but a word that, once it has been given the imprimatur of a famous author, takes on quite a different status. 'Songlines' becomes the title for an exhibition, the topic of common-room debate, something whose elusive meaning becomes part of the Western quest for the exotic in other worlds. It has become, like the Dreaming, a symbol of the difference of Aboriginal society.

Chatwin has quite a different relationship with anthropology to Harney. Harney the bushman was a guide to an earlier generation of anthropologists, introducing them to Aboriginal people and assisting them with their work. He was the kind of character that anthropologists often befriend in the field, someone who is a bit of an outsider, and whose sympathetic relationship with Aborigines sets him apart from the majority of Northern Territory whites. Most anthropologists, if they are honest, have their Bill Harneys, though the itinerant bushman or the pioneering missionary of the first half of the century have been replaced by the sympathetic schoolteacher or craft adviser of the second half.

Chatwin, in contrast, was clearly dependent on anthropology for his understanding of Aboriginal society. The paths he followed into Central Australia were paths that had been trodden by anthropologists and, interestingly enough, he combines in some respects the paths of different generations. Chatwin's overall quest has a bit of the nineteenth-century anthropologist's agenda about it, in that he seeks out the Australian Aborigines in order to discover something about the essential nature of man; in this case, his nomadic psyche. However, although this is reflected in the sets of quotations that he culls from a variety of different sources to illustrate his theme, most of the book is unaffected by it. Instead, the book focuses on the concept of Songlines as the metaphysical core of Aboriginal society, and juxtaposes this with a description of the conditions and politics of Aborigines in Central Australia today. It is this latter aspect of Chatwin's work that makes it so interesting, since he presents an accurate picture of the broader context in which anthropological data is obtained, a context that, until recently, was absent from most anthropologists' writings.

Chatwin's discussion of the Songlines themselves is overall quite unremarkable. 'Songlines' refers to what are generally known in the literature as Ancestral tracks or Dreaming tracks. These represent the journeys that mythological beings undertook across the different regions of Australia in the Ancestral past. We have already had an excellent example of one such track from Bill Harney. The tracks are an important component of the core structure of Aboriginal society, since they provide the mechanism for the association of people with land and provide the ideological basis for the regional interrelationships among people and groups (see, e.g., Morphy 1991). The Ancestral events resulted in the transformation of the earth's landscape into its present shape, and in the institution of the conventions of human social behaviour. The events and the journeys are commemorated in the forms of the landscape, in paintings, in ritual action, dances and song. Ancestral tracks, for example, are represented by the circle/line motif in Central Australian art that Munn's work (1973) has elucidated so brilliantly, and Ancestral tracks could be at least as accurately described as 'Paintlines' as they could as 'Songlines'. Songlines is a literary device, but it does not involve a major distortion, since any term chosen is likely to be an impoverished translation that fails to convey the complexity of the Aboriginal concept. As far as the concept of the Songlines is concerned, Chatwin remains true to the spirit of his contemporary anthropological sources in developing analogies that highlight the relationship between geographical space, culture and society:

> An expert songman . . . [is able] . . . to hear a few bars and say, 'this is Middle Bore' or, 'That is Oodnadatta' – where the Ancestor did X or Y or Z.
>   'So a musical phrase', I said, 'is a map reference?'
>   'Music', said Arkady, 'is a memory bank for finding one's way about the world.'

> (Chatwin 1987: 108)

Or, later, writing about sacred objects:

> A tjuringa . . . is an oval plaque made of stone or mulga wood. It is both a musical score and a mythological guide to the Ancestors' travels. It is the actual body of the Ancestor. It is man's alter ego; his soul; his obol to Charon; his title-deed to country; his passport and his ticket back in.

> (ibid.: 286)

Although it is impossible to assess such interpretative statements by any simple canon of factual accuracy, my belief is that the images that Chatwin develops are precisely of the kind that a literary popularising anthropologist would be content to have developed. At times when he attempts to elaborate the details of his model, he oversimplifies; on other occasions he stretches the evidence beyond what is known; but overall his work is consistent with anthropological writings. Chatwin's descriptions of the religious dimensions of Aboriginal society are in continuity with Harney's, but belong to a different anthropological generation. Whereas Harney's work is largely descriptive, Chatwin produces a synthetic analysis that is directed towards the discovery of a core structure. As representations of Aboriginal society, both are within the range of anthropological understandings of their time, wont to oversimplification and overgeneralization, but not seriously misleading.

The context that Chatwin presents is a very different one to Harney's, and it is one that anthropologists are much more familiar with. Chatwin arrives in Central Australia as an outsider. He enters the world that exists on the frontier of today's Aboriginal society; a world that hardly existed at all in Harney's time. This world is no longer that of the combo, of the Europeans who are pushing back the frontier. The frontier has stopped; it has been held up, and replaced by a bureaucracy. Spatially, the Northern Territory has been divided into Aboriginal and non-Aboriginal; conceptually, into Aboriginal and white Australia. The boundaries are more or less permeable and systems of permits, negotiating procedures, welfare practices and economic transactions create a constant flow of people across the borders. The boundary itself, however, is a world of its own, occupied by bureaucrats and politicians, cultural brokers, linguists and anthropologists, teachers and craft advisers. Sexual innuendo in *The Songlines* is restricted to the white Australian women who occupy this frontier: women of 'firm breasts', 'golden hair', or with their 'wet dresses flattened out'. The implicit sexism that it is possible to interpret in such descriptions may, in part, explain the antagonism of much of the Australian anthropological community to the book.

Chatwin describes the dual aspects of this frontier. There is the frontier occupied by the gatekeepers of Aboriginal society: the white people working for Aboriginal organizations, the advisers who know what is best for Aboriginal society and who protect Aborigines from outsiders in their own interests. Then there is the frontier where racism and hostility remain an ever-present and often dominant component of daily interaction. This frontier world often appears as a screen of half understandings which, though occupied in part by Aboriginal people, seems distanced from the Aboriginal world that it is ultimately all about. Chatwin conveys the sense of being on the frontier extremely well. He writes about the racism that Aborigines face every day in Alice Springs. He writes about the divisions within the white community. He also provides an ethnography of the world of European advisers, lawyers, linguists anthropologists and craft advisers who work for Aboriginal organizations, but who are forever set apart from Aboriginal society. In a marvellous account of casual conversation among whites at a Central Australian settlement, Chatwin shows how Aboriginal people and Aboriginal society enter as somewhat distanced topics of everyday life:

> We were standing behind the plate-glass window looking at the blank horizon. Water lay in sheets on the ground, flooding several

Aboriginal humpies to the depth of a foot or more. The owners had heaped their gear on to the roofs. The water was awash with refuse.

A short way off to the West was the old administrator's house, of two storeys, which had since been given over to the community. The roof was still on and there were floors and fireplaces. But the walls, the window sashes and the staircase had all been burnt for firewood.

We looked through this X-ray house into the yellow sunset. On both the upper and lower floors sat a ring of dark figures, warming themselves over a smoky fire.

'They don't give a fuck for walls' said Red, 'but they do like a roof for the rain.'

Arkady told him we were on our way to Cullen, 'Little dispute between Titus and the Amadeus mob.'

'I'll be out that way myself next week,' said Red. 'Got to go and look for a grader.'

Clarence Japaljari, the Chairman at Cullen, had borrowed the Popanji grading-machine to make a road from the settlement to a soakage.

'That was nine months ago' Red said. 'Now the fucker says he's lost it.'

'Lost a grader?' Arkady laughed. 'For Christ's sake, you can't lose a grader.'

'Well, if anyone is going to lose a grader,' said Red, 'it'll be Clarence.'

Arkady asked what the road was like up ahead. Red toyed with the buckle of his security belt.

'You'll be right' he said. 'Stumpy Jones nearly got bogged in the big storm Thursday. But Rolf and Wendy went through yesterday, and they radioed this morning they'd arrived.'

He was shifting uneasily from foot to foot. You could tell he was dying to get back to his weights.

'Just one thing,' said Arkady. 'You haven't seen old Stan Tjakamarra? We thought we'd take him along. He's on quite good terms with Titus.'

'I think Stan's gone on walkabout,' Red said. 'They've been initiating all week. It's been a right mess, I can tell you. Ask Lydia.'

Lydia was one of two school-teachers stationed here. We had radioed a message for her to expect us.

'See you in a while' Red said. 'She's cooking tonight.'

(ibid.: 135–6)

I think that this passage conveys the notion of the frontier as a screen very well. Aborigines are, in a sense, out there through the plate-glass window, observed as shadows in X-ray houses, not fully engaged in the world of the whites who are employed in part to manage their affairs. And, of course, the Songlines as a concept properly belongs to the screen rather than the world beyond it. It is a word to use when talking about Aborigines; it is a word from the 'how to understand them' tradition (cf. Elkin 1938) that signifies the mysteries that lie beyond, the mysteries that justify Aborigines' detachment from settlement life. It represents the world that the gatekeepers are protecting, it represents the value that Europeans see in Aboriginal society. And just as the idea that 'they don't give a fuck for walls' acts as a distancing mechanism, so too does the concept of Songlines, since this, too, is something that they don't share with us.

CONCLUSION

Harney and Chatwin belong to different periods of Northern Australia's history, and the gaps that they fill in the anthropological record reflect these changing times. Both reveal aspects of the contexts in which anthropologists work, but which are absent from their writings. Certainly in the case of the colonial relations of the nineteenth and twentieth centuries, anthropologists have recognized the gaps in their writings and have begun to fill them. Writings such as Harney's are among the sources for recovering the history of the Northern Territory. In Chatwin's case the gap is closer to contemporary anthropological practice and is both easier and harder to fill. Easier, in that the necessary information is part of the present. Harder, in that anthropologists are themselves so involved in the emotions and politics of the contemporary frontier that it is harder for them to achieve any distance from it. In the past, anthropological practice tended to distance the object of research from the contemporary world in which people actually lived. However, as a result of recent paradigm shifts in anthropology and the increased reflexivity of anthropological writings, such distancing has in itself, become unacceptable, and the broader context of fieldwork has become integral to anthropologists' writings.

Perhaps ironically, the position of anthropologists as participant observers still places them closer to Harney than it does to Chatwin. Anthropologists try to get beyond the glass screen to live in the X-ray houses and to be themselves treated as 'other'. In that sense, anthropologists are far more like Bill Harney than they are like Bruce Chatwin. And in their position on the frontier, anthropologists also share more in common with Harney the stockman than may at first seem to be the case. Anthropologists move back from Aboriginal society and into their own and, in so doing, in passing, they often occupy the frontier screen and contribute to its make-up. Indeed, the fact that they are, in a sense, Chatwin's informants may be what makes them resent him so much.

ACKNOWLEDGEMENTS

I am most grateful to Ingrid Skeels for her thorough reading of this text and for preparing it for publication.

REFERENCES

Berndt, R. M. and Berndt, C. H. (1954) *Arnhem Land: Its History and its People*, Melbourne: Cheshire.
Chaseling, W. (1957) *Yulengor Nomads of Arnhem Land*, London: The Epworth Press.
Chatwin, B. (1987) *The Songlines*, London: Jonathan Cape.
Elkin, A. P. (1938) *The Australian Aborigines: How to Understand Them*, Sydney: Angus and Robertson.
—— (1957) Preface in W. Harney, *Life Among the Aborigines*, London: Robert Hale.
Harney, W. (1957) *Life Among the Aborigines*, London: Robert Hale.
—— (1961) *Grief, Gaiety and the Aborigines*, London: Robert Hale.
—— (n.d.) *North of 23*, Sydney: Australasian Publishing Company.
Kuper, A. (1987) 'Primitive "chic"', *New Society* 3, July.
Morphy, H. (1983) 'Now you understand – an analysis of the way Yolngu have used sacred knowledge to maintain their autonomy', in N. Peterson and M. Langton (eds), *Aborigines, Land and Landrights*, Canberra: Australian Institute of Aboriginal Studies, pp. 110–33.
—— (1984) *Journey to the Crocodile's Nest*, Canberra: Australian Institute of Aboriginal Studies.
—— (1988) 'Behind the Songlines', *Anthropology Today* 4, 5: 19–20.
—— (1991) *Ancestral Connections: Art and an Aboriginal System of Knowledge*, Chicago: University of Chicago Press.
—— (1993) 'Cultural adaptation', in G. A. Harrison (ed.) *Human Adaptation*, Oxford: Oxford University Press.
Morphy, H. and Morphy, F. E. C. (1984) 'The myths of Ngalakan history: ideology and images of the past in Northern Australia', *Man (N. S.)* 19: 459–78.
Mountford, C. P. (1956) *Art, Myth and Symbolism: Records of the American*

Australian Expedition to Arnhem Land, vol.1, Melbourne: Melbourne University Press.
—— (1958) *The Tiwi: Their Art, Myth and Ceremony*, London: Phoenix House.
Munn, N. M. (1973) *Walbiri Iconography*, Ithaca: Cornell University Press.
Strehlow, T. G. H. (1948) *Aranda Traditions*, Melbourne: Melbourne University Press.
Thomson, D. (1949) *Economic Structure and the Ceremonial Exchange Cycle in Arnhem Land*, Melbourne: Macmillan.

Chapter 9

Women readers
Other utopias and own bodily knowledge

Judith Okely

WOMEN'S LIBERATION, THE SEXED BODY, AND POPULIST ISSUES

The search for alternative modes of being in the exotic other is often propelled by an internal critique. This is what inspired women after the Liberation Movement to look outside their own society in the early 1970s for resolutions and utopian answers to their questions. Women's subordination, gender divisions, the sexed body and women's bodily experiences became the subject of intense popular interest to the general woman reader. Examples from other cultures could possibly indicate the provisional nature of Western gendered culture. Given the undergraduate demand for courses which addressed these issues, they were also of interest to women and some men anthropology students. At the time, these concerns remained or had become largely peripheral to academic social anthropology. The vacuum was filled by a few popularist books which were addressed to a non-specialist readership and made use of cross-cultural examples. They were written from the margins or outside the anthropological academy.

The peripherality of these gendered issues may be explained by the gender of the practitioners and by the ambivalence towards scholarly research on gendered sexuality and the body. Although it is now a commonplace that the categories 'woman' or 'man' are not unitary, broad externally imposed categorizations have continuing implications for peoples' experience, access to and construction of knowledge. Knowledge and persons have been subject to gender demarcations and asymmetrical power relations.

Since the higher proportion of women to men students of anthropology has not been matched, and indeed has been reversed, at research and professorial level, the agenda of anthropological research has rarely, if ever, been set by women. Whatever the variation in their masculinist interests, men have formed the large majority in the power base where anthropological knowledge is generated and published.

Until the 1980s and after, concern with gendered bodily issues had a life of its own largely outside the anthropological academy. Here, I draw on material largely from Britain, but there are significant echoes in the United States. Although there were parallel movements world wide, the Women's Liberation Movement emerged in the West in the late 1960s, following a critique of Western capitalism. Prospects of relative full employment and a new youth consumerism empowered Paris students in 1968 to unite with industrial workers to challenge the *status quo*. Demands were made for greater political participation and the democratization of institutions. US students, and men faced with the draft, were backed by large sections of the Western intelligentsia in resistance to US involvement in the Vietnam War. The Black Power movement emerged to question racist majorities. Women were entering higher education and the labour force in greater numbers. New technologies of birth control helped change sexual mores. At the same time, women began to resist being treated as sexual objects rather than as persons. They objected to masculinist rhetoric and to being assigned mere servicing roles by the great white revolutionaries. At the Miss World Contest at the Albert Hall, London, flour was thrown at Bob Hope, the impresario. A Black Power spokesman, in asserting that the only position for women in the movement was 'prone', continued to represent women in terms of their sexed body. With a renewed consciousness, both black and white women embarked on a gendered critique.

Questions were again raised about the naturalness and fixity of gender divisions, sexuality, bodily experience and personal relations. Earlier, within anthropology, Margaret Mead had broached such topics, and written with popular appeal, but the profession largely ignored her, especially in Britain. Her work rarely, if ever, featured among the multiple course reading lists. Nevertheless, her *Male and Female* (1949) had become an important extra-curricular text for feminists in the 1960s. In the 1970s, de Beauvoir's *The Second Sex* (1972 [1949]) witnessed renewed popularity among women readers, especially in the States. De Beauvoir's assertion that 'woman is made not born' was rediscovered, to challenge the biological basis to difference. Although social anthropology had, at an early stage in descent and kinship studies, distinguished the social from the biological, these distinctions were scarcely developed in relation to gender.

With the Women's Liberation Movement, there was an interest in exploring the specificity of women's lived experience and their consciousness as women. Although in this multi-faceted movement some might have suggested that women naturally shared things in common, there was a concern for both differences and things shared. The notion of world sisterhood might have been a strategically useful polemical device, but among intellectuals and others there was an early scepticism about its reality (Oakley and Mitchell 1976: 10–13). The notion of some solidarity was exciting and inspiring when it took the form of all-women groups and conferences. Today, such groups and events are taken for granted. For women then it was a revelation to be in a hall or room filled entirely with women and where only women were the organizers and speakers. Previously, women had no choice but to assist in male-dominated meetings, whether trade unions, political gatherings or academic seminars. All-women meetings had, up to then, been insignificant or associated with organizations which reified women as servicers of men. But by the early 1970s, all-women seminars were seen as dangerously subversive by some academics. For example, at one university, anthropology postgraduates were not permitted to use the official premises for women-only seminars. Thus the marginality of women's issues was spatially reinforced.

The women in the Liberation Movement differentiated themselves from the earlier generation of post-suffrage 'equal rights feminists' who sought integration within the prevailing system. By contrast, the Women's Movement confronted and celebrated gender differences. They questioned the assumption that women should fit into existing institutions as honorary men. The private, they argued, could no longer be separated from the public. Sexual relations, domestic labour, child care and family structures were subjected to new political and theoretical scrutiny. The discussion of sexual experience had been smothered by the postwar 1950s ideology of the monogamous family and conflation of sexual pleasure with reproduction. Consciousness-raising groups in both the US and Britain focused on personal relations, pursuing ways in which the personal could be seen as political (Rowbotham 1990). Other themes included: notions of motherhood, relations with men and awareness of sexed bodily functions. Rowbotham, inspired by de Beauvoir, pointed to the problems implicit in rationalism, liberal feminism and Marxism which had treated women as merely human:

> The general cover of human-beingness camouflaged both the anatomical differences between men and women and concealed the manner in which the notion of the human being is male-defined in all forms of existing social organisation – including the revolutionary party. In fact this defensive denial of actual difference left the way wide open for a crude and mechanical reduction of feminine potential to the body. It was easy for the anti-feminists to determine a woman by her anatomy because the feminists persisted in ignoring that her anatomy existed at all.
>
> (Rowbotham 1973: 10–11)

Special emphasis was placed by the Women's Liberation Movement on recapturing the body. *Our Bodies Ourselves* (1976) and *Woman's Body: An Owner's Manual* (The Diagram Group 1977) were key texts. Women wanted knowledge about themselves which was bodily grounded.

In order to counter the Western ideological invisibility of the female genitalia, Western women experimented in self and mutual examination with the speculum, an instrument hitherto restricted to the medical encounter and the male gaze. Female anatomical self-observation was both empirically informative and symbolically subversive. The well-worn argument about phallic power that the protruding penis 'naturally' lends itself to superior representation, whereas the female genitalia is 'naturally' invisible, was challenged by the new feminists who, instead, suggested that the perception of the biological was recognized as ideologically selective. The tamed and domesticated portrayal of the female genitalia, women argued, was an historically and culturally specific obliteration, rather than anything essentially anatomical. Artists like Judy Chicago, in the cooperative work *The Dinner Party*, reinstated women's genitalia as aesthetic and as celebratory, highly visible objects. Mary Kelly, to public journalistic furore, framed behind glass and exhibited as art form a month's supply of her used tampons at the Institute of Contemporary Arts in London. Thus the usually hidden parts of feminine bodily identity and experience were brought to the public gaze.

Feminist scholars in other disciplines subsequently examined Western representations of the body. Walters's re-examination of the nude male in art raised questions about masculinity (Walters 1978). The male body from Greek statues, through Leonardo and Michaelangelo, she argued, has been taken as the norm against which the female body is deviant. Given that the male body is the taken-for-granted centring of existence, those who live in such bodies, including male anthropologists, may not be stimulated to be puzzled about them.

Consistent with this renewed curiosity in the sexed body was the search by Western feminists for alternative femininities in other cultures. Again I use the term femininity on the understanding that it is culturally constructed and neither universal nor innate. It was important to consider evidence from beyond the West. Such an enterprise has a long tradition, and has other political parallels. Bloch has lucidly suggested (1983) that Marx and Engels, drawing on others' writing, used pre-literate societies as a rhetorical device to argue that there were alternatives to capitalism, i.e. things could change in future if the study of the past showed fundamental differences from the present. Marx and Engels painted an idyllic inverse of capitalism in 'primitive' societies where, allegedly, mother right, sexual freedom and a form of communism existed with neither private property nor class conflict. The rhetorical use of other societies had populist implications, in that Marx and Engels also wrote texts for a popular readership, e.g. *The Manifesto of the Communist Party*.

Evans-Pritchard noted comparable uses of non-Western societies by Western religious theorists as a covert critique of the theorists' own society and religious ideology (Evans-Pritchard 1951). Nineteenth-century theorists of primitive religions and of the origins of religion in general were often writing in a context where it was awkward to question the truth of the dominant Christian religion, so they safely transposed their debates to the study of the 'other' and 'primitives'. By demonstrating the multiplicity of beliefs elsewhere, it could be suggested that Christian theology was not an inevitable universal. Male theologians, with the strategic advantage of the pulpit for a non-academic congregation, were also read beyond the academy and monastery.

Similarly, through the quest for answers outside the West, the androcentric academic restrictions on the discussion of gender relations, women's experience, their sexuality and reproductive practice were open to subversion or debate in wider popular circles. If Western women could find utopian solutions or alternatives elsewhere, there would seem to be hope for change in their own society. Some populist Western women writers have, in the same tradition as class politics and theological debates, used or imagined non-Western examples to offer alternatives to the Western gender *status quo*. But they were less easily absorbed into mainstream academic theories. This is in part because both writers and readers were of the subordinate gender and because the women writers' theoretical and methodological approaches rarely emerged from the 'malestream'. They were writing either from outside the discipline or from its margins. They were not always in a position to update their arguments in the light of current theoretical debates within the discipline. They had to appeal over the heads of the academy. In some instances, as in two examples I discuss in this chapter, other cultures were used to re-legitimate Western systems.

In the post-war period there had already been some signs of a demand for answers from women readers for critical discussion about gender relations and aspects of sexuality, reproduction and child care. De Beauvoir's *Le Deuxième Sexe* (1949) is an important example of a text which was read and absorbed by thousands of women through the anti-feminist 1950s and for decades later, and yet was condemned and belittled by mainly establishment male reviewers of all political leanings. Even the author was surprised by the enthusiasm of the response from her otherwise invisible female readers, who wrote to her in huge numbers. They said that the book had changed their lives (Okely 1986). The dialogue between the woman writer and women readers was conducted outside the academy. In this massive and scholarly work, de Beauvoir addressed such issues as women's subordination, its possible causes, sexuality and the sexed body. Whereas the women readers looked for identifications with themselves, de Beauvoir's largely generalized account was read as unseemly self and sexual exposure by François Mauriac, the novelist. In a letter to a writer at *Les Temps modernes*, he wrote 'Your employer's vagina has no secrets from me' (de Beauvoir 1965: 197). This tells us more about the culture of the male gaze than the writer's anatomy.

De Beauvoir gave an unusually negative and provocative view of maternity and child care (Okely 1986). She was writing against the prevailing postwar Western ideology which represented women primarily as housewives, stigmatized or obliterated women's extra domestic employment, and sentimentalized maternity. Despite the fact that a large number of women did have such employment, albeit part-time, women were exhorted to look to a husband for financial support. Questions as to their subordination within this contract were not up for debate. Only de Beauvoir raised them for her silenced women readers.

In contrast, the Women's Liberation Movement of the 1970s also focused attention on parenting. Since full employment had brought greater numbers of women into the labour force, increased numbers of college educated women were faced with decisions of maternity in conjunction with extra domestic employment and/or careers. This greater number of educated women readers looked for answers both within and outside their own cultures.

With some notable exceptions, social anthropology in Britain and the West had ceased to problematize the subordination of women and the construction of gender relations. It was generally taken for granted that women in non-Western societies were subordinate. The silence about comparisons with Western examples indicated some complacency in the Western anthropologists' own society. After the granting of the franchise to women, it was presumed that all Western gender relations were peaceably complementary, and that women were 'equal but different'.

SEXUALITY, THE FIELDWORKER, AND THE MALE GAZE

The constraints on the study of sexuality, menstruation and childbirth across cultures can in part be explained by the dominant masculine gender of the fieldworker. Male anthropologists, enjoying gendered privileges and academic power in their own society, were unlikely to be concerned with making connections or contrasts in gender relations their major focus of investigation elsewhere.

The character of anthropological fieldwork, entailing daily proximity, compounded the constraints. With the increasing professionalism of the discipline at the turn of the century, and the practice of participant observation fieldwork replacing armchair speculation and reliance on secondary sources, social anthropologists were keen to emphasize the objective scientific nature of their studies. Since sexuality in exotica was both popularly and academically interpreted as of sensational interest, anthropologists wished to distance themselves from amateur travellers' tales in which primitive peoples had been treated as objects of sexual voyeurism for Western readers.

The anthropologist was faced with an immediate dilemma of how to research and write about the intimate topic of sexuality which would not have remained hidden during the long-term immersion of participant observation. If, in addition, anthropologists have ever engaged in individual sexual relationships with 'the other', they have been loth to record, let alone consider, the implications in print. Such encounters, rather like much of the generalized topic of sexuality, have been confined to whispering in corridors or bar-room boasting (see, by contrast, Abramson 1993, Kulick and Willson 1995).

Like many of his subsequent students, Malinowski wished to distance himself from speculative stereotypes about primitive behaviour. Earlier accounts had included presuppositions of primitive promiscuity and other tantalizing inversions of the visitors' own morality. Sexuality and bodily matters were seen as subjects which risked sensationalism. Nevertheless, Malinowski was ambivalent. He played along with popular voyeurism in his melodramatic choice of title *The Sexual Life of Savages* (1929), despite the fact that a great deal of its contents was devoted to kinship, marriage and mortuary rites.

Malinowski was considerably handicapped as a male inquirer and in many instances tried to overcome this. Nevertheless, his text does not usually problematize his masculine perspective. The sections on childbirth devote considerable space to the mainly absent men rather than the presence of women (Malinowski 1932 [1929]: 194–5). His *Diary* (1967) explicitly reveals his major preoccupation with women as sexual objects for his repressed desire. When writing of seduction, the reader, both male and female, is drawn into his description of women as 'the fair sex' (1932: 257). While seeming indifferent to women's views of menstruation, Malinowski is at pains to inform the reader that men are not repelled by menstrual blood and that women washed daily in the public water hole. Men did so also (ibid.: 144). At key junctions he inserts himself into the text, in case his knowledge of 'the fair sex' appears to be at first hand; 'I am told that girls at the time of their first menstruation are tattooed round the vagina' (ibid.: 257). He feels compelled to find convoluted explanations for 'the undiscriminating way in which young and handsome boys will sometimes fornicate with old and repulsive women' (ibid.: 289). The reverse is not a matter for query, presumably because unions between 'old and repulsive' men and 'young and handsome' women are viewed as natural among the Western bourgeoisie. His text can now be read as a classical example of the male gaze.

Although Malinowski convincingly encouraged an approach which privileged the everyday rather than the sensational and exotic, if not the erotic, women's experience was not seen as part of what he called 'the imponderabilia of everyday life' (1922). Women's beliefs about menstruation, pregnancy and childbirth could have been seen as ethnographically important, yet they were marginalized.

Endless debates arose within anthropology as to whether sexual intercourse was understood by the 'natives', including the Trobrianders, to be connected with reproduction. Subsequently, Leach (1969) questioned whether Malinowski's material on the Trobrianders' alleged ignorance was nothing more than a public ideology. The Trobrianders' public denial that sex before marriage ever brought pregnancy could have been investigated in other practical ways. The reference to abortion magic suggests that pregnancies before marriage might have been systematically terminated by additional physical interventions, to which magic was an accompaniment. Although Malinowski denies the widespread practice of abortion (Malinowski 1922: 168), he is not in a position to prove this. The extent to which 'the natives' whom he questioned were female is often unclear. I suggest that he systematically underestimates the Trobrianders' need to conceal abortion from a white man, given the powerful censorship which missionaries had already imposed upon sexual customs (ibid.: 218; Okely 1975b).

The sensationalist title of Malinowski's (1929) book may have been addressed to a wider readership, but it had negative repercussions within the academy. At Cambridge University, the library copy was locked away after publication and only made available to postgraduates after special written permission from the appropriate professor (E. Leach pers. comm.) Thus, even this limited and somewhat androcentric study of sexuality was considered too controversial for scholarly enlightenment and further research within the academic canon. Decades later, it was an inadequate source for the understanding of women's bodily and sexual experiences in another culture.

WOMEN AS SUBJECTS OR OBJECTS

Up to the late 1970s (for exceptions see S. Ardener 1975b), and generally until the late 1980s, sexuality, if ever broached in the British anthropological academy, was more likely to be seen from masculine perspectives. Just as in Malinowski's texts women were less likely to be seen as subjects, and more likely as objects, so the same can be found in Lévi-Strauss. His celebrated discussion of a difficult childbirth (Lévi-Strauss 1967) concentrates on the role of the male shaman rather than the experience of the mother in labour. There was little study of women based on their accounts, interests and experience, in relation to sexuality and other issues. Edwin Ardener, in a now much quoted passage, noted that:

At the level of 'observation' in fieldwork, the behaviour of women has, of course, like that of men been exhaustively plotted ... When we come to that second or 'meta' level of fieldwork ... that social anthropologists really depend upon to give conviction to their interpretations, there is a real imbalance. We are for practical purposes in a male world.

(E. Ardener 1975: 1–2)

In some rare cases, especially in the work of the numerical minority of women anthropologists, women were treated as subjects or as active agents; their specific experience and standpoint were explored. Kaberry (1939) and Richards (1956) were among these exceptional examples. Nevertheless, even Richards's innovative focus on girls' initiation rites excluded the voiced experience of the neophytes. Douglas has never explicitly identified herself with feminist issues, but her attention to the daily practicalities associated, for example, with hygiene (Douglas 1966) reveals an eye for the detail of practices often associated with 'feminized' experience, such as domestic cleaning.

Earlier, Margaret Mead's pioneering work on aspects of gender identity, adolescent sexuality and child care (1928; 1935; 1949) was pilloried for her popular and proselytizing style. She was marginalized. 'Instead of making what she perceived as the male world of academia her focus, Mead made a conscious decision to centre her professional life at New York City's American Museum of Natural History, where she remained for almost fifty years' (Yans-Mclaughlin 1989: 252). Few of the questions she raised about gender issues were followed through in the years ensuing her publications.

Within the anthropological academy, these questions had to await the renewed enthusiasms and delayed effects of the Women's Movement upon social anthropology and a new generation of mainly women researchers (Rosaldo and Lamphere 1974; Reiter 1975; S. Ardener 1975a). These pioneering edited collections entirely from women (with the exception of E. Ardener 1975), were mainly the work of researchers without tenured positions. Rosaldo and Lamphere, it was said, were encouraged to waive their royalties, as it was suggested that the book would have only limited circulation. The articles in these pioneering volumes raised preliminary questions from the margins of the discipline.

Although these publications have subsequently been read and referred to widely, both within anthropology and across disciplines, and have been frequently reprinted, they neither reached nor were addressed to a popular readership. In the long run, their theories and ethnographies have percolated through other more popularist texts. Earlier, it was the less theoretically innovative books outside academia which reached the wider readership.

GENDERED INSTITUTIONS

While institutionalized androcentricism at the apex of the discipline may still exist, its implications in the 1970s were especially acute. Gender issues were being raised in the then ferment of feminist political circles, but anthropology was initially somewhat detached from these concerns. The tendency to universalize from only masculinist gendered perspectives (and from middle-class hetero-sexual ones) may in part be explained by the predominance of men at the research level. As social anthropology expanded as an under-graduate degree subject, it attracted a predominance of women students. This sex ratio continues to be reflected in most of the social sciences and the arts or humanities. Unlike science, where the majority of both staff and students are male, in the majority of other disciplines women students outnumber men, but again staff and the research elite are predominantly male. A specific example is available in British social anthropology.

A study (Barker 1978; Caplan 1978) in the 1970s over five years of the three main colleges at London University teaching social anthropology (the London School of Economics, University College and the School of Oriental and African Studies) revealed that 60 per cent of those gaining 'bachelor' degrees were women. Of those gaining 'master's' degrees, 52 per cent were women. From then on, the gender proportions were reversed: of those gaining doctorates, only 36 per cent were women, while 64 per cent were men. Among research staff, only 23 per cent were women (Caplan 1978: 547). The proportion of women anthropology lecturers was less than 10 per cent and, in the mid-1970s, there was only one woman as a full Professor of social anthropology in the entire United Kingdom. This was consistent with the overall invisibility of women in *all* subjects, i.e. science and the arts as well as the social sciences, in the mid-1970s: 'The proportion of university teachers who are women drops...to 9 per cent...women academics tend to be concentrated in the lower grades...only 1 per cent of professors are women' (Blackstone 1976: 207).

The reversal in gender proportions from undergraduate to research and professional practitioner is replicated in the relationship between reader and writer. The majority of the readers of key anthropological texts have tended to be female, while the majority of the anthropological writers have been male. Undergraduate enthusiasm for the study of social anthropology and other cultures has been found to be disproportionately among women.

When, in the early 1970s, women readers, both inside and outside the anthropological academy, sought alternative gendered information about other cultures, anthropology was not in a position to elucidate. Anne Oakley's *Sex, Gender and Society* (1972), a scholarly and multi-disciplinary overview which had scoured the available anthropological literature, was the nearest to answering questions about the construction of gender in other cultures. Significantly, it had emerged from a doctorate in sociology, where she had also found that women took 'the insubstantial form of ghosts, shadows or stereotyped characters' (1974: 1).

SUBORDINATION AND EVOLUTION AS POPULARIST ISSUES

A woman's contestation of male domination in evolution emerged as a riposte to Morris's androcentric and populist account, *The Naked Ape* (Morris 1967). In *The Descent of Woman* (1972), Elaine Morgan, a playwright and journalist with no known qualifications in anthropology, argued that *Homo sapiens* had evolved from the sea and that, once, females had been dominant. Influenced by a marine biologist, Alister Hardy, her utopian reconstruction (Morgan 1972: 30) of the past had similarities with feminist science fiction. Given the groundswell of new feminist interest, the text found its way into a first-year course on physical anthropology at an English university in the late 1970s. It was a popularist route to engaging female students with sociobiology rather than with feminist social theory.

Another text which reassessed gender hierarchy, the question of women's subordination and its possible causes, was provided by a woman anthropologist who had worked for years on the margins. While the few women anthropologists (Rosaldo and Lamphere 1974; Reiter 1975) with a first tentative toe-hold in the academy were debating the causes of women's subordination, without being able to point to an egalitarian or matriarchal past, Evelyn Reed offered the vision of an ancient and universal matriarchy. *Woman's Evolution* (Reed 1975) was the product of over twenty years of research. The extent to which it was produced outside debates in institutionalized social anthropology is exemplified by her uncritical comments on 'some savage groups in modern times' who 'still fail to make the distinction' between themselves and animals (ibid.: 274). Lévi-Strauss's influential *Totemism* (1962) seems to have passed her by. Similarly, Reed revealed a pre-Malinowskian theoretical perspective which still sought to explain customs in terms of their origins and as 'decayed forms' or as 'a vestige of its more ancient symbolism' (Reed 1975: 260).

Reed's work appealed to women readers outside contemporary anthropology as a massively detailed *Golden Bough* of women's activities in pre-literate societies. Certainly, Engels was being re-read sympathetically by the Women's Movement for his early association between gender divisions and the mode of production (Delmar 1976). Nevertheless, to the new generation of women anthropologists, Reed's thesis was considered to be an unconvincing reiteration of Engels's thesis that associated the subordination of women solely with the rise of private property, and which argued for a prior existence of gender equality. In Reed there are claims for an original matriarchy. So detached was Reed from the academy that she found herself out of tune with the emerging feminist anthropologists of the mid-1970s, describing them as having being 'brainwashed' when they presented her with evidence of female subordination even in hunting and gathering societies.

At a meeting at Durham University in the late 1970s which I attended, when Reed presented her matriarchal thesis, the response among the non-anthropological women in the audience was close to that of Christian revivalists as they grasped at this vision of a previous matriarchal utopia. Scepticism expressed by both male and female anthropologists was summarily dismissed. Some feminist sociologists on the fringes of the academy then developed her material and amplified Engels. They were invited by liberal male lecturers to address an alternative seminar in Durham.[1]

Reed's arguments were more original and grounded when she challenged popular and androcentric texts which used animal studies to argue that women were naturally subordinate (1978). The leap from observations and interpretations of animals and insects to Western humans proved highly appealing to many non-feminists. Fatalistic, innate and universalist explanations for domination of some categories of humans over others vied with women's search for non-universalist alternatives in other human cultures, rather than among animals.

Reed's critique of Ardrey, Lorenz and Morris challenged both the

assumptions of innate human aggression and their wholesale generalizations about gender, race and class divisions (Reed 1978). Implicitly,
in challenging the biological basis to gender difference, she also
engaged in notions of the sexed body. Morris, Reed argued, 'pumps sex
into his sexist book by devoting many pages to spicy accounts of the
private parts and private lives of primate females and the kind of erotic
stimuli that move naked apes into their body-to-body contacts' (ibid.:
70–1). In this popularist publication by Morris (1967), there is the
now familiar voyeuristic treatment of sexuality. Both women and
animals are treated as titillating objects for the male gaze and male
reader.

Reed challenged the work of popularist writers who, in contrast to
her own training, had very little anthropological education, but who
used the label 'anthropologist' to help legitimate their theories.
Feminist anthropologists within the academy have subsequently felt
free to explore socio-biology and primatology from an alternative and
rigorously academic perspective, using the intellectual traditions of
anthropology against sexism (Haraway 1989, Sperling 1991). There
were also earlier forays (Slocum 1975).

BODILY AND SOCIAL REPRODUCTION

I present three examples which addressed, in a popularized fashion in
the mid-1970s, aspects of women's sexuality or bodily reproduction
and child care. All remain in print in the early 1990s.

Menstruation

The Wise Wound: Menstruation and Everywoman by Penelope Shuttle and
her partner Peter Redgrove (1978) was the authors' first work of non-
fiction. They had previously published novels and poetry. Redgrove,
with a degree in Natural Sciences, worked as a research scientist and
scientific journalist. They acknowledge the influence of Layard,
anthropologist and psychoanalyst (see MacClancy 1986) with whom
Redgrove studied in the late 1960s. While strongly Jungian, the work
is not classified by the publishers as a psychology text, but is instead
located within sociology and anthropology. The links with either of
the latter subjects are somewhat tenuous. However, the work aims to
answer some of the questions sought from other cultures by women in
the 1970s, in this case the search for some universal, pan-cultural
meaning to menstruation, 'a blessing or a curse?' (Shuttle and

Redgrove 1978: 13). It addresses what is seen as a conspiracy of silence.
'It will, we hope, encourage women to ask these questions themselves,
and to begin building up a body of information which is about what
women actually experience and not what they are told they should
experience by doctrinaire authority' (ibid.: 13).

The authors drew attention to the neglect of writing and
attention to:

> Two of the most basic experiences in human life . . . Both of these
> belong to feminine experience. One is the experience of bearing a
> child, and the child's experience of its mother in being born; and the
> other is the woman's experience of herself during menstruation.
>
> (ibid.: 16)

They argue that it should be up to a woman herself to determine her
'own labour experience' (ibid.: 17) as well as her wishes towards the
experience of menstruation. Through the mass of cross-cultural
examples, the authors thus appeal to a search for women's bodily
self-determination.

As with other texts which appeal to a non-specialist readership, the
material is not necessarily simplified. The work is packed with
detailed, near encyclopaedic data, mainly from Western historical
sources, folklore and psychoanalytical literature, although hostile to
Freud. There are references to anthropologists, especially those of the
pre-fieldwork generations, such as Briffault, but also to E. Ardener,
Benedict, Buxton, La Fontaine, Skultans (a rare article [1970] on
menstruation practices in Britain) and Turner. The ethnographic
material in *The Wise Wound* is rarely discussed in a rounded social
context, whether or not it was originally so presented in the few
anthropological studies cited.

For an anthropologist reader, used to a specific theoretical
organization of empirical material, the text becomes increasingly
bewildering with the accumulation of examples. The organizing
argument, when it can be identified, appeals to universalist assumptions which are thoroughly ethnocentric. The authors look to something beyond the prevailing hegemony of a predominantly
technological society. Readers are invited to escape the *status quo* by
affirming an underlying, lost set of beliefs or power. Other cultures are
referred to in so far as they support the theme of Western malaise.

The major appeal is to the Western woman reader looking to
subjective experience and to her own body for mystical answers to
depression, especially that apparently related to pre-menstrual tension

or powerlessness. The prologue is explicitly addressed to a female reader, in that the authors suggest that 'This implies a change of attitude towards and a reassessment of *one's* femininity' (ibid.: 14; my emphasis).

The underlying assumptions in the text presume a universal and essential 'feminine' and an unproblematized link between all women and the biology of bodily process. Contrary to cross-cultural examples, the authors argue that 'witchcraft is the natural concern of all women ... the natural craft of all women ... because witchcraft is the subjective experience of the menstrual cycle' (ibid.: 209). The authors assert that a creative process of 'descent and return ... was learnt by the women from their first menstrual cycle and imparted to their male partners who have taken it for their own and forgotten their teachers' (ibid.: 274). Thus the anti-biologism of feminist and Women's Liberation writing was overridden. In the hands of these authors, the resurgent interest in the female body moves from the material to a mystical and ahistorical universalism. While the text makes use of other cultures, the potential answers from social anthropology are largely absent.

The book was marketed for the wider non-academic readership. The cover suggests that it tackles:

> a subject that has been forbidden for centuries. It is the first study of its kind, and in unveiling taboos both ancient and modern, it will change the way women – and men – view themselves. The journal *Psychology Today* [quoted without reference] suggested that 'It could bring about a major change in our understanding of the sexes.'
>
> (1978 cover)

A quote from *The Observer*, also reproduced for marketing purposes, captures the inherent Frazerian tradition and gives anthropological legitimacy: 'An Aladdin's cave of scientific, psychological and anthropological insights ... all quite irresistible' (ibid.).

Birth

The study of the experience of childbirth by women, called for by Shuttle and Redgrove, was addressed by Kitzinger in a number of publications. *Women as Mothers* (Kitzinger 1978) made extensive use of cross-cultural examples, in this case to challenge the notion that the modern Western experience was ideal or essential.[2]

The book is presented and 'marketed' as challenging any innateness of maternal instincts. The underlying theme is to demonstrate through multiple cross-cultural examples that maternity can be different. There are also echoes of Mead in Kitzinger's contrast between cultural practices in America and the 'African bush', in this instance of childbirth rather than adolescent sexuality.

Kitzinger was registered for a higher degree in social anthropology at a British university in the 1960s. She had been inspired by a visit by Margaret Mead, who 'validated what I wanted to do' (Kitzinger pers. comm. 1995). She says that she found it difficult for her thesis topic on 'Pregnancy, birth and motherhood in Jamaica' to 'be accepted as a "valid" subject'. She had strong support from one male examiner. But such topics, she claims in an interview years later, were generally regarded 'as female trivia . . . women's networks were not seen as relevant' (ibid.). Certainly, among the subsequent generation of women postgraduates, of which I was one, the belief – right or wrong – was that topics like childbirth were considered inappropriate for a doctorate. Women anthropology postgraduates of the early 1970s, both in the UK and the USA (Jane Szurek pers. comm.), had the impression that they had to prove their ability by studying areas and topics classically validated as gender free, or in effect 'masculine'.

There is critical irony in Kitzinger's genderized observations about choices of topic:

> Anthropologists do not write much about birth – possibly because they are usually men and are not permitted to take part in the rituals surrounding labour. They have, however, written so extensively about the disposal of the placenta that one might be forgiven for believing that this must be one of the most important rites in primitive and peasant childbirth.
>
> (Kitzinger 1978: 105)

Kitzinger presents the image of the male anthropologist, waiting outside the birth hut to take notes when the placenta is brought out for disposal. I find her observations confirmed in Malinowski's discussion of childbirth. He can write little about the experience of birth, but gives relatively detailed comments on the afterbirth (Malinowski 1932: 195–6).

Kitzinger makes a general point about the anthropological neglect of 'the private world' of women:

> Anthropologists have tended to discuss women as objects involved

in transactions between social groups and to see society largely in terms of relations between men, referring to women only when they affect men's behaviour. In Evans-Pritchard's brilliant studies of the Nuer of the Sudan, women come into the books rather less often than cows.

(Kitzinger 1978: 13–14)

Kitzinger is acutely aware of the belittling by the canon of the cultural anthropology of Mead. She quotes Evans-Pritchard's paternalistic comments on the popularizing style of *Coming of Age in Samoa* (Mead 1928): 'a discursive, or perhaps I should say chatty and feminine book ... Nevertheless, it is ... written by a highly intelligent woman' (Evans-Pritchard 1951, cited in Kitzinger 1978: 14). In this way, Kitzinger invites the reader to notice the explicit gender marking of style and author in the male commentary and canon.

That childbirth 'is a cultural act in which spontaneous physiological processes operate within a context of customs' (Kitzinger 1978: 105) is a major organizing argument. Given the earlier biologistic texts, and despite the work of de Beauvoir and Mead, this would still have been a relatively novel approach to non-social-science readers. As with de Beauvoir before her (see Okely 1986), there is sometimes the tendency towards universalisms (Kitzinger 1978: 80).

At the time, they had a didactic worth and appealed to women readers looking for both similarities and differences with other women (cf. Okely 1986). Kitzinger engagingly moves from universalisms to examples selected for their exotic contrast with anything Western:

In parts of East Africa ... a woman who is having a long and arduous labour may have her vagina packed with cow dung. It is an act which has significance in pastoral societies where the main economic value is cattle. The dung is meant to encourage the birth of the child by letting it smell how wealthy the father is.

(Kitzinger 1978: 109)

Women as Mothers is consistent with the popularist style of producing a mass of cross-cultural examples, often extracted from the total ethnographic context. The experience of maternity is examined chronologically, commencing with an awareness of the Women's Movement within which there was 'ambiguity in the approach to motherhood. It represents for some a biological trap ... and for others an opportunity for achieving something which a man manifestly cannot do' (ibid.: 47). The examples confirm women's ambivalences, adding a cross-cultural dimension to the then Euro–American ethnocentricity of some feminist texts.

In contrast to other popularist texts, there are some references to the few anthropological texts about and by women anthropologists at the time, e.g. Woolf (1972), du Boulay (1974), Ortner (1974), and Rosaldo and Lamphere (1974). But in the mid-1970s, especially for a woman then writing on the fringes of the anthropological academy, there was little opportunity for an overall theoretical perspective. The sociologist Anne Oakley's anti-biologistic discussion of maternity and use of cross-cultural examples (Oakley 1972) is not referred to. This is another indication of the isolated context then of feminist social scientists.[3]

The cover of *Women as Mothers* draws attention to the current malaise:

> At a time when mothers in the West feel their role as an increasingly challenged and difficult one... Sheila Kitzinger shows that maternal behaviour, far from being inborn and unchanging, is a direct response to the society the mother lives in... Conception, pregnancy and childbirth itself are surrounded by quite different kinds of ritual and expectation.
>
> (Kitzinger 1978 cover)

Kitzinger's text lived up to the popularist expectations at the time. Other cultures were seen to provide critical alternatives for Western women readers.

Child care

Liedloff's *The Continuum Concept* (1975) addressed a need to examine other cultures for utopian answers to questions about child care in the industrial or post-industrial capitalist West. Again, the legitimacy of anthropology is invoked in this publication and, like Shuttle and Redgrove, the author has no qualifications in the discipline. The Penguin paperback edition classifies the work under sociology and anthropology. Quotes of approval come from five men, including professionals such as Leboyer and the psychiatrist Storr, but no anthropologists. Connections with anthropology are invoked simply because tropical forest Indians as exotic others are the object of study.

Liedloff's career, as a university dropout, artist and poet who turned down the offer to model for Dior, is vicariously appealing to the general woman reader. On a trip to Florence, she met by chance two

Italians who invited her to Venezuela to hunt for diamonds. After such an expedition, and acquaintance with some Tauripan Indians, she was inspired to spend more time with the latter.

She increasingly focused on their child care. She describes the Indian practices, and identifies the 'in-arms phase' during which, until babies can crawl, they are in continual physical contact with the mother. There are some detailed observed incidents of the Indians' daily life in relation to children. But these are detached from an ethnography of the total context. The Indians, who have machetes, are persistently described by the term 'Stone Age'; the presumption is that they have had no independent history and that they are vestiges of early 'Man'. The Indians are represented as having no hang-ups, no word for work, no competitiveness. Their rituals are described ethnocentrically in the following way:

> Ritual is another form of relief from the burden of choice-making. One's mental state is very like that of an infant or another species of animal. During the ritual, especially if one has an active part, such as dancing or chanting, the organism is run under a flag far older than that of the intellect.
>
> (ibid.: 136)

The text is full of evolutionists' theories and uncritical comparisons with primate behaviour, more specifically with the monkeys whom the author had as occasional pets in the woods. Lorenz's theory of 'imprinting' on the part of geese makes its appearance. There is no awareness that other non-Western cultures may have a multiplicity of different forms of child care. Although some comparisons are made with another group, these Indians are not compared with other non-Western groups elsewhere in the world. It is implied that they are the embodiment of all non-Western others.

The main advice transposed from the tropical forest is that Western mothers should continuously hold their babies during the 'in-arms phase':

> Once a mother realises that seeing that her baby is carried about for the first six or eight months will ensure his self reliance . . . even her self-interest will tell her not to spare herself the 'trouble' of carrying him while she is doing her housework or shopping . . . once a mother begins to serve her baby's continuum (and thus her own as a

mother), the culturally confused instinct in her will reassert itself and reconnect her natural motives.

(ibid.: 155, 156)

Liedloff has to answer the problem of women's work outside the home. The mother is exhorted not to do it:

> very often these jobs are matter of choice; the mothers could, if they realised the urgency of their presence during the baby's first year, give up the job in order to avert the deprivations which would damage the baby's entire life.

(ibid.: 156)

There is no suggestion that fathers could be a substitute. Where a mother 'must work', babysitters are advised to hold the baby on their laps while watching television or doing homework. Again, it is presumed that all carers, even in the case of grandparents, should be female.

There are some quite forceful directives:

> Holding a baby while doing housework is a matter of practice . . . Dusting and vacuum cleaning can be done mainly by one hand. Bedmaking will be a little more difficult, but a resourceful mother will find a way . . . Cooking is largely a matter of keeping one's body between the cooker and the baby when there is danger of splashing.

(ibid.: 156–7)

There is no recognition of the problems a mother might face if she has to watch over other children, perhaps toddlers, at the same time.

In contrast to the new feminist concerns to describe and to make visible domestic activities as exploited, unpaid labour (Oakley 1974), Liedloff lumps cooking and cleaning with 'walking and talking with friends', and advises mothers, 'It would help immeasurably if we could see baby care as a non activity. We should learn to regard it as nothing to do' (Liedloff 1975: 157). Baby care is reduced to nappy-changing and breast-feeding. Bathing the baby can apparently be done alongside the mother.

Whereas Kitzinger had pointed to the ambivalences in the Women's Movement towards the institution of motherhood, Liedloff is uncompromising towards any new ambivalence or challenge to the *status quo*. Not only are mothers made to feel guilty for working outside their home, but their time and personal space must be entirely baby-centred. A new, more refined perfectionism is asked of mothers in the name of the natural. The female body which gives birth is now to be linked without a break for several years to the growing baby. The father's body is not recruited likewise for care. Liedloff's ideal mother depends entirely on the earnings of a husband who, whether in that role or as a father, is largely absent from her text and programme. Here the mother's bodily and economic autonomy is subordinated entirely to the infant and to the male earner.

In effect, the main themes and messages of Liedloff's book resurrect the 1950s Bowlby thesis (Bowlby 1951): that mothers should remain at all times with their offspring. Bowlby is one of the few writers referred to at length (Leidloff 1975: 80–1). De Beauvoir's resistance (1949) to maternity and her critique of domestic labour is unmentioned. The gender division of labour is never questioned. Predictably, the language has no self-consciousness of gender. The baby is always referred to as male. Thus the elementary questions of the new feminism and existing gender scholarship are passed over. The primitive other is used selectively by Liedloff to reaffirm the Western patriarchal nuclear family. Any search by women readers for alternatives to gender asymmetry re-exposed by the Women's Movement is answered by a new orthodoxy disguised as a liberation from modern capitalism.

CONCLUSION

In the late 1960s and the early 1970s, gender divisions were challenged by the Women's Liberation Movement. The so-called Swinging Sixties, with greater sexual licence, were experienced ambivalently by women, who began to question the extent to which they were being treated as objects rather than subjects. Women began to investigate the political in the personal, to seek for specificities in sexed bodies, and for experiences which might be associated with their gender. Consciousness-raising groups encouraged the recognition of similarities as well as possible differences. There was a curiosity about female bodies, female heterosexualities, maternity and child care. If alternatives might be found in other non-Western cultures, what was once thought to be natural could be unmasked as contingently social and cultural.

Social anthropology was not in a strong and informed position to provide the ethnography and answers to these questions, either within the academy or for a popular readership. First, such genderized areas had hardly been studied by the mainly masculinist academic hegemony. Women anthropologists at postdoctoral level and with academic power were a tiny minority and had not been encouraged to examine genderized issues. Second, any gender research in progress was understandably addressed to the academic community. Feminist anthropologists had to legitimate their research in erudite language and presentation. The long-popular Frazerian tradition of presenting bits and pieces from other cultures out of total ethnographic context was no longer the theoretical priority within the discipline. Some women experimented with this on the fringes of the academy.

Shuttle and Redgrove drew on aspects of anthropology as incidental adornment to their arguments. Eurocentric Jungian universals were the organizing principles to their varied historical and non-Western examples. The 'Feminine' was understood as pan-cultural and universal. The unproblematized biological fact of menstruation among females was appealed to as a source of mystical power. The varying cultural perceptions and constructions of the female physiology were not addressed. The woman reader, in a time of cultural change and critique in the 1970s, was encouraged to see menstruation and aspects of female bodies as an escape from worldly powerlessness.

Kitzinger, with postgraduate experience in social anthropology, by contrast used the many examples of maternity from other cultures to show its cultural rather than any essentialist biological context. She treated the reader as female and invited her to think about alternatives. Both implicitly and explicitly, there was a critique of the technologized and dominant Euro–American view of birth. Her agenda was non-directive, in contrast to that of Liedloff, whose use of one non-Western culture resulted in a reaffirmation of the Western patriarchal nuclear family, in conjunction with new bodily constraints upon a mother. The example of Liedloff reveals how critical questions raised by the Women's Movement were also open to re-appropriation by the prevailing Western ideology. Moreover, the gender of the writer does not guarantee any specific gendered standpoint. It cannot of course be presumed that any woman anthropologist may be an expert on or even interested in gender (E. Ardener 1975). But a critical mass of women anthropologists in positions of academic and intellectual authority has innovative consequences.

Subsequently, feminism has had greater influence within social anthropology. Whereas in the 1960s or 1970s women anthropologists had to conceal their feminist or gender interests to examination and appointment boards, since the late 1980s the concept of gender has almost become gentrified.

Despite some contributions in Britain and the USA in the 1970s by a few women anthropologists (La Fontaine 1972; Paul 1974; S. Ardener 1975b; Faithorn 1975; Okely 1975a; Rubin 1975; Callaway 1978; Hastrup 1978; Hirschon 1978), it was only in the late 1980s that sexuality and the related experience of women as sexual and reproductive subjects have been recognized as academically acceptable topics.[4] Questions of sexuality and gender in reproduction are now the subject of new, fertile research: for example, Caplan (1987) and, to some extent, Ortner and Whitehead (1981). Martin's detailed monograph (1987) exposes Western medical textbooks on menstruation, reproductive organs and the management of birth as culturally specific and androcentric. Detailed anthropological texts on menstruation cross-culturally have emerged (Buckley and Gottlieb 1988; Gottlieb 1990; Marcus 1992). Strathern (1992) has unravelled the legal presumptions in reproductive technology, showing them to be ethnocentric rather than scientifically neutral.

Sexuality, the gendered body, the gendered division of labour, and an attention to gendered voices and experiences, masculine and feminine, are now part of some academic agendas. Nonetheless, there are areas of sexuality which remain controversial, as women and some men have extended their anthropological gaze to masculine sexuality, especially heterosexuality (Arnold 1978; Cornwall 1994; Hart 1994).

There continues to be a populist demand for overall and daring overviews, something which anthropologists, trained in micro-studies, have been reluctant to attempt. Consequently, the ethno-graphies of anthropologists may be raided, especially when approaching the ever-sensationalist areas of sexuality. *Sex and Destiny*, Greer's dense and mass-marketed tome on sex and fertility (1986), invited readers to consider alternative non-Western forms of birth control and female circumcision from a culturally relativist perspective.[5] Greer, like her cohort of feminists now confronting middle age, found a paucity of literature on yet another taboo subject of women's sexuality, the menopause (Greer 1991). Here there is less use of cross-cultural material, partly because even the earlier reporters of exotic erotica lacked any consideration of this topic. This absence of material is possibly because menopause has been thought to be about the loss of female sexuality, not just fertility, and therefore only of concern to the subjects who experience it, rather than to those male subjects who perceive women primarily as sexual objects.

In the context of the 1990s, in a different political and economic climate, populist demands from women readers about other cultures will inevitably have changed. The extent to which women wish to popularize gendered anthropological research from within the discipline remains open to question. In any case, gendered research continues to be affected by institutional structures. Even in the 1990s, the majority of undergraduates, whose task it is to read the academic publications, are largely female, yet women researchers relative to men are still grossly under-represented, and the proportion of women in university positions in British social anthropology remains minuscule. Women, whatever their research interests and standpoints, are still not writing half, let alone the majority, of academic anthropological texts.[6]

NOTES

1 The one woman sociologist in the department, Ruth First, joined me in scepticism. Her pioneering work and political struggle, which eventually led to her assassination, embraced the analysis of sexuality, racist, gender and class divisions in apartheid South Africa.
2 In the late 1970s, I found it a useful addition to my reading list.
3 Oakley's *Sex, Gender and Society* (1972) was published under the auspices of *New Society* rather than via academic publishers.
4 Moore's overview (1986) does not address questions of sexuality and the body, despite the literature by then available.
5 It was hailed by Fay Weldon in *The Times* as one of the greatest books of the twentieth century, to be compared to Marx's *Das Kapital*.
6 Julie Marcus puts it more starkly: 'Today, the major arguments within the discipline of anthropology remain arguments among men and about men, arguments about the matters men consider important; those matters remain those of the past – relations between men' (Marcus 1992: viii).

REFERENCES

Abramson, A. (1993) 'Between Autobiography and Method: Being Male, Seeing Myth and the Analysis of Structures of Gender and Sexuality in the Eastern Interior of Fiji', in D. Bell, P. Caplan and W. J. Karim (eds) *Gendered Fields*, London: Routledge.
Ardener, E. (1975) 'Belief and the Problem of Women', in S. Ardener (ed.) *Perceiving Women*, London: Malaby.
Ardener, S. (ed.) (1975a) *Perceiving Women*, London: Malaby.
—— (1975b) 'Sexual Insult and Female Militancy', in S. Ardener (ed.) *Perceiving Women*, London: Malaby.
Arnold, K. (1978) 'The Whore in Peru', in S. Lipshitz (ed.) *Tearing the Veil*, London: Routledge and Kegan Paul.
Barker, D. (1978) 'Women in the Anthropology Profession – 1', in R.

Rohrlich-Leavitt (ed.) *Women Cross-culturally. Change and Challenge*, The Hague: Mouton.

de Beauvoir, S. (1949) *Le Deuxième Sexe*, Paris: Gallimard. English edition, (1972) *The Second Sex*, trans. H. Parshley, Harmondsworth: Penguin.

—— (1965) *Force of Circumstance* (translation), Harmondsworth: Penguin.

Blackstone, T. (1976) 'The Education of Girls Today,' in J. Mitchell and A. Oakley (eds) *The Rights and Wrongs of Women*, Harmondsworth: Penguin.

du Boulay, J. (1974) *Portrait of a Greek Mountain Village*, Oxford: Oxford University Press.

Bloch, M. (1983) *Marxism and Anthropology*, Oxford: Clarendon Press.

Bowlby, J. (1951) *Maternal Care and Mental Health*, World Health Organisation.

Buckley, T. and Gottlieb, A. (eds) (1988) *Blood Magic: The Anthropology of Menstruation*, Berkeley: University of California Press.

Callaway, H. (1978) '"The Most Essentially Female Function of All": Giving Birth', in S. Ardener (ed.) *Defining Females*, London: Croom Helm.

Caplan, P. (1978) 'Women in the Anthropology Profession – 2', in R. Rohrlich-Leavitt (ed.) *Women Cross-culturally. Change and Challenge*, The Hague: Mouton.

—— (ed.) (1987) *The Cultural Construction of Sexuality*, London: Routledge.

Cornwall, A. (1994) 'Gendered Identities and Gender Ambiguity among *Travestis* in Salvador Brazil', in A. Cornwall and N. Lindisfarne (eds) *Dislocating Masculinity*, London: Routledge.

Delmar, R. (1976) 'Looking again at Engels's *Origin of the Family, Private Property and the State*', in J. Mitchell and A. Oakley (eds) *The Rights and Wrongs of Women*, Harmondsworth: Penguin.

The Diagram Group, (1977) *Woman's Body: An Owner's Manual*, London: Paddington Press.

Douglas, M. (1966) *Purity and Danger*, London: Routledge and Kegan Paul.

Evans-Pritchard, E. (1951) *Theories of Primitive Religion*, Oxford: Oxford University Press.

Faithorn, E. (1975) 'The Concept of Pollution among the Kafe of the Papua New Guinea Highlands', in R. Reiter (ed.) *Toward an Anthropology of Women*, New York, London: Monthly Review Press.

Gottlieb, A. (1990) 'Rethinking Female Pollution: The Beng Case (Côte d'Ivoire)', in P. Reeves Sanday and R. Gallagher Goodenough (eds) *Beyond the Second Sex*, Philadelphia: University of Pennsylvania Press.

Greer, G. (1986) *Sex and Destiny: The Politics of Human Fertility*, New York: Harper and Row.

—— (1991) *The Change*, London: Hamish Hamilton.

Haraway, D. (1989) *Primate Visions*, New York: Routledge.

Hastrup, K. (1978) 'The Semantics of Biology: Virginity', in S. Ardener (ed.) *Defining Females*, London: Croom Helm.

Hart, A. (1994) 'Missing Masculinity? Prostitutes' Clients in Alicante, Spain', in A. Cornwall and N. Lindisfarne (eds) *Dislocating Masculinity*, London: Routledge.

Hirschon, R. (1978) 'Open Body/Closed Space: The Transformation of Female Sexuality', in S. Ardener (ed.) *Defining Females*, London: Croom Helm.

Kaberry, P. (1939) *Aboriginal Woman: Sacred and Profane*, London: Routledge and Kegan Paul.

Kitzinger, S. (1978) *Women as Mothers*, London: Fontana.

Kulick, D. and Willson, M. (1995) *Taboo: Sex, Identity and Erotic Subjectivity in Anthropological Fieldwork*, London: Routledge.

La Fontaine, J. S. (1972) 'Ritualization of Women's Life-crises in Bugisu', in J. S. La Fontaine (ed.) *The Interpretation of Ritual*, London: Tavistock.

Leach. E. (1969) 'Virgin Birth', in *Genesis as Myth*, London: Cape.

Lévi-Strauss, C. (1963) *Totemism* (translation), Harmondsworth: Penguin.

—— (1967) 'The Effectiveness of Symbols', in *Structural Anthropology* vol. 1. (trans. 1968), London: Allen Lane.

Liedloff, J. (1975) *The Continuum Concept*, London: Duckworth.

MacClancy, J. (1986) 'Unconventional Character and Disciplinary Convention: John Layard, Jungian and Anthropologist', in G. Stocking (ed.) *Malinowski, Rivers, Benedict and Others*, Madison: University of Wisconsin.

Malinowski, B. (1922) *The Argonauts of the Western Pacific*, London: Routledge and Kegan Paul.

—— (1929) *The Sexual Life of Savages*, London: Routledge and Kegan Paul. (1932 edition referred to in text).

—— (1967) *A Diary in the Strict Sense of the Term*, London: Routledge and Kegan Paul.

Marcus, J. (1992) *A World of Difference: Islam and Gender Hierarchy in Turkey*, London: Zed Press.

Martin, E. (1987) *The Woman in the Body*, Boston: Beacon Press.

Mead, M. (1928) *Coming of Age in Samoa*, Harmondsworth: Penguin.

—— (1935) *Sex and Temperament in Three Primitive Societies*, Harmondsworth: Penguin.

—— (1949) *Male and Female*, Harmondsworth: Penguin.

Moore, H. (1988) *Feminism and Anthropology*, Cambridge: Polity Press.

Morgan, E. (1972) *The Descent of Woman*, London: Souvenir Press.

Morris, D. (1967) *The Naked Ape*, New York: Dell Publishers.

Oakley, A. (1972) *Sex, Gender and Society*, London: Temple Smith.

—— (1974) *The Sociology of Housework*, London: Martin Robertson.

Oakley, A. and Mitchell, J. (1976) 'Introduction' to J. Mitchell and A. Oakley (eds) *The Rights and Wrongs of Women*, Harmondsworth: Penguin.

Okely, J. (1975a) 'Gypsy Women: Models in Conflict', in S. Ardener (ed.) *Perceiving Women*, London: Malaby.

—— (1975b) 'Malinowski's Interpretation of Sex and Reproduction: A Reappraisal'. Paper for the Women's Anthropology seminar, Oxford. Unpublished ms.

—— (1986) *Simone de Beauvoir; A Re-reading*, London: Virago and New York: Pantheon.

Ortner, S. (1974) 'Is Female to Male as Nature Is to Culture?', in M. Rosaldo and L. Lamphere (eds), *Woman, Culture and Society*, Stanford: Stanford University Press.

Ortner, S. and Whitehead, H. (eds), (1981) *Sexual Meanings: The Cultural Construction of Gender and Sexuality*, Cambridge: Cambridge University Press.

Our Bodies Ourselves (1976), London: Simon and Schuster.

Paul, L. (1974) 'The Mastery of Work and the Mystery of Sex in a Guatemalan Village', in M. Rosaldo and L. Lamphere (eds) *Woman, Culture and Society*, Stanford: Stanford University Press.

Reed, E. (1975) *Woman's Evolution: From Matriarchal Clan to Patriarchal Family*, London: Pathfinder.

—— (1978) *Sexism and Science*, New York, London: Pathfinder.

Reiter, R. (ed.) (1975) *Toward an Anthropology of Women*, New York, London: Monthly Review Press.

Richards, A. (1956) *Chisungu*, London: Faber and Faber.

Rosaldo, M. and Lamphere, L. (eds) (1974) *Woman, Culture and Society*, Stanford: Stanford University Press.

Rowbotham, S. (1973) *Woman's Consciousness, Man's World*, Harmondsworth: Penguin.

—— (1990) *The Past is Before Us*, Harmondsworth: Penguin.

Rubin, G. (1975) 'The Traffic in Women: Notes on the "Political Economy" of Sex', in R. Reiter (ed.) *Toward an Anthropology of Women*, New York, London: Monthly Review Press.

Shuttle, P. and Redgrove, P. (1978) *The Wise Wound: Menstruation and Everywoman*, Harmondsworth: Penguin.

Skultans, V. (1970) 'The Symbolic Significance of Menstruation and Menopause', *Man*, 5, 4: 639–51.

Slocum, S. (1975) 'Woman the Gatherer: Male Bias in Anthropology', in R. Reiter (ed.) *Toward an Anthropology of Women*, London, New York: Monthly Review Press.

Sperling, S. (1991) 'Baboons with Briefcases: Feminism, Functionalism, and Socio-biology in the Evolution of Primate Gender', *Signs* 17, 1.

Strathern, M. (1992) *Reproducing the Future*, Manchester: Manchester University Press.

Walters, M. (1978) *The Nude Male*, Harmondsworth: Penguin.

Woolf, M. (1972) *Women and the Family in Rural Taiwan*, Stanford: Stanford University Press.

Yans-Mclaughlin, V. (1989) 'Margaret Mead', in U. Gacs, A. Khan, J. McIntyre and R. Weinberg (eds) *Women Anthropologists: Selected Biographies*, Illinois: University of Illinois Press.

Chapter 10

A *bricoleur's* workshop
Writing *Les lances du crépuscule*

Philippe Descola

Nowadays everyone is aware that a text, of whatever kind, may be read independently of its author's intentions. The author's personality, the motives which shaped the work, the circumstances in which it was written, all these biographical traces count for very little in the way it will be received. Each reader will take it as they wish, reading and interpreting it according to their temperament, mood and prejudices. It is, therefore, after much hesitation that I have yielded to the editors' requests to provide a written version of the oral paper I gave on my book *Les lances du crépuscule* (Descola 1994), which was then nearing completion. I finally took this decision, not out of authorial conceit, but from an obscure wish to justify to my peers the project of writing an anthropological book 'for the general public'. The unease I felt about this undertaking in fact reveals a more general problem in the practice of anthropology: how can one explain anthropologists' reluctance to reach an audience wider than just the specialists of the discipline, when their scientific approach is based on an experience in principle open to everyone, and when their works are for the most part written in ordinary language?

The technicalities of anthropology are not such as to make the lessons we draw from the field untranslatable for the uninitiated. Besides, the pantheon of anthropology includes personalities who have belatedly but swiftly acquired the rudiments of a profession which we still manage to teach to astute minds in two or three years. The greatest physicists of this century have not felt this sense of propriety towards popularization. Their most successful popular works well show that a passionate vocation combined with a poetic sense of metaphor can enable a large number of people to appreciate the interest of an area of research normally inaccessible without a substantial training in mathematics. Historians, who specialize like us in explicatory accounts and cultural contextualization, are not to be outdone either: the most famous among them have known how to draw a huge public audience, without at the same time abandoning the demands of rigour particular to their discipline. What, then, is the cause of this haughty attitude among anthropologists which leads us to write exclusively for the 'happy few'? Why do we discourage the very real desire of the uninitiated to share our knowledge of highly original cultures, thereby leaving the task of popularizing in the hands of those specializing in cheap trash and exoticism? Could it be that, in abandoning the comfort of our jargon and the security of the literary conventions for monographs, we would be too afraid of revealing the fragility of the scientific precepts on which our claims to truth are based?

I have embarked on this essay in order to answer this question and, in so doing, to allay my professional scruples. In analysing the reasons which led me to write *Les lances du crépuscule*, the techniques that I employed, the role attributed to the book and the way in which it might contribute to the better understanding of our profession, I proceed in the manner of an ethnographer: from a singular experience I endeavour to bring out a lesson of a more general significance. I go forward, therefore, unmasked, in a manner unusual in our profession which usually reserves confessions to the posthumous publication of field diaries.

Les lances du crépuscule is a commissioned work, the result of the meeting and reconciling of two aims. In 1980, just after my wife and I had spent nearly three years with the Achuar, a group of Jivaro Indians of the Ecuadorian Amazon, Jean Malaurie asked me to write a book for the 'Terre Humaine' series which he was in charge of at the publishing house Plon. Claude Lévi-Strauss, whose pupil I had been, recommended me. He himself had previously published *Tristes Tropiques* (1955) in this same collection. Some sixty titles strong to date, 'Terre Humaine' is a unique undertaking which, over time and despite the diversity of its authors, has come to embody in France a distinct narrative genre as well as an original, though diffuse, trend of thought. The series began in 1955 with *Les Derniers Rois de Thulé* by Jean Malaurie, and since then the series has been dedicated to exploring different aspects of *la littérature du réel* through ethnological accounts, life histories, autobiographies and travelogues. Contributions to the series are drawn as much from scholars and reputed writers as from more anonymous witnesses of both European and exotic cultures in the process of being marginalized. The coal miner from the north of France rubs shoulders with Victor Segalen, and the primary school teacher from Anatolia follows Margaret Mead. Nearly half of the titles are translations, sometimes of classics, but more often of works which had passed unnoticed when they appeared in their original language but which have gained the readership they deserve through 'Terre Humaine'. Indeed, some books have achieved phenomenal success (two million copies of *Le Cheval d'orgueil* by Pierre Jakez Hélias!), thereby contributing to the very great acclaim of the series in France – in most of the large bookshops the series is displayed in its entirety on a separate shelf – and providing strong grounds for the director of the series to impose difficult and demanding manuscripts on a large publishing house otherwise very sensitive to commercial considerations.[1]

Malaurie's proposal threw me into a state of both intense excitement and dread. I was flattered that I, a young and unknown researcher recently back from the field, had been asked to write for such a prestigious series, but at the same time I was terrified at the idea of having to have my talents measured against those of some of the greatest French anthropologists. At the time, I was writing up my doctoral thesis,[2] and ultimately what made me accept the commission from 'Terre Humaine' was the gulf I saw between the rich diversity of a still fresh ethnographic experience and the systematic exercise I was undertaking in order to obtain my professional credentials. Without repudiating in any way the value of a scientific approach which I continue to believe in, I was struck by the existence of a residue, of a wealth of meanings and personal experiences, for which the orthodox nature of my academic work offered no outlet. The conventions of monographic writing have been fixed now for more than sixty years. These rules require any ethnologists aspiring to the recognition of their peers to adopt a style of writing which they absorb very early in their careers, thanks to reading their seniors, and which they very often end up by taking as natural. The results are a certain standardization of the forms of description, the more or less exclusive use of the analytical categories recognized by the profession, and the self-imposed avoidance of the expression of too obviously subjective opinions. There is nothing in itself wrong with this for a science which aims to produce valid generalizations through the comparison of ethnographic materials drawn from widely differing cultures; one can understand that such an ambition accords with a homogeneity in the manner of presenting the facts.

By proscribing all reference to subjectivity, however, classical ethnology condemns itself to leaving in the dark what is distinctive about its approach among the other human sciences, i.e. a form of knowledge, based on the personal and continuing relationship of a particular individual with other particular individuals and which arises from a combination of circumstances that is different each time. Although this knowledge is not devoid of legitimacy, the conditions under which it is obtained are seldom made explicit to the uninitiated. Historians take care to refer to the archives they have used, which others are free to consult and to interpret differently. Sociologists describe the questionnaires and the statistical procedures which allowed them to reach their conclusions. Psychologists do not hesitate to describe at length their experimental protocols. In brief, only ethnologists consider themselves free from the obligation to explain how, on the basis of a unique experience, they have been able to arrive at a body of knowledge which they expect everyone to accept as valid. The workshop of the ethnologist is himself and his relationship with a given population, his blunders and his cunning, the tortuous development of his intuition, the situations he has found himself in by chance, the role that often unknowingly he is made to play in local politics, the friendship which ties him to the person whom he makes into his main informant, his reactions of enthusiasm, anger, or disgust – a whole complex mosaic of feelings, qualities and events which give to our 'research method' its particular character.[3] Now, it is this whole dimension of our scientific approach which the precepts of ethnographic writing force us to pass over in silence. Certainly one always finds at the start of a monograph some indications of time and place, but these lack any existential substance, and only function to establish an introductory guarantee of truth: 'I have lived in a certain village or a certain community at a certain time and, therefore, I speak with full knowledge of the facts.' Save for this standard clause, references to the conditions of fieldwork only appear in the rest of the text in allusive ways, clear enough to those who have been through similar experiences, but upon which it would be considered unseemly to dwell.

To write for 'Terre Humaine' offered an opportunity to react against this state of affairs and to try to restore to ethnological writing the subjective dimension which had been excluded by convention. I was driven in this endeavour by the assumption that our discipline could come out of the ghetto in which it had allowed itself to be shut away while remaining faithful to its primary aim; the assumption that ethnology could simultaneously instruct, edify and entertain, produce scientific results and question itself on the state of its practice, retrace a personal journey and make known all the richness of an unknown culture. It is true that this assumption rested on several remarkable precedents: the books by Lévi-Strauss, Georges Condominas, Georges Balandier or Pierre Clastres published in 'Terre Humaine' justified my project by providing proof that the expression of a personal sensibility or of a militant point of view were not incompatible with theoretical rigour. The problem, therefore, did not present itself in the form of a basic choice between *Geisteswissenschaften* and *Naturwissenschaften*, as is the case at the current time in North American anthropology, but rather a choice between modes of expression according to the topics and the intended purpose of the text. The French 'essayist' tradition has for a long time now allowed scholars to avail themselves of a double language: that of the paradigms and the concepts of their discipline, the tools of a specialized knowledge constantly being regenerated, and that of the philosophical critical implications of their work, tools for putting into perspective the values and principles which govern our behaviour. *Tristes Tropiques* (Lévi-Strauss 1955) is not in contradiction with *Les Structures élémentaires de la parenté* (Lévi-Strauss 1949), just as *L'Afrique fantôme* by Michel Leiris (1934) cannot be dissociated from the learned books which this great ethnographer has devoted to the secret language of the Dogon or to Ethiopian possession cults. The two kinds of books are necessary, and it takes some naivety to believe, after the fashion of the disciples of postmodernity, that the former will survive long after the disappearance of the latter.

It was with these ideas in mind that I undertook to write *Les lances du crépuscule*. My aim was twofold: on the one hand, to write a monograph on an Amazonian people dear to me that would be accessible to a wide public without, for all that, lapsing into oversimplification; and, on the other hand, to enable the uninitiated to understand how an ethnographer builds his understanding of an exotic society. The first objective echoes a concern common to all ethnologists. Our work imposes on us a twofold social responsibility: a responsibility to a people who have placed their trust in us over several years and whose originality we are able to celebrate more faithfully than professional travel writers, and a responsibility to our co-citizens who can at least expect us to show them some return from research which they finance through their taxes. The ethnologist's duty in regard to these two constituencies makes his work the more uneasy, as the expectations of one do not necessarily correspond with those of the other. The people with whom he has lived hope that their existence may be recognized by the dominant society, even indeed legitimated with the backing of a book; in other words they expect that their culture will be accurately represented and even protected from decline by the magical power of writing. But they, of course, resent their secrets being betrayed or some unpleasant aspects of their social practices being too bluntly revealed. With the spread of literacy, some of them will even be able to read the ethnographer's work and verify if he has properly fulfilled his side of the implicit agreement he had with them. He had better watch it if he betrays their trust! Not only will any return to the field be impossible for him, but also, in a time when tribal minorities have fortunately acquired the means to make themselves heard in international fora, the news of his betrayal of them will spread rapidly among his peers, bringing with it disgrace and ostracism. The Western public, on the other hand, experience some difficulty in going beyond the exotic stereotypes which shape their outlook and which they expect to find in a book explicitly written for them. It is necessary, then, to make extensive efforts to contextualize unfamiliar institutions and customs so as to obviate the danger of misunderstandings. These conflicting demands necessitate a balanced style of exposition, neither complaisant nor condescending, a rare literary skill which is without doubt the key criterion for the success of this type of work.

My second aim, to give an insight into how an ethnographer over time acquires an understanding of another culture, was intended to shed light on what is without any doubt the great blind spot of our discipline. This aim was born out of a disquiet I experienced even as a student, and which I find today among my own students: prior to leaving for the field no one is able to explain to the neophyte exactly what it is they have to do. Once one is sure that the student knows how to collect a genealogy, keep a field journal carefully, take a census and map the village, record linguistic features such as tones and glottal stops, they are then left to their own devices. What does one say to students who ask you why it is essential to have carried out fieldwork before launching into theoretical and comparative anthropology? You may answer that it is necessary to have been through the experience of learning another culture oneself before being properly able to decipher and assess the significance of one's colleagues' writings on other cultures, in the same way that historians carry out a critical appraisal of their sources. Doubtless it is necessary to have been through the experience of fieldwork, but what is the source of this flair or intuition which we apply to the reading of others' work by having tested it out for ourselves? This is the question that, quite rightly, sociologists and historians do not cease asking us: what are the procedures that you use in the steps between 'participant observation' and the final monograph? What proof for the validity of your findings do you offer? On what basis do you feel justified in moving from the particular to the general? My own field experience has convinced me that it is not possible to give a definite response to these kinds of questions, as each ethnologist, in his solitary workshop, builds his understanding of a society from the disparate elements that circumstances offer.

It was necessary, then, to take a different tack, that is to say, to consider the particular aspects of the situation: in other words, to give an idea of the tricks the *bricoleur* has recourse to, by retracing the ins and outs of key phases of the process of discovery that ethnographic research sets in motion. Besides, I was surprised that, up to now, this had been so little attempted. The accounts of fieldwork that the Anglo-Saxons have elevated to the level of a genre teem with pertinent and ironic comments on the mistakes, inadequacies and misunderstandings of the narrator, but they rarely dwell on the sequence of chance happenings, intuitions and strategies that enable the ethnographer to build an understanding of an event, a behaviour, an institution or a practice.[4] The accounts of failure – such as *Un Riche Cannibale* by Jean Monod (1972) – are in this regard more instructive: in explaining incompatibilities and misunderstandings they trace *a contrario* the conditions of progress for a successful investigation. To let the readers enter our workshop, and to enable them to assess the value of the models which we do our best to depict: these, then, were the two goals I was aiming for. They opened before me a vast ground littered with pitfalls, the most perilous being the spectre of narcissism and literary conceit, symptoms of that missed vocation as novelist for which, to paraphrase Leach, most anthropologists still yearn.

To manage a building site one needs not only a clear picture of the building to be constructed, but also some ideas about how to build it; in my case these were derived from a literary education rather than from anthropological theory. *Les lances du crépuscule* is divided into three unequal parts. The first part, a long prologue written in the past tense, succinctly recounts the circumstances which led me to spend a small part of my life with an almost unknown tribe in the Amazon. It contains the few pieces of information on my education and disposition which I felt the reader needed in order to understand my behaviour in the field. But it also retraces the stages of my approach, describes the shadowy pioneer frontier on the fringe of the

Amazon forest, and constitutes, as it were, an invitation to accompany me on my journey at the same time as providing a familiar and accessible model for the reader to identify with: the ethnologist is scarcely better prepared than anyone else to set off into the depths of the jungle. The prologue, having served its purpose, ends on the very day when I finally arrive among the Achuar, after a long journey.

There follow twenty-four chapters written in the present tense, organized into chronological order and divided into three roughly equal parts. Each chapter follows the rule of the three unities inspired by Aristotle's *Poetics*: unity of time (the day), unity of action (a single event and the various situations which are thematically subordinated to it) and unity of place. The uses of the present tense and of the classical model represent a device for structuring the account according to the criteria of theatrical performance, and thus give it an immediacy of tone equivalent to a fieldwork diary; it is also a somewhat parodical method of reinstating the famous 'ethnographic present'. Each chapter is therefore built around one or two vignettes painting the picture of an event (a visit, a hunting party, a raid, a ritual, a conversation, or even a mere joke) which provides the pretext for an elaboration of the theme it illustrates. Several themes are generally linked together as logical developments of the main theme; this is to prevent the principle of the unity of action imposing too great a rigidity on the ordering of the material and thus to avoid ending up impoverishing the material by forcing it into an *a priori* set of compartments. In the same way, the extensive use of 'flashback' gets around the constraints imposed by the unity of time and place by allowing the present situation to be paralleled by a previous one in which an analogous interaction led to a different message or interpretation. The work ends with an epilogue which constitutes a sort of key for a retrospective reading of the book, at the same time as providing a more general reflection on the lessons that an ethnological experience of this kind can contribute to the understanding of the problems of modernity. Here, I tackle several methodological and epistemological questions central to ethnographic writing: the gap between the time of action and the time of writing – common to all ethnological monographs, but amplified here by the recounting in the present tense of events which happened sixteen years previously; the translation of a lived reality into a reality reconstituted and interpreted in writing, a translation which introduces a fictitious dimension into all ethnographic work and which situates it on the level of verisimilitude rather than truth; finally, the question of the scientific virtues of exotic decentring, understood as an experience of thinking by which the ethnographer simultaneously becomes aware of a double relativity – of the culture which shaped him and of the one he is studying – the first reflexive step in any comparative approach.[5]

The construction of the book is, then, classical enough, particularly in the division of the contents into the three parts which make up the body of the work. The first ('Taming the Forest') recounts my apprenticeship among one local group in the customary practices of daily life, of the lived environment and the ways in which nature is socialized. Under the title 'Matters of Affinity', the second part begins a period of moving into other local groups – and thus the first attempts at generalizing through comparison; this part is mainly devoted to social and political life and the cultural encoding of emotions: the relations of kinship and ritual friendship, love and seduction, war and vendetta, moral authority and the mechanisms of social relationships, indigenous conceptions of misfortune and of ethnic identity, etc. The last part, entitled 'Visions', addresses notions of cosmology, theories of the person and of knowledge, and dwells extensively on the visionary experience such as occurs in the shaman's trance and in the encounters, under the influence of hallucinogens, with ghosts and the souls of the ancestors.

One will have recognized in this outline a sort of transposition of the conventional layout of earlier monographs into three successive parts: economy, society, religion. These divisions of a society into self-contained and functional levels have quite rightly been strongly criticized: it is true that no single sphere of social life can be considered independently from others, and that an analysis in terms of the main categories of descriptive sociology makes it almost impossible to grasp a culture as a whole and to bring out the ordering principles and systems of values which give a society its originality.[6] But for now, having experienced the inevitability of this triadic narrative structure myself, I believe that it does not so much reflect theoretical assumptions as the simple chronological unfolding of ethnographic inquiry, dressed up in the form of analytical categories. If most ethnological monographs used to begin with descriptions of 'subsistence practices', this was not only because this domain was deemed to be the foundation of the whole social system, but also because material culture is the first aspect of an exotic society to which the newly arrived ethnographer has immediate access. Unable to master the language, for the first few months one is deaf and dumb, confined to observing behaviours, the uses of space, techniques, the ritualization of daily life. One is attentive to sounds, to smells and to an unfamiliar environment, forced to adapt one's body to entirely new habits and ways of living. One only emerges gradually from this immersion in the material aspects of life when eventually snatches of dialogue become intelligible: one is then able to glimpse the complexities of social life, not at first in terms of its rules, but in the game of individual strategies, the clash of interests and ambitions, and in the expression of passions and the interplay of emotions. Finally, much later, when one has acquired some command of the language and when, through repetition, certain beliefs and rituals have lost their strangeness, only then does it become possible to enter into the twists and turns of modes of thinking. In many of the classical monographs, these inescapable stages of ethnographic research were transformed into a descriptive format thanks to which the authors, without always being aware of it, found an appropriate correspondence between the process by which they arrived at their understanding and the way the results of this understanding were presented. Now, it is exactly this kind of correspondence that I have aimed at in *Les lances du crépuscule*, to get the uninitiated reader to grasp how the unfolding of the fieldwork experience directs one's understanding of a culture. Consequently it was inevitable that the distribution of the contents would somehow reflect a long-established threefold division.

In contrast, however, to earlier monographs, in which the unconscious diachrony of structure was accompanied by a synchronic presentation of material, in *Les lances du crépuscule* I have sought to recount the chronological process by which my understandings developed. With the help of my field journal, and while remaining faithful to the pace of discovery, I have tried to introduce little by little throughout the text the information that I had obtained in a discontinuous manner and the interpretations which I gradually arrived at as a result of particular circumstances. Apart from necessitating much self-restraint, if one is willing to assume at the start of the work the level of ignorance and naivety corresponding to the situation experienced at the beginning of fieldwork, this aim has to grapple with the time-lag between the ethnographic experience itself and the subsequent writing up of this experience: the person I had become was not entirely the same as the one who had discovered the Achuar some fifteen years earlier. Like all who have attempted autobiography, I have not been able to stop myself superimposing feelings and ideas from my subsequent life experience over the emotions and opinions that are contained in all their ingenuousness in my field journal. I like to think that these interpolations are less retrospective embellishments than plausible developments of what I would then have expressed; the fact remains that they were thought of and written after the event, just as all ethnological works are thought and written after the event.

Some of the techniques I have used were specifically intended to limit the effects of the temporal de-synchronization characteristic of ethnographic writing. The first technique is inspired by the methods of the 'whodunit', a typically English literary genre which also shows some clear similarities to the way in which fieldwork unfolds. This method implies that the explanation of a fact, the understanding of a situation or the interpretation of a cultural phenomenon will be preceded by a series of clues, slipped into the narrative at regular intervals in order that their accumulation, together with the final clue which triggers the problem-solving process, will enable readers to appreciate the intellectual pathway of the ethnographer just as though they had been there themselves. The whole skill of the great 'whodunit' writers is to give the reader the clues to the mystery to be solved, but in such a diffuse way that one very seldom arrives at the solution before the hero of the book. In this instance, by contrast, the great difficulty is that, whereas the 'whodunit' presents the enigma to be solved at the outset, the ethnographer's awareness of the significant or problematic nature of a situation results from the accumulation of clues that are revealed to him. I have proceeded in this way on several occasions. In some instances, indeed, closely following the methods of the 'whodunit' was especially apt: this was the case, for example, in the piecing together of the guilt of a murderer in the context of a vendetta. At the moment the truth came out, and thanks to the recapitulation of the pieces of evidence, this situation served retrospectively to reveal the strategies employed by some of those concerned to hide the name of the culprit from the relatives of the victim and to incite other equally plausible accusations. But I have also used this method in other domains, notably to recount the successive stages that led me to an interpretation of shamanic trance. In this case it was a matter of reconstructing the 'critical mass' effect which occurs when the accumulation of heterogeneous and not always initially well understood pieces of information finally combine with a better understanding of the language, and with the insights of a reliable informant, to trigger the chain of retrospective understanding.

Another technique used to reconstruct the stages in the process of discovery is also drawn from the arsenal of the writers of 'whodunits':

the exposition of false leads. Obviously here it is not a matter of deliberately deflecting the reader from the solution to the mystery so as to maintain the suspense, but to enable the reader to gain a real appreciation of the process of trial and error which leads to the understanding of a phenomenon. In the classical monographs, ethnographers placed themselves in the role of the God of Leibniz and presented as self-evident a view of a society that, in reality, they took a long time to construe synthetically. In contrast, in several instances I have tried to retrace the sequence of my often erroneous or incomplete interpretations, while describing each time the specific circumstances which led me to revise them. These progressive revisions, divided up between different chapters in order to reflect their chronological sequence accurately, will perhaps better allow the reader to grasp the cumulative effect of time and of luck on the way we reach our ethnographic conclusions. I also wanted to bring out the confused and disparate character of the rough data from which we build our interpretations. The uninitiated often imagine that we proceed after the fashion of the natural sciences, with systematic techniques for collecting data and with clearly formulated hypotheses. Now, apart from some exceptions (kinship, classification, material culture, demography . . .), it is circumstances, over which we have very little control, which dictate the course of our inquiry. The 'facts' we gather rarely take the form of an ordered knowledge or discrete body of evidence susceptible to methodical treatment; they appear most often as a heterogenous flood of unsolicited utterances and unprovoked interactions which belong more to a chronicle of news items than to an experimental protocol. I have tried to bring out this diversity, confused and embedded in the vagaries of daily life, in order that too credulous a reader may be able to judge on actual evidence the kind of intellectual *bricolage* to which the ethnographer has to resort.

I said at the start of this essay that, in writing *Les lances du crépuscule*, I set myself two ambitions: to enable the readers to enter into our workshop and to enable them to appreciate the beauty of the societies we try to depict. The second aim is implicit in the majority of ethnological monographs. In these works one can discern an admiration tinged with narcissism for the complex and original culture with which the researcher, after considerable difficulties, has over time developed a relationship of complicity, even empathy. The anthropologist 'as hero', as we all know, is someone who makes the scene of their heroism appear as worthy of admiration. But such a goal becomes trivial if it is not accompanied by a higher aim; and besides, it is difficult to achieve when one assumes a non-specialist readership. In fact, one cannot prejudge the knowledge of the reader and thus it is necessary to proceed as though the reader were totally ignorant of some of the mental attitudes of our discipline that we too easily assume to be obvious to everyone. To get round this problem, without resorting to a didactic style, there is no other recourse than the use of comparative generalizations. The first steps here are typical of the approach of classical monographs such as flourished in the functionalist tradition. An initially strange custom or belief is first situated in its local context in order to dispel its strangeness, by showing its place in the domains of meaning in which it is embedded. Then the custom is shown to be a variation among a larger body of analogous facts found in neighbouring societies in the same culture area which, taken together, thus exhibit a characteristic 'style' in relation to which the initial custom no longer appears as exceptional. The famous Jivaro custom of shrinking the heads of their enemies can provide us with an example, albeit almost a caricature of one. This practice can be made to appear less strange or less sinister in the eyes of an uninitiated public if one interprets it as an element in a politics of otherness, playing on a continuum between the near and the far, and on a dialectic of affinity and consanguinity that one finds at work among many of the Amazonian societies practising headhunting or ritual cannibalism. However, this fundamental principle of ethnological explanation does not succeed in completely dispelling the strangeness of an institution for an uninformed reader: in situating the exoticism of a local custom within a regional context, one contents oneself with diluting a particular strangeness in a wider, more encompassing strangeness.

The second stage of this approach allows us to counterbalance the narcissism of ethnographic writing, and consists, then, of attempting to derive an analytical lesson from the phenomenon under consideration. This is done by taking it at a higher level of abstraction and relating it to what we ourselves know about the way it is manifest in our own culture. When I compare the treatment of the dead or the notions of the individual among the Jivaro with those found in the West, I do not restrict myself to leading readers into a landscape in which they feel at home; I also attempt to make them become aware of the relativity of the practices and ideologies which have shaped their opinions. I hasten to add that this ambition is not at all motivated from a fanatical adherence on my part to the theory of cultural relativism, but rather from the wish to make ethnology play the critical role that is almost necessarily implied by the nature of the knowledge it produces. Incidentally, there is nothing very new about using the comparison of customs to expose the transience of facts and institutions that a triumphant modernity would too often wish to make out as eternal; Montaigne, in his famous essay 'Des cannibales', or Montesquieu, in *Les Lettres persanes*, do just this. Some may object that it is not the place of ethnology to cast blame or to edify through exotic parables. Certainly, but why should ethnologists refrain from using their knowledge to shape the views of their contemporaries, given that they can draw from their incomparable experience of otherness an inspiration analogous to that formerly drawn by the moralists from travel accounts? Have not these same travel accounts been at the source of a vocation for many of us, who, as children, were 'fond of maps and engravings'? Did they not teach us to love imagined countries long before returning from them as bearers of wise utopias?

It was indeed the liking I had as a child for the 'Le Tour du Monde' series, or for the Hetzel editions of the stories of Jules Verne, that has prompted me to try to recreate in *Les lances du crépuscule* the atmosphere of poetic mystery that the engravings used to give to travel accounts.[7] It seemed to me that an ethnological book with claims to originality had to rediscover the relationship between text and image appropriate for this genre, and so I looked for a new inspiration by drawing on the models provided in earlier works. Most ethnologists' photographs, and mine in particular, are technically mediocre; they are in no position to rival the superb professional photographs of exotic peoples which, through magazines, have influenced the public's tastes. In actual fact, they chiefly serve as a tangible proof that we have been where we claim to have been and that we have really seen what we are reporting. Such proof is not without some value; I have, therefore, complied with the tradition of the series which has commissioned my book by providing some sixty photographs. However, in order to provide a counterpoint to these photographs, I also commissioned an artist to illustrate a dozen or so scenes from the book in a style and with a technique that echoes the engravings of Riou, but in a style sufficiently modern to exclude any impression of pastiche. Although ethnographically very accurate, based as they are on documents which I had provided to the illustrator, these drawings will doubtless shock some of my colleagues, so firmly rooted is the idea that only photography, with its supposed truthful realism, is suitable for the ethnographic genre. Indeed, this prejudice is merely the corollary of the positivist point of view which would have it that a monograph paints an exact picture of reality. The line drawings I wanted for this book are not only intended to recreate an atmosphere or to cater to nostalgia; my intention was to draw attention to the element of artifice that enters into all ethnological monographs while making immediately apparent an artifice at another level. The art of anthropological writing consists precisely in disguising this artifice under the appearance of a faithful account in which, by contrast with travel writing, the element of exoticism is carefully reduced by detailed interpretations. In trying to bridge with words the obvious gulf between Us and Them, however, we do not always consider that, in the eyes of an uninformed reader, a vast range of conspicuous differences still remains. By providing illustrations evocative of old-fashioned engravings, I wanted to render manifest this irreducible sphere of differences. Because it is differentiated from photography by its depiction of reality in an obviously less realist manner, a pen drawing has the effect of qualifying the realism of the descriptions and analyses it accompanies. Furthermore, because it has fallen into disuse in our discipline for almost a century, and because it therefore carries the marks of historical conventions, this form of illustration highlights the elements of arbitrariness and invention our prose conceals; it is well suited, then, to produce the distancing effect which ethnographic writing seeks to overcome.

The aims I set myself in undertaking to write *Les lances du crépuscule* made it inevitable that I would serve up something of myself to the readers. I have not done this without reluctance, a reluctance, moreover, that I still keenly feel as I finish this essay entirely devoted as it is to an individual's experience. My unease is not to do solely with a matter of temperament. If I have found it particularly difficult to shed the reserve that I have until now found to be an accommodating refuge, this is also because of the intellectual training inculcated in us by ethnology. This training allows us to accept as legitimate the expression of personal ideas, provided that such ideas are given the analytical and critical trappings that situate them in the midst of a recognized theoretical debate. On the other hand, this training leads us to ban any reference to the existential circumstances which have contributed to engendering these ideas in us. A patiently internalized atavism keeps us within the neutral confines of scientific discussion. This stance condemns us to run against the current of all we hold acceptable from the moment that we wish only to show that ethnographic inquiry – from which, nevertheless, ethnology unreservedly draws the materials for its inductive comparisons – is first of all a singular experience of the diversity of others. All ethnologists will have been able to test out this self-censorship for themselves. What inner pressures do we not have to withstand in order to slip from the use of the indefinite pronoun or the formal 'we' to the blunt and impertinent 'I', whose intrusion indicates a lack of reserve? What prejudices do we not have to overcome when we venture to paint the picture of an individual's character – which nevertheless partly affects the nature of the information they give us – whereas no one finds improper the hidden evaluations of a people's character, a much more hazardous form of judgement in fact, but one which can be concealed behind the objective screen of general issues. These precautions are doubtless necessary to prevent ethnology from floundering in introspective gossip. To take them too literally, however, runs the risk of blurring the distinction between genres that is essential for the pursuit of our discipline. If anthropology has no need of a subjectivity which would tend to weaken the import of its explanatory ambitions, ethnography – and to a lesser extent ethnology – cannot be detached totally from the personal context within which its propositions originate. To forget this necessary division of labour which operates within each of us is to confuse two intellectual enterprises of different kinds, and thereby to contribute to making this original form of understanding of others that we have the good fortune to have as our profession, more abstruse in the eyes of the uninitiated.

NOTES

1 See Malaurie (1993) for a discussion of his views of his collection and an overview of the books it includes; the publication of a second volume is planned for 1996.
2 Subsequently published under the title *La Nature domestique. Symbolisme et praxis dans l'écologie des Achuar* (Descola 1986).
3 When advancing general statements on the nature of the anthropologist's experience, I have chosen to use the masculine gender rather than a clumsy mixture of her/him or she/he. My main reason for doing so – apart from semantic technicalities pertaining to the status of grammatical genders in French – is that these statements are generalizations stemming from my personal experience. They are thus probably coloured by my bias as a male anthropologist, a limitation I fully acknowledge.
4 I am thinking here in particular of Francis Huxley (1956), Elenore Smith Bowen (1964), David Maybury-Lewis (1965), and Nigel Barley (1983).
5 Some of the arguments of this essay have been taken up in the epilogue of *Les lances du crépuscule*.

6 It is precisely because I felt such ways of dividing up the material to be obsolete and invalid that, in *La Nature domestique* (Descola 1986), I attempted to analyse Achuar ecology and the way they represent it in a single framework, without according greater priority to technical determinism than to cultural determinism.

7 Published during the second half of the nineteenth century, *Le Tour du monde* was a periodical devoted to exploration and travel accounts, a kind of equivalent to what is now the *National Geographic* magazine. It was beautifully illustrated with engravings by well-known artists such as Riou, who also illustrated the original Hetzel edition of the works of Jules Verne.

REFERENCES

Barley, N. (1983) *The Innocent Anthropologist*, London: British Museum Publications Ltd.

Bowen, E. S. (1964) *Return to Laughter*, New York: Doubleday.

Descola, P. (1986) *La Nature domestique. Symbolisme et praxis dans l'écologie des Achuar*, Paris: Foundation Singer-Polignac/Editions de la Maison des Sciences de l'Homme. English translation (1994) *In the Society of Nature. A native ecology in Amazonia*, Cambridge: Cambridge University Press.

—— (1994) *Les lances du crépuscule. Relations Jivaros, Haute-Amazonie*, Paris: Plon. English edition (1996) *The Spears of Twilight*, trans. J. Lloyd, London: Harper Collins; New York: The New Press.

Hélias, P. J. (1975) *Le Cheval d'orgueil*, Paris: Plon, 'Terre Humaine'.

Huxley, F. (1956) *Affable Savages*, London: Rupert Hart-Davis.

Leiris, M. (1934) *L'Afrique fantôme*, Paris: Gallimard.

Lévi-Strauss, C. (1949) *Les Structures élémentaires de la parenté*, Paris: Presses Universitaires de France. English edition (1969) *The Elementary Structures of Kinship*, trans. J. Bell, J. von Sturmer and R. Needham, London: Eyre and Spottiswode.

—— (1955) *Tristes tropiques*, Paris: Plon, 'Terre Humaine'. English edition (1976) *Tristes Tropiques*, trans. J. and D. Weightman, Harmondsworth: Penguin.

Malaurie, J. (1955) *Les Derniers Rois de Thulé*, Paris: Plon, 'Terre Humaine'.

—— (1993) *Le Livre Terre Humaine*, vol. 1, Paris: Plon.

Maybury-Lewis, D. (1965) *The Savage and the Innocent*, London: Evans.

Monod, J. (1972) *Un Riche Cannibale*, Paris: Union Générale d'Editions.

Chapter 11

Fieldwork styles
Bohannan, Barley, and Gardner

Jeremy MacClancy

Every generation has its anthropologists, every epoch its ethnographers. Whether self-promoted or picked up by the public, candidates emerge in every period as the popular representatives of our discipline. Turnbull's work on the Ik was taken as an illuminating commentary on the human condition; Castaneda's first book confirmed hippies' hopes about the mystical value of their drug-induced visions. Books which seem too much of a piece with their time, however, die with the passing of that time. *The Mountain People* is now scorned, *The Teachings of Don Juan* has come to be regarded as no more than an ingenious fake.

While the more dated of popular works have now been buried within the history of the discipline, the words of those who have tried to touch more enduring themes hold the promise of living a little longer. Among fieldwork accounts intended for a non-academic readership, Laura Bohannan's *Return to Laughter* was an early contribution to the genre, and it remains the definitive example. Nigel Barley's *The Innocent Anthropologist*, though perhaps too novel to be yet regarded as an established classic, continues to sell well and has helped to make its author the most well-known anthropologist in British non-anthropological circles.

In this chapter I wish to speak of both these works and of a more recent account, Katy Gardner's *Songs at the River's Edge. Stories from a Bangladeshi Village*, which I believe may well prove to be a great popular success. All three works speak of the rigours of a prolonged stay among exotic peoples. All three reveal to us something about both the anthropologist and the anthropologized. But beyond these basic similarities, this trio of books, published in 1954, 1983, and 1991 respectively, are popular for very different reasons.

Laura Bohannan's *Return to Laughter*, the fictional account of her time among the Tiv of Nigeria, is one of the best-selling descriptions of fieldwork ever written. Since its publication in 1954 it has been reprinted over twenty times and has now become a permanent part of introductory courses in anthropology. In the United States especially, students first learn about the subject via Bohannan. The question, of course, is why *her* book?

It is not merely that *Return* was one of the first introspective accounts of life in the field. Rather, it is because she deals in a straightforward yet engaging manner with the central moral problems of sharing a protracted length of time with people apparently very different to Westerners. For the primary focus of her novel is not the Nigerians she lived with but, as she states, 'the sea change in oneself that comes from immersion in another and savage culture'.

The protagonist (let us call her 'Elenore', after the pseudonym Bohannan used for her novel) is a well-read American brought up in an urban Catholic household. A highly disciplined and determined neophyte, she regards her fieldwork as an uncomplicated means towards a fixed end: getting a doctorate from Oxford. However, despite her academic training in anthropology, she remains innocent about the lived reality of other cultures. Prefiguring the Tiv as Whites in black skins, she imagines that they 'would differ only in externals of dress and custom, that their basic reactions to the same basic situation would be the same as mine' (Smith Bowen [Bohannan] 1954: 144). Since she, presumably, knows how to cope with Westerners, there should be no problem dealing with the Tiv.

In the field, Elenore does not want to get involved, merely to be accepted. She does not wish to be caught in a web of social obligations, but to be free to go her own way with their full confidence. Instead of letting untidy emotions mess her work, she intends to maintain a neat, scientific detachment. To her, it is important 'to regard impersonally and analytically' (ibid.: 145). Academic objectivity required nothing less. Living with the Tiv will give her facts, and only facts; for there is no question of testing Western values in comparison with theirs, no question of doubting that the West is not the best of all possible worlds. During fieldwork she will only be her 'real self' while reading alone in her house at night. 'What these people had to say to me went into my notebook. It was the lessons I could learn from Locke and his fellows that I would write into my heart' (ibid.: 146)

In her first weeks, all goes reasonably well. She assiduously compiles genealogies, lists of botanical terms, and other vocabularies;

she maps the homesteads within her patron's influence; she names a child, jots down recipes, and joins women's weeding parties. She is learning. But Elenore is discontented:

> My dissatisfaction lay wholly in the part I was being assigned. I was rapidly being absorbed in the life of the women and children. All the magic, all the law, all the politics – over half the things professionally important to me – were in the hands of the men, and so far not one man had been willing to discuss such matters with me . . . I had been identified with the women: unless I could break that association, I would leave the field with copious information on domestic details and without any knowledge of anything else.
>
> (ibid.: 78–9)

And so her real troubles begin.

In order to learn about politics, she becomes a politician; in order to be told the details of witchcraft, she is not scared to be thought a witch. At first manipulated, she becomes adroit at manipulation. Treated as a pawn by rival elders, she turns into a queen able to check them both. But this sort of manoeuvring is common the globe over. It does not question one's understanding of the world.

What does prove subversive is her increasing awareness of Tiv values and her deepening emotional involvement with some of them. She realizes she cannot pigeonhole her neighbours into Western stereotypes (the *grande dame*, the crusty old man, the giddy matron, the Mr Milquetoast, etc.) for their emotional reactions to events may be different to ours. The culturally constituted consequences of a couple's adultery show her she must judge local acts by local, not by Western, standards. On learning the details of polygamy, she is surprised to find herself sorry for a man henpecked by five wives. At a wedding she is forced to make a choice:

> 'You must make up your mind,' Udama announced loudly, so that all could hear, 'whether you wish to be an important guest or one of the senior women of the homestead. If you are an important guest, we will again lead out the bride, so you may see her. If you are one of us, you may come inside, but then you must dance with us.'
>
> . . . my hesitations were gone almost before she stopped speaking. I went inside the hut.
>
> (ibid.: 123)

Watching over a close but mortally ill friend, she tussles with the professional standard of detachment and then rejects it for the sake of possibly saving her companion. On this and other occasions Red-woman (as she is called) loses her coolness and waxes passionate. During a smallpox epidemic she at first resists being 'infected by their fears', and then succumbs. Scared of the consequences of assisting the ejected scapegoat blamed for the epidemic, she stays indoors and suffers her conscience instead.

> There was no doubt in my mind – and there is none now – that by leaving him to his fate I denied the greatest of our moral values: one must not withhold help which it is in one's power to give. The dilemma was naked before me, and before it I shrank back in naked inadequacy... Fear made us all cruel.
>
> (ibid.: 273, 277)

In the early stages of her stay with the Tiv, Elenore had noted and appreciated their easy laughter, their proud bearing, and their grace of speech and movement. Later she had come to regard these cultural attributes as superficial, as cloaking an ugly harshness and cruelty. People prepared to laugh at the trials of a blind man lost in the jungle could not be admired. Now, on her return after fleeing the epidemic, she feels diminished and painfully aware of her own fallibility. It is her friends who show her the error of her self-judgement.

The disease gone, the homestead re-established, they stage an evening of story-telling. As a variety of participants act out a hilarious series of local fables, Elenore is forcibly reminded of the ethics underpinning their society. One trio play the roles of litigant, interpreter, and administrator. As the case becomes ever more involved, the colonial officer becomes ever more confused, so the final judgement he passes is an entirely irrelevant decision based on wholly erroneous grounds. The audience are laughing so much they cannot hear the speakers and the chief, almost choking on his chuckles, comments, 'That is the way it is ... They judge us, but they do not understand us, and what can we do?' (ibid.: 293). The next skit is of a blind man stumbling about the bush. The impersonator plays his part so well that even Elenore, despite herself, starts to laugh. 'That is the way it is,' remarks the chiefs' brother, himself partially blinded by the smallpox, 'Indeed it is so. What can one do?'

Now Redwoman's eyes have been opened. She sees that the Tiv are not, as she had earlier thought, callous and indifferent to suffering. Though tragedy, in their harsh environment, is genuine and frequent, they do not try to avoid their grim reality, but to face it – with laughter. This mirth is not a form of humour, but a lively, and often embittered, acceptance of their lot. 'It is the laughter of people who value love and friendship and plenty, who have lived with terror and death and hate.' If they could not look death in the face, and smile, they would go insane.

Her account may end at this point, but Elenore now knows that she herself is unfinished. Though an adult Westerner, she was as a child among her Tiv acquaintances. They have taught her some things, and she will go on learning. She has discovered that there are some moral values she cannot compromise, even though she will be unable always to live up to them, even though they might clash with the dictates of her academic discipline. She has admitted her own weakness and embraced humility.

Elenore's training at the hands of the Tiv may help her to qualify as a professional academic, but her fieldwork is in fact more a process of spiritual, rather than of anthropological, education. For Elenore is concerned about the state of her soul – at that time still a current concept – while the central theme of Bohannan's book is the crooked progress of her protagonist as she painfully stumbles her way towards some sort of self-knowledge and spiritual realization. In this sense, *Return to Laughter* is, as David Riesman suggests in the introduction, a kind of modern *Pilgrim's Progress* (ibid.: xv). Elenore may not be as unswerving as Bunyan's Christian, nor may she meet capital-lettered characters with abstract nouns for names (Ignorance, Discretion, Mr Valiant-for-Truth, etc.), but she does set out on a journey which, like Christian's, is much more a psychological than a geographical excursion. Like her seventeenth-century model, but in metaphorical mode, she passes through Valleys of Humiliation and of the Shadow of Death, survives a Slough of Despond, and manages to escape from the clutches of Giant Despair. In both cases, exciting action is tempered by conversation, and both pilgrims have long, improving discussions with those who befriend them. In both books the progress of the protagonist is measured in part by skill in solving puzzles, whether Tiv or biblically based.

The literary parallels between this pair of religious allegories is further implied by Bohannan's frequent use of archaic terms, phrasing and cadence. Children are 'begotten', a local's hatred 'waxes stronger', and almost no one uses apostrophic abbreviation in their negative questions: ' "Was it not that of which you started to speak just now?" I asked bluntly' (ibid.: 149).

Bohannan's academic models may come from the world of Boas and Evans-Pritchard, but her stylistic ones derive from that of the Bible and Shakespeare – both the sacred text and the Collected Works are on Elenore's bookshelf. She is not an unschooled traveller, but an educated pilgrim steeped in the traditions of her tribe. Her quest for herself, though pursued in an exotic setting, proceeds down an already well-beaten path.

Either way, whether by content or by form, the point, I think, is plain: Bohannan is a bush Bunyan for her times.

Laura Bohannan seeks to understand the social role of laughter; Nigel Barley, in contrast, does not wish to investigate humour, but to produce it. The point of his fieldwork accounts is less to portray the anguish of the soul in an exquisitely wrought prose than to puncture the pretensions of sanctimonious anthropologists and to amuse the reader. Instead of the over-solemn books written by these serious characters, Barley wants to dwell on precisely those aspects of fieldwork usually regarded as 'irrelevant', 'unimportant', 'not anthropology'. He does not want to be part of a supposedly discipline-wide cover-up, but to lay the subject bare.

In *The Innocent Anthropologist* (1983) and *A Plague of Caterpillars* (1986), Barley gives us the low-down on his two field-trips to the Dowayo, mountain pagans of northern Cameroon. On neither excursion do things go well. He is, by turns, lonely, bored, depressed, diseased, injured, cheated, exhausted. The only time he experiences hysterical joy is the day of his departure from the village. Persistently pestered by goats, termites, mice, cicadas and scorpions, he has also to cope with the demands of locals thirsty for beer and hungry for money. He tries to ingratiate himself with the villagers but fails to make more than one or two Dowayo friends; most regard him as at worst a harmless idiot, and at best an entertaining curiosity, a 'jester in shorts'. Unsure of his command of their tonal language, he wonders whether he has ever done more than teach them his pidgin version of it. When he does try to do his job, Dowayo are vague and evasive about what they know and, despite his assiduity, he only learns the local lore in a haphazard, spasmodic manner. Rites are confusing, magical practices are secret, goats eat his notes, rivers wash his films, and mould patterns his lenses. Fieldwork is difficult and discouraging, and Barley chronicles the obstacle course well.

Barley does not restrict himself to happenings in the villages, but delights in detailing the Cameroonian middle-ground where the First World meets the Third in an unpredictable, usually unproductive manner. He enters a hospital looking for a dentist and ends up with a white-coated mechanic who removes his two front teeth. He is harassed by enthusiastic prostitutes and constantly thwarted by equally energetic officials, ones who have learnt the bureaucratic lessons of their former colonial masters all too well. Prices are outrageous, the roads lethal, the pop music raucous, and the food – unfortunately – all too describable. Among the varied stock of characters he befriends are an Afro–American anthropologist surprised that the homeland of his dreams does not match his expectations, a Cameroonian teacher who, on visiting Barley, promptly copulates with a villager's wife in the man's hut, and a clinging baboon whom the author is forced to take to the cinema. For an expatriate to fare well in this sort of environment, it is best to be either less than sane, or an anthropologist.

Barley's idea of writing up the parts other ethnographers leave out sounds an eminently laudable aim. It is also a highly marketable one. His five popular books are all still in print and the first one is now in its seventh impression. His literary ability and productivity have made him so well known that his popular fame has shunted Lévi-Strauss and lesser figures into the academic shade. He is feted in the national press and has even been given his own television series. Yet, though social anthropology thrives on competing viewpoints and alternative approaches, and though all but the most dour practitioners of the subject enjoy a laugh at themselves, Barley is not liked by his peers. Indeed, the antipathy towards him is such that, at times, Barley-baiting appears to be the only blood-sport British anthropologists would not wish to see banned. What, exactly, has he done to annoy them so?

His detractors deny that envy of the successful is the motivating force underlying their aversion. They claim not to begrudge the fact that he was prepared to say what others were scared, or insufficiently talented, to write. These academics might be suspicious of the popular, but they do not regard that in itself as sufficient grounds for damning his books. Instead, what they complain about is the way he laughs at those who cannot answer back, and his apparent readiness to reinforce pejorative stereotypes.

It is true that Barley tends not to let professional ethics get in the way of his sense of fun. His portrayal of the Dowayo, while often sympathetic, is fundamentally unflattering: their way of life appears to be crude, their lived environment smelly and squalid, and their magician's technical equipment a joke. If I were the village chief who acted as Barley's host, I would not like to be remembered by many thousands of Britons as a beer-swilling sluggard who only took pains to avoid unwelcome visitors. Nor would I like to be the most powerful rainmaker of the area, a locally revered man whose impotence is now the laughing-stock of Barley's readers. Since this pair and most of the Dowayo are illiterate, they have no redress. They have been mocked and they have no possibility of offering alternative representations in the written medium that Barley was able to utilize. Furthermore, even if they could write, the chances of them having access to the same market as Barley is unlikely. A learned guest should not perhaps portray his hosts in a completely uncritical light, but that does not mean he should exploit their lack of defences to produce an image of them which they cannot contest.

Barley's sins become blacker, however, when he moves from the particular to the general. For he regards some of his specific fieldwork difficulties as typical of those experienced by most anthropologists living with peoples low on some Western developmental scale. He opens, for instance, the section dealing with his attempt to elucidate kinship terms from villagers with a comment on how much has been written 'on primitive peoples' ability or inability to deal with hypothetical questions' (Barley 1983: 91–2). Later, when discussing his efforts to learn remedies from local healers, he states that 'in primitive society knowledge is seldom freely available' (ibid.: 105). When not comparing the Dowayo with other technologically under-developed peoples of the globe, he regards the villagers he lived with and the Cameroonians he met on the way as providing him with enough evidence to comment on a whole continent. He thinks, for example, that analysing data and pursuing the demands of abstract thought without interruption or distraction 'most un-African' (ibid.: 113). His perhaps most insulting generalization is reserved for his page on copulatory customs: 'Sexual encounters in Africa are so unromantic and brutish in their nature that they serve rather to increase the alienation of the fieldworker, not to moderate it, and are best avoided' (ibid.: 162–3). It is all the more ironical, then, that it is Barley himself who states that 'Africans go in for heavy over-statement' (ibid.: 47).

He commits the same sins in his novel about the colonial encounter on the Niger Coast in the last century, and in his book about bringing four Torajan villagers from the Indonesian island of Sulawesi to the Museum of Mankind. In his novel, he likes to detail the physical nature of the local women:

Akwa taste favoured ladies of Junoesque proportions and behinds came equipped with a shelf on which books might have been kept.

(Barley 1990: 37)

In one scene, the clerical protagonist contemplates a near-riotous group of locals:

The women fought back with mighty sweeps of their huge behinds and meaty forearms. Truscot thought unwillingly of Irish washer-women in London. Somewhere ... he had heard the witticism, 'Irish women have received a dispensation from the Pope allowing them to wear their arms upside down so that they grow thicker towards the wrists.' So, it seemed, had Akwa ladies.

(ibid.: 16–17)

In his book about his trip to Sulawesi, he feels at liberty to make nationwide generalizations such as the one about Indonesians' 'inability to cope with abstract, formal relationships' (Barley 1988: 39). When he finally reaches Torajaland, he relaxes and then reveals his condescending self: 'It felt good to have got away from the tourist round and met these good, simple people' (ibid.: 84). Back in London, he patronizes his four Torajan visitors by seeing their mutual relationship as akin to that between a father and his four children. In a recent newspaper article, Barley admits he might be criticized for presenting a one-sided vision of Indonesia, but tries to justify his prejudices in terms of addiction:

Friends ask, 'But what about East Timor, Irian Jaya, army dictatorship, corruption, exploitation? How can you enjoy Indonesia with such blatant evils? By going there, you are supporting all that?' There must, you feel, be something in the argument.

Then you walk into a noodle shop where you have never set foot before. The waiter, a complete stranger, rushes up and hugs you. 'Hello,' he says. 'My name's Otto. I've got four children, all of them boys. My wife says that proves I'm too highly sexed. What do *you* think?' You melt. You are hooked.

(Barley 1992a)

As he candidly reveals, Barley is so emotionally involved in the country, he is unable to let evil or politics get in the way of his pleasure. In his eyes, the Indonesians are typecast as kind, generous, warm people and no counter-evidence – whether of East Timorean massacres or the disastrous effects of the mass transmigration schemes – is going to change his mind.

One worry about Barley's typecasting is that his public may come to think his crass stereotyping and gross insensitivity are standard anthropological practices. In other words, this successful author, by consistently stereotyping others, aids the stereotyping of his own profession. And since he is so successful, the danger is that, with the decline generated by postmodernists in the authoritativeness of those anthropologists previously regarded as exemplars, his readers may begin to regard him as on a par with true masters of the discipline such as Evans-Pritchard and Lévi-Strauss.

Given Barley's approach to exotic others, it should come as no surprise that Auberon Waugh, son of Evelyn, thought *A Plague of Caterpillars* (Barley 1986) 'quite simply the funniest book to have come out of Africa since...*Black Mischief*. However, if Evelyn Waugh's novel about the tribulations of middle-class Englishmen in black Africa can be read with any enjoyment today, it is *because* the novel is such a product of the 1930s. Were it to be written by one of our contemporaries its perpetuation of stereotypical attitudes towards 'the primitive' and 'Africans' would most likely be branded as racist. And precisely what Waugh's comment implies about the racial attitudes of Barley's fans is unlikely to be flattering.

Defenders of Barley might claim that his mocking comments are tolerable because they are directed at everyone – including the author. Throughout his books he is, it is true, more than ready to laugh at himself and to underline the occasionally ridiculous nature of his fieldwork investigations. But, while the wisdom of the locals, the sanity of the expatriates, and the value of anthropology may some-times be placed in doubt, the one thing that is never questioned in Barley's books is his intelligence. No matter what happens to him, no matter how horrific, squalid, or demeaning the situation, his prose style unfailingly displays his invincible IQ. He may at times make a fool of himself but, at the end of each volume, he always makes sure he comes out on top.

We could say that, if Bohannan portrays Elenore as a pilgrim seeking enlightenment, then Barley presents himself as a peacock seeking an audience. For, to many, he is an object of wonder whose colours and strut are to be admired, while to others he is a nasty squawker whose cry is to be avoided.

According to the reviewer of *Return to Laughter* for the *Times Literary Supplement*, 'The author makes it quite clear that her Africans are not more stupid, lazier or more superstitious than illiterate peasants elsewhere, nor, once their fairly simple basic ideas are grasped, more difficult to understand.' In this sort of context, where supposedly learned reviewers could make such primitive comments, we should not perhaps underplay Bohannan's wish to enlighten and to educate the ignorant of her tribe.

By 1979 – the year Barley started his fieldwork – large sections of the Anglo–American public had become much more informed about the aims of social anthropologists and about the peoples they went off to live with. Unlike Bohannan, Barley did not feel the need to prove that his hosts were as human as he. And so, instead of trying to educate his public, he chose rather to entertain them, by scoffing at the pretensions of his self-important peers.

Gardner, compared to Barley, is not peahen-proud. In *Songs at the River's Edge. Stories from a Bangladeshi Village*, she does not place herself at centre-stage, nor does she confine the locals to bit-parts. Instead of using them as foils in amusing anecdotes, she lets stories of their lives take up the greater part of her text. The point of her literary production is not to deflate fellow academics, but to portray the cultural reality and the common humanity of the villagers she stayed with. Unlike Bohannan, however, Gardner is not concerned about depicting the lives of *all* the different sorts of people within her homestead. For, in contrast to the works of both Bohannan and Barley, Gardner's fieldwork account is most emphatically one by a woman about women, and the unstated aim of her book is to correct the androcentric bias of the genre.

Gardner opens and closes her *Stories* with chapters on the twin pains of arrival and departure. Otherwise she fills her text with the problems and predicament of the female villagers themselves. Different chapters describe the lot of a servant, the anguish of a bride who has yet to meet her groom, the labour of birth, the fears of a barren wife that her man will desert her, an impoverished woman's improvident purchase of a new sari and her subsequent beating by her husband, the devastation caused by the monsoon, and the ease with which death comes. It is, on the whole, an empathetic catalogue of female woes in a distant, though highly comparable, setting. Western women readers can contrast their own fate and count their blessings, or note their common damnation.

The men who appear in the episodes Gardner narrates are, almost without exception, wretched, insignificant, selfish, ugly, laughable or brutal. The titular heads of households, they can try to organize others, can batter their women, and may administer barbaric punishments. She curses men for the privileges they are granted, and only one man is ever commended in her text: a young savant of local lore, praised by her as being 'more mature and wiser than any of my university-educated men friends back in Britain' (Gardner 1991: 131). The point of her praise, however, is soon revealed, as it serves to highlight his downfall in the city where he is regarded as an illiterate bumpkin and is promptly duped by an unscrupulous middle-man. It is significant that the sole aspect of the village which makes Gardner laugh is the graffito penned by an overzealous student, 'It is not pelt and power or high titles that make a man immortal. It is the patriotic zeal in a man which brings undying glory for a man' (ibid.: 112).

The local women, in contrast, do not scribble such pomposities, and Gardner lets their down-to-earth virtues shine through her stories. Though they have to rear large families, prop up households, and submit to their husbands, they survive; some thrive and are, at times, exemplars of strength to their Western readers. Born 'stunningly beautiful', they may, despite decades of wearying hardship, remain radiant:

> She had once been pretty, but years of childbirth and bitter poverty had totally erased any lingering traces of her youthful looks. Her teeth were rotten from insufficient food and reddened with *pan*-chewing, her greying hair was thin and brittle, and her body was so skinny that her breasts had almost totally disappeared and her legs stuck out from her worn sari like twigs. But still, like so many of the village women, she had a kind of beauty, and her face usually beamed with smiles. Everyone liked Matoc Bibi.
>
> (ibid.: 114)[1]

Gardner is uninterested in brotherhood. It is not that the village men are unfriendly, rather that she feels she does not, and never would, belong with them. What she wishes to nurture is a sense of sorority. And she tries to feed it in spite of her new-found friends' possible desires to the contrary. She insists on serving herself at mealtimes and, when in the first month of her fieldwork her dirty clothes are snatched from her, she cries, 'Aren't I a woman? Aren't I equal? Why shouldn't I wash my own clothes?' (ibid.: 18). Her female hosts are prepared to accede to these demands, but even Gardner has to admit, from the very beginning, that her supposed equality with the local women-folk is but a polite form of play-acting they are courteous enough to perform.

In a setting of such poverty and destitution, the anthropologist is a rich interloper who has the power to accept, or reject, the local rules whenever it suits her. Though Gardner calls the daughters of the Muslim family she lives with 'my new sisters', and though she 'wanted more than anything to be one of them', she does not stall in resisting those aspects of the village culture which grate against her personality. She refuses to wear a veiled cape, does not dress smartly on important occasions, and is disrespectful to a young male student of the Qur'an (ibid.: 20, 25, 39, 52, 91). As she confesses in the conclusion, 'my transformation into a Bangladeshi woman had never been more than a surface veneer of habits and appearances which for the most part had remained entirely within my control' (ibid.: 154). Unlike Bohannan's Elenore, whose personality underwent a sea-change because of her time with the Tiv, Gardner is able to slough off what she has learned as easily as a snake shedding its skin. The metaphor she applies to herself is of a dry sponge which can soak up behaviours and, later, quickly squeeze them out (ibid.) All that stays with her at the end is an emotion – her love, reciprocated, for Sufia, her best Bengali friend.

Unlike Bohannan, Gardner does not appear to care about her soul, or at least she does not mention its existence. Unlike Barley, she is not self-regarding, though all fieldwork accounts are necessarily narcissistic to some degree. Perhaps, if we wished to pigeonhole her, she could be classed as a Woman of Her Time.

It is a commonplace among anthropologists that ethnographies are usually boring, and most of them virtually unreadable. These days the most revealing question to ask one's colleagues is not whether they have read *Kinship among the X*, but whether they have finished it. While there have been some recent attempts to modify the genre, the sad truth still seems to be that, if academic anthropologists were not paid to read these weighty tomes, most of them wouldn't.

In order to be professionally correct, the neophyte just back from the field has to submit to the literary laws of the discipline. If she, or he, wishes to be accepted by her superiors as a potential equal, she has to follow the already established ethnographic guidelines of her department. Until very recently, that entailed producing a text which was meant to appear objective, thorough, and dehumanized. In the process the locals under study were all too often transmuted into the two-dimensional victims of a social determinism, as though they were puppets whose movements are all culturally prescribed. Their describer was under no obligation to recount the way she carried out her fieldwork, the specific people she relied upon, the sorts of difficulties she faced, nor those aspects of local life she could not, or did not wish to, study. Instead of cataloguing her inadequacies, failures and omissions, she could make herself appear omniscient, omnipresent and omnicompetent. In these circumstances, it is not surprising that many ethnographies seem unbelievable, and are unbelievably boring.

Personal accounts of fieldwork were, and are not, confined by such constraints. Their authors can portray the locals as characters in the round. In these volumes the indigenes need not be depersonalized but may be described as individuals, each with his or her own strengths, idiosyncrasies and foibles. Unlike the stick-men of standard ethnographies, their particular personalities are not lost within some abstract and generalizing analysis. They can be shown as the emotionally complex and psychologically subtle characters they may well be. They can also be revealed as people with individual life-histories, ones whose sustained interaction with one another unfolds in an intricate manner over time. In personal accounts, the sequential narration of events is not forsaken for the synchronic analysis of structure.

Personal accounts are doubly personal, for they can expose the personalities both of the locals and of their scribe. Rather than confine herself to a confessional sketch in the introduction of her ethnography, the fieldworker can chronicle the crooked, uneven course of her investigation. Instead of appearing all-knowing, ever-resourceful and totally unflappable, she may detail her ignorance, blunders, and occasional inability to control her moods. Elenore loses her temper over the unsuccessful attempts of Tiv medical techniques to save the life of her friend; Barley rails at the swindling ways of local merchants; Gardner reacts to the condescending manner of a Bengali hotel-keeper by calling him a 'patronising git'. Since she delivers the epithet in English and accompanies it with a saccharine smile, the man does not even raise his eyebrows. In these accounts, the lofty academic can appear engagingly human, at times all too human.

Fieldwork is the distinctive method of social anthropology. It is thus surprising that it has remained, until relatively recently, a mysterious process whose secrets were not discussed in print by the initiated. The authors of personal accounts of the experience have chosen to buck this code of silence by revealing just how aleatory fieldwork can in fact be. The ethnographer may have a well-organized, cleverly constructed schedule of work, but these plans are often shredded as the locals refuse to comply with their guest's expectations. Writers like Bohannan and Barley expose the central role of chance and of their own personalities in influencing the course of their research. By focusing on the personal, they emphasize the ethnographers' reliance on those locals who, for some reason, have come to enjoy the newcomer's company. And, as these authors reveal, when friendship fails to deliver the goods, their investigatory procedures may take a more indirect turn; they may decide to learn about the ways of their hosts by employing subterfuge, manipulation, and what Rabinow calls 'symbolic violence' (Rabinow 1977). On the example of these writers, fieldworkers need to be as cunning as they are resourceful.

Personal accounts try to engage the public in a way staid ethnographies do not attempt to achieve. By itemizing their feelings and reactions, warts and all, writers in this genre can present themselves as mirrors for their readers to look into. Armchair travellers can play at identifying with the protagonist: how would *they* have responded to life in the bush, to the rigours of the Cameroonian highlands, or to the pervasive poverty of rural Bangladesh? Could they have coped with an over-affectionate primate, an accusation of witchcraft, or sharing a small house with fifteen others during the monsoon?

Sedentary voyagers can also reassure themselves that what they are reading is 'the real thing'. Barring missionaries and exceptional characters such as Charles Doughty, most literary travellers have neither the time nor the knowledge to make other than superficial comments. In contrast, an anthropologist is supposed to have spent sufficient time in one place to get to know the locals as well as she can. Her words are meant to be authoritative, and her literary product veridical. Her experience is so rich she has no need to pad her text with tales.

The practice of ethnography emerged from the tradition of travel-writing (Thornton 1983; Herbert 1991: 150–203) and today some anthropologists seem keen on a partial return to their literary origins. They wish to see written more experientially rich accounts of fieldwork, ones in which neither the position of the fieldworker nor the sensuality of the surroundings is forgotten. Marcus and Fischer (1986: 17–44) speak of recent experiments in reflexive ethnography; Wheeler (1986) propounds the synthesis of travelogue, ethnography and autobiography; Stoller (1989: 15–34) calls for 'tasteful ethnography', in which an author describes how things look or smell in the land of others and the ways the senses are there conceived. As all these anthropologists admit, relatively little of what they moot is radically new: Malinowski and Firth, to name two examples, were both concerned to convey in their books the atmosphere of local life; in the last three decades many ethnographers have written reports of their experiences and of the way it made them reflect on their life back home. Further, as any anthropological reader of Doughty's *Travels in Arabia Deserta* (first published in 1888, and still in print) knows, the idea of combining sophisticated narrative with nuanced analysis is not one restricted to the ethnographers of the late twentieth century. The 'postmodernist moment' in anthropology does not amount to a clean break with the past of the discipline, rather an extolling of certain traditions within it which, in recent decades, have been relatively submerged. Bohannan felt forced to use a pseudonym for *Return to Laughter*; today that would be considered unnecessary. To these extents postmodernist anthropologists are not so much blurring genres as revaluing some of them.

This revaluation is, however, an impoverished one. For literary postmodernists recognize neither the all-important moral dimension of fieldwork nor the central role of fieldworkers as moral agents:

> The much touted slogans of empowerment, emancipation, authentication and dialogical or polyphonic discourse, often borrowed from literary studies as more or less apt metaphors, have not led to a greater awareness of moral ambiguities and concrete decisions of the field-workers, but to a plethora of literature which tries to deal with moral dilemmas on the level of rhetorical tropes.
>
> (Koepping 1994: 10)

In other words, fieldworkers get on with the job, literary fieldworkers talk about the troubles of getting on with it, and postmodernists talk about talk about it.

While postmodernists busy themselves thinking that they are mapping out the moral universe of anthropologists, literary fieldworkers demonstrate the ultimate futility of that task. For what Bohannan and Gardner both reveal in their own ways is the inadequacy of any pre-established code of professional ethics, no matter how comprehensive it pretends to be. Each of them has to face unforeseen moral quandaries, and each has to resolve them in order to be able to remain in their field-community. Bohannan forsakes standards of detachment in order to help save a friend. Gardner loses her cool when a townsman tries to cheat a villager. Also, both of these writers reveal that, despite moral differences, a form of human solidarity may be attained, that a human bond, born of intimate contact, may unite fieldworker and fieldworked. Perhaps it is for these reasons that Barley is so disliked by his peers: by pointedly omitting any ethical dimension to his work, he underlines his determination to let nothing get in the way of a joke; by playing the solitary role of jester, he denies the possibility of a human bond which could bridge cultural divides – and so denigrates his hosts all the more. As for postmodernists, they are silent on this matter.

Postmodernists might wish to produce reflexive and critical texts but, unless they are careful, may well end up writing books as unreadable as those they are reacting against:

> Some of these new 'experimental ethnographies' seem even less accessible than the old realist texts. Such texts are sometimes filled with ethnographers ruminating over the epistemological problems of studying 'the other'. Experimental ethnographic texts derive their authority from the author's tone and posture as a reflective, skeptical, philosopher-poet. Unfortunately, surrealist and post-modernist ethnographies, like surrealist and post-modernist art, can be as opaque as they are imaginative . . .
> Although often more engaging than much social scientific writing, ethnographies are rarely as touching and intimate as good literature and cinema.
>
> (Foley 1990: xvii–xviii)

In this context of postmodernism and its critics, what distinguishes the few genuinely popular authors from the majority of those who have chosen to write personal accounts of their own fieldwork is their literary ability. The old adage might have been that anthropologists were closet novelists, albeit second-rate ones, but it is depressingly clear that most do not even rank as third-rate. British practitioners used to pride themselves on their use of the English language. They liked to contrast their style with the impenetrable prose of their sociological counterparts, pseudo-scientists who seemed to mask even the smallest idea in a profusion of polysyllabic abstract nouns. But few anthropologists would dare to be so literarily arrogant today, and whatever they may think of Barley's attitudes towards Third Worlders, they have to concede that the man knows how to write.

Part of the reason for the success of Bohannan and Barley is their relative degree of innovation. To my knowledge, *Return to Laughter* was the first book-length treatment by an anthropologist of her fieldwork. Subsequent contributors to the genre who have wished to write of the trauma and anguish of the experience have had to use her book as their reference point. In a similar fashion, any anthropologist who today describes their fieldwork in a jokey, disrespectful manner can be immediately termed 'Barleynese'. What distinguishes Gardner's *Songs at the River's Edge* from many other recent accounts of fieldwork among women by women is that it steers away from a confessional mode, which tends to produce 'embarrassingly uncontrolled or unedited' results (Okely 1992: 11).

Each of this literary trio does something different, each in its own way defines a variant of the genre, and each is very much a product of its time. Bohannan's phrasing of fieldwork as a spiritual quest for oneself was particularly appropriate for her postwar peers: in the Oxford of her days, the largest society in the University was the Christian Union, while existentialism provided succour for anguished undergraduates who were unattracted by established creeds. Barley's first book came out at a time when Lévi-Straussian structuralism had raised anthropology to a new level of public prestige and pomposity. Susan Sontag's much-quoted characterization of the anthropologist 'as hero' had become a pretentious trope waiting to be mocked, and Barley saw no reason to leash his tongue. Also, while 'no one would want to concede that his is an anthropology of a more discriminatory and insensitive 1980s ... perhaps Barley's self-promotionalism may be taken as a by-product of the individualist and entrepreneurial Thatcherite decade' (Stewart 1992). The publication of Gardner's book reflects, of course, the developing encounter between feminism and anthropology. Though it is put out by the Virago Press, *Songs . . .* is not a strident text penned by a termagant. Gardner does not rage constantly against the ills of a male-dominated world, nor, for that matter, does she wear her heart on her sleeve and let it bleed all the time. Instead, she has recounted some of the events she witnessed, in a sophisticated yet accessible manner which appeals to a broader audience than feminists tired by theoretical tomes and anthropologists bored by the anecdotes of their male colleagues. Her book is not a sermon but a seductively subversive text for the as yet unconverted.

The fieldworker as pilgrim, as peacock, as woman of her time – a successful trio of roles chosen by three different anthropologists of different generations. This triad of literary guises does not, however, exhaust the potential of the genre: there is a fecund variety of other parts for writers of fieldwork accounts to play: for example, the anthropologist as trickster, as advocate, as shaman, as detective, as victim, as cultural missionary, as spouse, or even as reconstructed male. Which role or roles will prove popular in the future is not something to be predicted by a commentator, but to be decided by the public.

ACKNOWLEDGEMENTS

My remarks on Bunyan are indebted to Keeble (1984) and Hill (1988). My thanks to the late Godfrey Lienhardt and to Rodney Needham for comments.

NOTE

1 *Pan* is a green spicy leaf, chewed with betel-nut, spices and lime.

REFERENCES

Anon (1954) Review of *Return to Laughter*, *Times Literary Supplement* 10 December: 798.
Barley, N. (1983) *The Innocent Anthropologist. Notes from a Mud Hut*, London: British Museum.
—— (1986) *A Plague of Caterpillars. A Return to the African Bush*, London: Viking.
—— (1988) *Not a Hazardous Sport*, London: Viking.
—— (1990) *The Coast*, London: Viking.
—— (1992a) 'Fatal Attraction', *The Guardian 'Weekend'*, 14–15 March: 25.
—— (1992b) *The Duke of Puddle Dock: Travels in the Footsteps of Stamford Raffles*, London: Viking.
Bohannan, L. (1954) 'Miching Mallecho: That Means Witchcraft', *London Magazine 1*, 5 June.
Foley, D. E. (1990) *Learning Capitalist Culture. Deep in the Heart of Tejas*, Philadelphia: University of Pennsylvania Press.
Gardner, K. (1991) *Songs at the River's Edge. Stories from a Bangladeshi Village*, London: Virago.
Herbert, C. (1991) *Culture and Anomie. Ethnographic Imagination in the Nineteenth Century*, Chicago: University of Chicago Press.
Hill, C. (1988) *A Turbulent, Seditious, and Factious People. John Bunyan and his Church 1628–1688*, Oxford: Clarendon Press.
Keeble, N. H. (1984) 'Introduction' to *The Pilgrim's Progress* by John Bunyan, The World's Classics, Oxford: Oxford University Press.
Koepping, K.-P. (1994) 'Introduction: Commitment and Context. Ethical Issues in the Anthropological Encounter', *Anthropological Journal on European Cultures*, Special Issue on 'Anthropology and Ethics', 3, 2: 7–19.
Marcus, G. E. and Fischer, M. M. J. (1986) *Anthropology as Cultural Critique*.

An Experimental Moment in the Human Sciences, Chicago: University of Chicago Press.

Okely, J. (1992) 'Participatory Experience and Embodied Knowledge', in J. Okely and H. Callaway (eds) *Anthropology and Autobiography*, ASA Monographs 29, London: Routledge, pp. 1–28.

Rabinow, P. (1977) *Reflections on Fieldwork in Morocco*, Berkeley: University of California Press.

Smith Bowen, E. (pseudonym of L. Bohannan) (1954) *Return to Laughter. An Anthropological Novel*, New York: Harper and Bros.

Stewart, C. (1992) 'The Popularization of Anthropology', *Anthropology Today* 8, 4: 25–7

Stoller, P. (1989) *The Taste of Ethnographic Things. The Senses in Anthropology*, Philadelphia: University of Pennsylvania Press.

Thornton, R. (1983) 'Narrative Ethnography in Africa, 1850–1920: The Creation and Capture of an Appropriate Domain for Anthropology', *Man* 18, 3: 502–20.

Wheeler, V. (1986) 'Travellers' Tales: Observations on the Travel Book and Ethnography', *Anthropological Quarterly* 59, 1: 52–63.

Index